Intellectuals and

For my late father,
Makrand B. Desai

Intellectuals and Socialism
'Social Democrats' and the British Labour Party

Radhika Desai

Lawrence & Wishart
LONDON

Lawrence & Wishart Limited
144a Old South Lambeth Road
London sw8 1xx

First published 1994 by Lawrence and Wishart

© Radhika Desai 1994

ISBN 0 85315 795 2

Set in Monotype Baskerville by Ewan Smith,
Printed and bound in Great Britain
by Redwood Books,
Trowbridge

Contents

Acknowledgements

I would like to thank Jane Borges for her friendship and hospitality in London while I did my research there. Also in London, many people – politicians (Social Democratic, Labour), activists, writers and journalists – jogged their memories for my benefit, giving generously of their time and often, their hospitality. Funding for the research was provided by the Skelton-Clark Committee of the Queen's University at Kingston, Ontario. My most important intellectual debt is to Professor Colin Leys. He has taught me a great deal – demandingly and stimulatingly – about politics and about (as he once put it) 'putting theories to work'. I hope I have imbibed, over the years, some of his exemplary intellectual rigour and incisiveness.

Earlier drafts of the book benefitted from Colin's close editorial and analytical scrutiny. Laurie Adkin critically commented on penultimate drafts of several chapters. Alison Acker generously helped with last minute proofreading. Responsibility for all remaining errors, inconsistencies and stylistic gaffes remains mine, of course. Erin Richmond's efficient, accurate and cheerful help with the typing greatly speeded the process of completing the manuscript.

The book is dedicated to the memory of a loving father who died just as I was beginning work on this book and who would have read it as much with interest and critique as with fondness.

R.D.
July 1994

Introduction

It is now widely appreciated that an era in the history of European socialism has decisively ended. It began with the rise of the mass working-class social democratic parties of the Second International and led, in the twentieth century, both to 'actually existing socialism' in the USSR and eastern Europe, and under different political and ideological coordinates, to social democracy in the West. With the exhaustion and collapse of both, no 'emancipatory' strategy with serious prospects of policy success seemed any longer to exist.

The exhaustion of social democracy was at once economic (the end of Fordist-Keynesian accumulation), political (the decline of mass-based working-class parties), and ideological (the end of the post-war 'consensus'). This book argues, however, that one of the most important and unappreciated facets of this brand of socialism and its denouement was its relationship to intellectuals. Intellectuals imparted to socialism both the overarching theory and the policies that identified it as such. Both its greatest achievement – 'the Welfare State' – and its characteristic limitations – its bureaucratism and abject reliance on the pace of capitalist growth – can be traced to the role of intellectuals. In at least apparent correspondence, the decline of socialism was accompanied by a crisis of this role. This book explores this dimension of the history and crisis of social democracy by studying the relationship between the post-war British Labour Party and its principal intellectuals, the 'revisionist' social democrats, and the breakdown of this relationship in the 1970s. Eventually the intellectuals broke from their party to form the Social Democratic Party (SDP) in 1981. The philosophical poverty and policy drift of the Labour Party since the split demonstrates, more clearly than many other cases, that the role of intellectuals had been critical for social democracy; the split itself, which formally marked the end of the relationship, shows that the emerging difficulties of this role were central to social democracy's decline. Thus, apart from providing insights into an important element of socialism's past successes, and into at least the intellectual requirements of any socialist renewal, which

I

are of wider import, this book also hopes to illuminate a hitherto neglected aspect of Labour's post-war trajectory and current impasse.

Some may well object to my tendency to use the word 'socialism' interchangeably with 'social democracy' in this book. But, as Perry Anderson has remarked, '[f]or all their mutual disclaimers, [western social democracy and eastern Communism] were joined as heirs of the ideals of nineteenth century socialism', and 'the collapse of Communism in the East, far from strengthening its historical rival, has for the moment further weakened it.'[1] There is also a widely maintained distinction between social-democracy and some 'true' (but not Stalinist) socialism. But even in its Western Marxist high-theoretical version, the latter has amounted to an impressive set of theories and noble intentions, which, however, have yet to form the basis of any practical strategy. Moreover, in some respects at least, the distance between socialists and 'mixed-economy' social democrats seems, if anything, to have diminished.[2] As Eric Hobsbawm has pointed out, the question 'whether there is an actual line separating non-socialist mixed economies from socialist ones, and if so where it is to be drawn ... is, at least for the present, a highly academic question.'[3] In short, the impasse of the left has stripped many issues and controversies to their bare essentials: and as the left, Marxist or otherwise, seeks new directions for a progressive politics, the scrutiny of the experience and exhaustion of social democracy, in its intellectual just as much as other aspects, is unavoidable.

Intellectuals and Socialism

Like much recent analysis of the role of ideologies and philosophies in politics, the role of intellectuals can most fruitfully be theorised within Antonio Gramsci's conception of hegemonic politics. However, while the role of intellectuals is clearly central to any theory of political hegemony, a preoccupation with the *effectiveness* of hegemonic ideologies (with the question of 'consent'), combined with a misdirected anti-elitist and anti-intellectual bias, has prevented most Gramscians from analysing the role of intellectuals in politics and socialism effectively. Yet, as a close examination of Gramsci's work makes clear, their centrality to hegemonic politics must be traced to ideology's *directive* function, just as much if not more than to its consent generating one. Intellectuals provide hegemonic historic blocs, including socialist ones, with their overarching theory and strategy.

Gramsci accorded a centrality to intellectuals (and culture generally) which is apparent throughout his writings. His concept of 'organic intellectuals' (closely linked to the working class), which was a singular attempt to bridge Marxism's basic strategic antinomy between ultra-democratic ideas of the self-emancipation of the proletariat and vanguardism, has attracted most attention. And not surprisingly. As a concept it is embedded in, and a most characteristic expression of, Gramsci's penetrating fragments of a radically *social* theory of culture and politics. What is often forgotten however, is that the 'organic intellectual' is more a programmatic than a historical category; that while it has served to raise important issues of politics and culture, any search for organic intellectuals in the history of European socialism probably obscures more than it clarifies. The intellectual function in socialist politics hitherto has actually tended to be performed by those Gramsci called 'traditional' intellectuals (not linked to either capital or labour) who were capable of elaborating larger visions of social order which could form the basis of its hegemonic ambitions.

Typically they had become attached to the Europe's working-class parties as a result of a general bifurcation of intellectual life into marked conservative and critical tendencies and were central to their development and direction. They also brought with them their independently conceived (*dirigiste*) conceptions of socialism. While the social distance which separated these critical traditional intellectuals from the culture, institutions and experience of the working classes they sought to direct in politics accounted for some of its important limitations, their services also enabled important socialist advances.

Labour's Intellectuals

Tracing the historical relationship of Britain's traditional intellectuals to the Labour Party requires an understanding of the broad historical evolution of Britain's intellectuals and their political allegiances. Britain's national specificity, in this regard as in many others, verged on the exceptional: the absence of revolutionary rupture in modern British history marginalised and stifled its only truly theoretical Enlightenment intellectual tradition: Benthamite Utilitarianism. In politics, it permitted an unintellectual conservatism to persist. In such circumstances the principal *intellectual tradition* to emerge was tamely empiricist, eschewing any ambitions of broader social theory. While thus supporting only more modest forms of political action, it became linked, in politics, with successive parties of the left – from Philosophic Radicalism to the Liberal Party and finally Labour – setting the agenda of British politics through them. The relationship of the revisionist or social democratic intellectuals to the Labour Party can be traced to the turn of the century when their intellectual forebears, Fabians and progressive liberals, first began to move toward Labour.

During the interwar period the political allegiances of the intellectuals had been in flux. With the decline of the Liberal Party after the Great War and the absorption of the project of the New Liberals into that of the Labour Party, large numbers of British intellectuals shifted their political allegiance to Labour. However, many others remained sceptical of the Labour Party as an acceptable political home: Keynes, who stayed with the Liberals, is a notable example. During the 1930s others still experimented with alternatives such as Fascism (the New Party), Communism (the CPGB) and in the 1940s the short-lived wartime Commonwealth Party. However, a key group of intellectuals in the Labour Party, mainly Fabians, worked in the aftermath of the political crisis of 1931 to produce the distinctive programme which, later supplemented by Beveridge and Keynes, informed the 1945–51 Labour government. While the intellectual tradition which Labour thus inherited contained important deficiencies, until the first major intervention in party policy-making by these intellectuals in the 1930s, the Labour Party lacked an effective or distinctive economic programme.[4] Labour's intellectual weakness had manifestly compounded the difficulties of its second (minority) Labour government, already faced with civil service and capitalist opposition and the debacle of 1931 was only its most dramatic demonstration. The new programme of the 1930s eventually came to occupy a sacred place in the folklore of the Labour Party and in effect defined the meaning of 'socialism' for both the right and left wings of the party.[5]

By the 1950s the achievements of the Attlee governments, with their combination of radical purpose and moderate methods, and ultimately, the ameliorative effectiveness of its new strategy, finally cemented the link between the Labour Party and Britain's principal intellectual tradition. The further marginalisation of the Liberals, and the support given by their remaining parliamentary leaders to Conservatism in the 1950s, also worked to break the link between the principal intellectual tradition and Liberalism; this tradition now adopted the Labour Party and sought to dominate it, and through it to set the agenda for British politics as a whole once again. The principal tradition of social theory in Britain, which had historically been allied to the critical political tendency (most recently to Liberalism), was firmly linked to Labour. Labour now laid its rightful claim to the mantle of the 'thinking man's [sic] party'. After the fulfilment and exhaustion of the programme of the 1930s, the legatees of this intellectual tradition worked to produce a new and (in the altered post-war situation) revised programme for the party. Thereby they came to be known as 'revisionists', and later as 'social democrats'.[6]

The ascendancy which the revisionists came to enjoy in the post-war Labour Party, best symbolised by the election of one of them, Hugh Gaitskell, as leader, tended to obscure the basic conditionality of the intellectuals' relationship to it. The shift in the intellectuals' political allegiances from Liberalism to Labour was crucially predicated upon the promise of political influence. And, in the 1920s and 1930s at least, this seemed radically uncertain for the largely middle-class intellectuals in the defensively working-class Labour Party. Keynes, for example, had chosen not to join the Labour Party because he believed that 'the intellectual elements in the Labour Party will never exercise adequate control'; for those that did join, the contrary hope was the *raison d'être* of their new political affiliation. But one of the main conclusions to be drawn from the trajectory of these intellectuals in the Labour Party – which ended in the 1981 split – is that Keynes's judgement proved, as so often, correct.

In 1981, when the social democrats left the Labour Party to form the SDP, the link between Labour and what had been Britain's principal intellectual tradition finally ended. While critical for the Labour Party, this break also had profound implications for British politics as a whole. The link between the principal intellectual tradition and the critical political tendency (as the 'party of advance')[7] had set the agenda of politics in modern Britain, and now the junction between intellectual life and high politics was radically reconfigured. Beginning with Mrs Thatcher, political influence belonged not to the mainstream of British intellectuals but to a small group of sectarian neo-liberals,[8] who even at the end of 1993 seemed to face no immediate prospect of an organized, intellectually coherent political challenge. This forms, at the very least, the cultural terrain on which any progressive or socialist politics must regroup.

The 1981 Split in the Labour Party

The social democrats' departure from the Labour Party in 1981 marked the close of a longer trajectory traced by the post-war – 'revisionist' – generation of intellectuals in the Labour Party. As the recognised heirs of the architects of the programme of the 1930s, as the only group of intellectuals in the Labour Party to produce a new programme for Labour in the post-war period, and as the beneficiaries of a close alliance of top trade unionists and the party leadership, they enjoyed an easy ascendancy – an ascendancy, moreover, unmatched previously, or since, by any group of intellectuals in Labour's history. The programme they produced for the party eventually proved deeply flawed – based on untenable assumptions. Nor, given its conformity with the particularly conservative political and cultural conjuncture which constituted its moment, was it notable for its radicalism as a programme for socialism. But it seriously attempted to re-theorise socialism for the clearly changed circumstances of post-war Britain and was the only major attempt of its sort. As such it must be critically understood on its own terms.

But, whatever the flaws or political inclinations of this programme, its authors' fate as intellectuals in the Labour Party was actually determined by the specifically *political* project which also went with it. Quite apart from fashioning a new programme for the party in the 1950s, as their intellectual predecessors had done in the 1930s, the revisionists had to engage in the unprecedented task of rethinking its goals and strategy and giving the party an explicit doctrinal basis. They also needed, by the same token, to hegemonise it. But Labour was, as Tom Nairn noted in his synopsis of Labour's history, a profoundly unintellectual party: it had emerged 'not ... in response to any theory about what a socialist party should be; it arose empirically, in a quite piece-meal fashion, like so much in British society before it'.[9] As such it was indifferent, if not actively hostile to, theories – to any theorization of its programme and strategy; and as Keynes, for one, had clearly sensed, a hegemony based on ideas and a group of intellectuals was impossible. Lacking an independent institutional base in the party, the revisionists' political power – based on essentially Labourite unions – could only contain such contradictions temporarily. The party which they sought to (re)direct in accordance with their theories resisted such treatment, preferring to adhere to its Labourist traditions. This is the lesson to be derived from Gaitskell's failure to delete Clause Four from the party constitution in 1959, leaving intact historic ambiguities surrounding Labour's aims and strategy.

The eventful years of Gaitskell's leadership thus themselves revealed that a revisionist leadership could not continue to rely on the handful of leaders of large trade unions to sustain its power and Gaitskell's death in 1963 only set further back any prospects for revisionist hegemony in the Labour Party. Without a clearly ascendant leadership figure to rally around, the revisionists lost much of their cohesion. And the decline of their political position in the party, already apparent during the Wilson governments of the late 1960s (during which, moreover, revisionism, which by default formed the tacit basis of the government's strategy, also came unravelled), became even more precipitous after 1970. The reasons were, once again, political. Public and trade union disillusion with the Wilson Labour governments generated a grass-roots upsurge against the parliamentary leadership which constituted itself as the new Labour left. While its more radical impulses also embodied important critiques of the tacitly revisionist strategy of the party (and by implication of the traditional intellectuals' role as it had come to be practised by the revisionists), it primarily represented a deep-rooted shift in the balance of power in the Labour Party, swinging the disaffected and militant unions towards the left. The purely parliamentarian revisionists were far more seriously affected by this than the centrist leadership.

Unable to transcend the limits of labourism, and squandering the opportunities for a clearly class-based socialist politics, the new Labour left joined with various centrist elements in an essentially populist movement to oppose British entry into the European Common Market. The Common Market had long been central to the revisionist modernising strategy, and the social democrats (as the revisionists had now chosen to call themselves) staked their political position in the party on the issue. This stand was also a demonstration of their attitude to the changing Labour Party. This had irreversible political consequences. By leading a group of sixty-nine Labour MPs in breaking a three-line Labour whip and voting with the Tory government for entry into the Common Market in October 1971, the former revisionists re-crystallised into an identifiable political tendency. But ironically, now bereft of the centrist and trade union support they had formerly enjoyed, their new narrower identity became at the same time a hallmark of their increasing marginalisation in the Labour Party and, as their position only continued to decline further through the 1970s, it closely prefigured the 1981 SDP split. Their preoccupation with the Common Market issue and their political marginalisation now excluded them, for the first time since the 1930s, from the process of policy-making, which became dominated by the left. By the late 1970s the social democrats' political position had declined to a point where any hope of influence over the party had faded, and their decision to leave the Labour Party was based much more on this perception than on particular policy differences between themselves and the rising new Labour left.

In 1981 the social democrats broke away from the Labour Party after having fought a rearguard battle in the party over the previous ten years. With the resurgence and political successes of the new Labour left after the defeat of the Labour government in 1979, the political conclusion that they had tried to avoid throughout the previous decade, in the hope that they might still pull the party out of the mire of its difficulties with its trade union base, and away from the increasingly successful new Labour left, had to be faced at last: the Labour Party could no longer serve as the instrument of the political role they had inherited and wanted to continue to play: that is, setting the agenda for British politics.

The social democrats hoped to make the Social Democratic Party (SDP) into a new vehicle of their inherited political role. Their power to set the agenda was now to derive from their ability to hold the balance of power in a three party system, especially under proportional representation (a central plank in the SDP platform). Early prospects looked promising. By December 1981 some polls put the SDP's support at over 50 per cent in an electorate unhappy about the depth of the recession and alienated by the polarisation then evident in the

Conservative and Labour parties; and, despite the hostility of the first-past-the-post electoral system to third parties, the SDP and Liberal Party Alliance polled 26 per cent of the vote in the 1983 general election. But the subsequent merger of the majority of the SDP with the Liberal Party after a poorer electoral performance in 1987 led to the scattering of the forces of the Social Democrats. They no longer retained any politically or philosophically distinctive presence in politics. Yet this story is not merely one of the tribulations of fourth parties under the British electoral system. The exhaustion of revisionism as a viable socialist strategy, already apparent in the 1970s, was a major factor. The social democrats, politically marginalised and embattled in the Labour Party throughout the 1970s, had also failed to attract a younger generation of intellectuals of sufficient stature to take over from the older. They also failed to regain the intellectual initiative outside the Party, in the much altered and variegated intellectual atmosphere of the 1980s. After the merger, the Social Democrats who agreed to it were outnumbered and found it extremely difficult to retain a distinctive presence in the merged Liberal Democratic Party.

The 1981 split, then, signalled the exhaustion of an important political heritage – important for the British left, and for British society as a whole. The SDP was a terminal manifestation of this. Although launched under the banner of 'breaking the mould' of British politics, as the only force representing novelty (and sanity) in a tired and inefficient two-party system, its true agenda was a vain attempt to *preserve* a political mould in which intellectuals had occupied a central place. The rise of Labour's 'market research socialism' in the late 1980s, after the defeat of the new Labour left, belatedly underscored this. Labour (and the left in Britain more widely) was now bereft of an important element in its past successes and, I would argue, also bereft of something essential to its future renewal.

Such concerns, however, are not reflected in the literature on the SDP split. Left-wing commentators tended to see the SDP as an irrelevance, now thankfully past. After the bitter conflicts of 1979–81 within the Labour Party, which pitted the influential new Labour left against the future Social Democrats, this is no doubt understandable. Many have even refused to recognise what happened as a split, pointing out (correctly enough) that the SDP did not take any trade unions with it; but in taking this view they have failed to grasp the significance of these events as an *intellectual* break. If the event was commented upon at all on the left, the accounts spoke of opportunism, betrayal and 'good riddance'. For example, while tracing with some dexterity the intellectual development of the social democrats (if only to accuse them, correctly if not necessarily pertinently, of reneging on their own promises), Ken Coates, in his zeal to condemn, conflates the social democrats with the unintellectual labourist centre of the party, blaming them for the compromises of the 1974–79 Labour government.[10] However, although the social democrats may legitimately be accused of intellectual failure in these years, the main responsibility for the political vacillations of these years would seem to lie elsewhere, especially in the powerful pragmatic and unintellectual centre of the party.

To identify the 1981 split as a break in the relation between the Labour Party and its intellectuals is not to claim that all those who joined the SDP were intellectuals, even if it gained more support amongst so-called professional sections of the electorate than any other. An important right-wing working class populist tendency, headed by Stephen Haseler and Douglas Eden (who had formed the rabidly anti-left and authoritarian Social Democratic Alliance [SDA] in the mid-1970s) also ranged itself behind the SDP. Mainly based in local politics, this tendency had always been distinct from the parliamentary social democrats.[11] While the diffuse policy moderation of the SDP, itself a symptom of the intellectual exhaustion of the social democrats, was accompanied by a political and sociological vagueness or lack of definition in the new party, this should not obscure the fact that the SDP was the *creation* of those who had been Labour's foremost intellectuals. Because they no could no longer hope to play their self-assigned role in it, they had to attempt, at least, to play it outside. Most accounts of the SDP concentrate on the more proximate plans and events which led to the creation of the SDP.[12] But while these accounts may help to understand *how* the SDP was formed, they fail to convey enough about *why* it was formed, and why it was formed by those who formed it. When the split occurred, a widespread impression was created that at its root lay disagreements in the years immediately preceding the split on issues, such as defence, or incomes policy, or the EEC, or the level of public expenditure. To be sure, all such issues became fronts of division between the social democrats and the then ascendant new Labour left, and as these fronts multiplied, so a case may be made that the social democrats felt bound to leave because of these differences. But while policies and issues were important, what was decisive was their obviously declining and indeed, by 1980, seemingly unrecoverable, position in the party. The social democrats' performance of a traditional intellectual role in British politics, through the Labour Party, was dependent upon their retaining a fairly powerful political position in the party. This was now under attack and the social democrats had few resources with which to resist. But such complex reasons could hardly be easily acknowledged, still less expressed.[13]

For an understanding of the true significance of the intellectual project which the social democrats represented, and for any attempt to reformulate the ideals and strategy of socialism in the future, a deeper, more accurate analysis of 'those who went and those who stayed' (to use Coates's phrase) is important. This book seeks, therefore, to understand the general relationship of intellectuals to socialism within a wider theory of ideology and hegemony, within which the making and unmaking of the relationship of intellectuals to the Labour Party can be more adequately grasped.

Notes

1. Perry Anderson, 'The Light of Europe', *English Questions*, Verso, London, 1992, p 324.

2. A representative piece rethinking socialist perspectives on the market is Robin Blackburn, 'Fin de Siècle: Socialism after the Crash', *New Left Review*, Number 185, January–February 1991.

3. Eric Hobsbawm, 'The Crisis of Today's Ideologies', *New Left Review*, Number 192, March – April 1992.

4. K.O. Morgan, *Labour in Power 1945–51*, Oxford University Press, Oxford, 1985, pp 11–12.

5. K.O. Morgan, *op.cit.*, pp 1–5. On Labour's programme in the 1930s and its making see Elizabeth Durbin, *New Jerusalems: The Labour Party and the Economics of Democratic Socialism*, Routledge and Kegan Paul, London, 1985.

6. These intellectuals of the post-war Labour Party have been identified variously as 'revisionists', 'Gaitskellites', the 'radical right' (of the Labour Party), the 'Hampstead Set', the 'intellectual right' and later the 'social democrats'. Two of these terms are best adapted to the present purpose. The first label, 'revisionists', refers to the architects of Labour's (revised) programme in the 1950s and will be used to identify them up to about 1970. Thereafter, they became known as the 'social democrats' (lower case) as the issue of British entry into the EEC became more central and the identification of these modernising intellectuals with their social democratic counterparts on the continent became more prominent in public debates. It was largely under this rubric that they left the Labour Party. The upper case 'Social Democrats' will be used only in referring to the members of that party after 1981. It is also important to point out that these labels refer only to the *intellectual* revisionists and social democrats to the exclusion of other (mostly) right wing Labour Party members and trade unionists who may have come within their political ambit over time.

7. The phrase is Roy Jenkins'. See his *The Pursuit of Progress*, Heinemann, London, 1953.

8. On this see Radhika Desai, 'Second-Hand Dealers in Ideas: Think-tanks and Thatcherite Hegemony', *New Left Review*, Number 203, January–February 1994, pp 27–64.

9. Tom Nairn, 'The Nature of the Labour Party – I', *New Left Review*, Number 27, September–October 1964, p 38.

10. Ken Coates, *The Social Democrats: Those Who Went and Those Who Stayed*, Spokesman, Nottingham, 1983.

11. David Marquand explained the subsequent relationship of the SDA and the social democrats thus: 'Haseler's invective is all working class.... He's

invented a history of a sort of populist radicalism, Norman Tebbitry in a way, and it's been a very consistent thing. I remember being involved in a television thing in the early 1970s on Europe where he opposed it on a sort of proletarian solidarity, populist-nationalist ground. The working class wasn't interested in all this sort of rubbish. I remember him commenting on something I said, 'Well, that's a typical remark of the parlour-pink intelligentsia in the PLP'. I've always regarded Haseler with some suspicion when he later emerged as a figure in the SDP. There's a splendid phrase in Roy Jenkins' *European Diaries* where he says Haseler and Eden came to see him and he was very suspicious of them, "They look like hard-faced men who've done badly out of the Labour Party". That sums it up, actually.' (Interview with David Marquand, 13 October 1989.)

12. This applies especially to Hugh Stephenson, *Claret and Chips*, Michael Joseph, London, 1982.

13. Interview with David Marquand, 13 October 1989.

2

Intellectuals in Ideology and Hegemony

If '[t]he *problem* of ideology is to give an account, within a materialist theory, of how social ideas arise',[1] in writing about intellectuals, this chapter is a contribution to a 'supply-side' account of ideology. It does not ask how ideas are internalised: whether, or how, such things as class, race, or gender determine the people's acceptance of ideas. While these are important questions, it is doubtful whether for society as a whole a fully supportable account of this 'demand side', the consumption of ideology, has yet been provided. But this difficulty does not mean that some no less important questions about the conditions in which ideas are generated, and the manner in which they come to structure particular political projects and struggles, cannot be answered either; and it is this side of the problem – how ideas attempt to define, structure and limit particular political projects, and confront, efface or subsume alternative ones – that this book is concerned with. If, as the work of Antonio Gramsci has demonstrated, ideologies shape political projects, the role of intellectuals as producers and peddlers of ideas, theories, plans and values is clearly central.

Ideas and political ideologies are not only the forms of consciousness which reflect social conflict. They are also the templates, however incomplete and imperfect, of the social (re)construction envisaged by each party in any struggle. It would thus also be true to say that the scale of the social transformation envisaged by any political project would correspond to the scope of the intellectual function in it. However, despite the great transformative ambitions of socialism, Marxists, including those working within a Gramscian perspective, have largely ignored the role of intellectuals in it, apparently out of a deep-seated anti-elitist/anti-intellectual bias.[2] It is true that the involvement of Marx and Engels in the political struggles of their time gave many of their pronouncements on the historical role of intellectuals a polemically anti-intellectual cast.[3] The role of intellectuals in the later Marxism of the Second International, while acknowledged, was understood to be purely organisational and pedagogical: that is, essentially to confirm, and perhaps correctly anticipate, an already generally known onward march of history, not to play a fundamentally creative role in it. It was left to Gramsci, who radically reformulated the Leninist conception of hegemony to include a theory of ideological struggle, and who was deeply concerned with questions of culture, to develop a theory of the role of intellectuals; and the theoretical framework which follows is thus primarily based on a reflection on Gramsci's concepts of 'hegemony' and óf 'organic' and 'traditional' intellectuals. While of course, much recent Marxist (and 'post-Marxist') work on the subject of ideology has been prompted by Gramsci's work, it has nowhere reflected the centrality that Gramsci attributed to the role of intellectuals. This chapter therefore tries to give the role of intellectuals its due place in the theory of ideology and hegemony.

Hegemony and its Functions

In Gramsci's thought 'hegemony' is the central organising concept. At the society-wide level (or the 'national' level in Gramsci's account) politics is essentially a struggle for hegemony. Hegemony is seen variously as 'political, intellectual and moral leadership over allied groups',[4] or 'the entire complex of practical and theoretical activities with which the ruling class not only justifies and maintains its dominance but manages to win the consent of those over whom it rules'.[5] While references to hegemony are scattered throughout Gramsci's *Prison Notebooks* without there being one full definition, Gwyn Williams' early explication is both accurate and sympathetic to Gramsci's concerns:

> By 'hegemony' Gramsci seems to mean a socio-political situation, in his terminology a 'moment', in which the philosophy and practice of a society fuse or are in equilibrium; an order in which a certain way of life and thought is dominant; in which one concept of reality is diffused throughout society in all its institutional and private manifestations, informing with its spirit all taste, morality, customs, religious and political principles, and all social relations, particularly in their intellectual and moral connotation. An element of direction and control, not necessarily conscious, is implied.[6]

As a concept hegemony does not refer to the sway of a dominant class throughout whole epochs. Rather, each, like the capitalist epoch, is a series of particular hegemonies based politically in a powerful class or class coalition and punctuated by periods of crisis. Each hegemony has a specific set of material conditions including, in the capitalist epoch, a specific 'strategy of accumulation' or specific 'growth model', complete with its various extra-economic preconditions, which outlines the general strategy appropriate to its realisation.[7] The elaboration of such a strategy, like the other principal themes of any hegemony, is evidently an intellectual project, calling for an appropriate theory of accumulation (such as, for example, Adam Smith's *The Wealth of Nations*, or Keynes's *General Theory*).

Intellectuals play a crucial role in the generation, organisation and dissemination of the hegemonic ideology. It is possible to isolate at least two functions within this role. First, intellectuals must help to prompt the 'spontaneous consent given by the great masses to the general direction imposed on social life by the dominant fundamental social group [i.e. the dominant class]'.[8] This formulation of Gramsci's is well-known, but the adequacy of our understanding of this 'consent-procuring' function is debatable. It usually amounts to a 'trickle-down' model of the relationship between the theoretical propositions of intellectuals and the notions which articulate people's everyday experience of the world, a model once popularised by Louis Althusser in his work on 'Ideological State Apparatuses'.[9] But this is surely too simple and must be qualified in several ways. Firstly, a selection process of some kind must filter that which, from the often abstract pronouncements of intellectuals, is actually absorbed at the level of popular consciousness – a selection governed both by the requirements of 'common sense' and by the topicality of public concerns. There is, secondly, the extent to which intellectuals are able to articulate – both to express and to make coherent – the lived experience of the people.[10] And, finally, the acceptance of ideologies varies according to the differences in the material circumstances, and therefore the experiences, of people: hegemonic ideologies may have only a quite limited purchase among subordinate classes and groups (of women, for example).[11] Indeed, hegemonic ideology considered as one that has secured 'consent' is clearly too simplistic: there are also significant kinds of 'non-coercive acquiescence and obedience' to be considered as well.[12] For present purposes, however, it is enough to note that the importance of the 'consent-procuring' function of intellectuals may be exaggerated; hegemony often has a less consensual aspect than is usually supposed.

The second hegemonic function of the intellectuals is to give intellectual direction to the dominant class; intellectuals 'give it homogeneity and an awareness of its own function, not only in the economic but also in the social and political fields'.[13] This is arguably the most important function that intellectuals perform in relation to the hegemonic ideology. Indeed, it is plausible that the most significant function of the hegemonic ideology is to subject to it the subordinate ranks of the *ruling classes*, and secure the congruence of *their* practices to its requirements.[14] This means, in effect, that the most important groups for whom the dominant ideology must become 'common sense' may be a quite limited stratum. Such a narrowing of the *necessary* 'interpellative scope' of the hegemonic ideology – the range of people who must accept it – also helps explain the relative ease with which one hegemonic ideology may replace another. This process would be far harder if it required the effective interpellation of an entire population at each critical conjuncture. In practice, this interpretation suggests, it only needs to interpellate the most essential sectors of the hegemonic class itself – its 'opinion leaders', 'decision-makers', 'agenda-setters' – while marginal and subaltern ideological processes may constitute tensions within the hegemonic order which may lead to ideological and social change.

Thus, while the element of consent is what has chiefly fascinated theorists of ideology and interpreters of Gramsci, the directive function of hegemony, the organisation of the dominant and allied classes, the historical bloc, into a hegemonic project in a way that 'gives it homogeneity and an awareness of its own function' is at least as important if not more so. Hegemonic political struggles are invariably 'structured' in terms of ideologies/theories produced at one time or another by intellectuals. Intellectuals, theorists and philosophers combine existing ideological elements or create new ones in theories and ideologies that have the scope, coherence and elaboration required both to inspire and organise social and class forces for the organization of a hegemony, and the struggle for it and to elaborate its social plans and programme. They thus play a central part in the organisation and direction of social movements or in their hegemony.

Organic and Traditional Intellectuals in Gramsci

For Gramsci, the role of intellectuals lay at the core of any Marxist conception of politics, ideology and revolutionary strategy:

> [T]he exploration and refinement of the concept of the unity of theory and practice is still only at an early stage ... people speak about theory as a 'complement' or an 'accessory' of practice, or as the handmaid of practice. It would seem right for this question too to be considered historically, as an aspect of the political question of the intellectuals. Critical self-consciousness means, historically and politically, the creation of an *elite* of intellectuals. A human mass does not 'distinguish' itself, does not become independent in its own right without, in the widest sense, organising itself; and there is no organisation without intellectuals, that is without organisers and leaders, in other words, without the theoretical aspect of the theory-practice nexus being distinguished concretely by the existence of a group of people 'specialised' in conceptual and philosophical elaboration of ideas.[15]

His *Prison Notebooks* routinely dwell on their role as, for example, in his remarks on the lack of a true hegemony in Italy and the *Risorgimento* and the influence of petty clerical intellectuals over the South. A list of topics which Gramsci drew up as an agenda for his writings in prison indicates the centrality of intellectuals – they, and the culture they produced, were his point of departure for the analysis and understanding of hegemony and society.[16]

Gramsci confronted the basic antinomy in the Marxist conception of the role of intellectuals in socialism between the idea of the 'self-emancipation' of the proletariat, where their role is absent or minimal, and that of the 'scientific' status of Marxism, where the organisational and educative role of intellectuals was central. One important result of Gramsci's attempts to resolve these tensions by working out the rather abstract and philosophical Marxist ideas on the nexus of theory and practice for the concrete social level, was his idea of 'organic intellectuals':

> Every social group, upon coming into existence on the original terrain of an essential function in the world of economic production, creates, together with itself, organically, one or more strata of intellectuals which give it homogeneity and an awareness of its own function not only in the economic but also in the social and political fields. The capitalist entrepreneur creates alongside himself the industrial technician, the specialist in political economy, the organisers of a new culture, of a new legal system, etc.[17]

Thus organic intellectuals are defined by their origins in and links to the *political and economic organisation* of the fundamental classes. They are both the agents, emblem, and measure of that self-organisation. The production of a stratum of organic intellectuals of the Italian working class was an important part of the project of the journal *Ordine Nuovo* which Gramsci edited.

Gramsci clarifies that, initially at least, these organic intellectuals 'are for most part "specialisations" of partial aspects of the primitive activity of the new social type which the new social class has brought into prominence'.[18] But the society-wide scope of any more ambitious hegemony, as envisaged by Gramsci at least, required more encompassing, not to say totalising, world-views. In order to pass from the specialised stage to being capable of articulating a proletarian struggle for hegemony, therefore, organic intellectuals, while distinctive in that they participate in the technical labour process, must also become capable of articulating wider concerns, 'political and directive': 'from technique-as-work one proceeds to technique-as-science and to the humanist conception of history, without which one remains "specialised" and does not become "directive" (specialised and political).'[19] However, quite how one 'proceeds' from being a technically qualified worker to having 'the humanist conception of history' he did not specify; evidently, he envisaged a transition from being a routine functionary to an intellectual who is able to 'give [the proletariat] homogeneity and an awareness of its own function not only in the economic but also in the social and political fields'. While such a transition remained unspecified, Gramsci was very clear about the effects he expected a stratum of organic intellectuals to have on its class of origin:

> The intellectual stratum develops both quantitatively and qualitatively, but every leap forward towards a new breadth and complexity of the intellectual stratum is tied to an analogous movement on the part of the mass of the 'simple', who raise themselves to higher levels of culture.[20]

At least with regard to their intimate connection to their class of origin, Gramsci's organic intellectuals are counterposed to the stratum of already existing 'traditional' intellectuals. In contrast to the fusion of theory and practice, of politics and philosophy, which the organic intellectuals represent, traditional intellectuals are detached from any immediate connection with the fundamental classes, though they may have had a connection to a fundamental class in the past.[21] As a consequence they see themselves as an autonomous social group, with a long history. In capitalist society, Gramsci says, the intellectuals under the label 'traditional' include 'the *noblesse de robe*, a stratum of administrators etc., scholars and scientists, non-ecclesiastical philosophers etc.'[22] who have replaced the ecclesiastical intellectuals of feudal society as secular organisers of culture in modern capitalist society. The traditional intellectuals lacked the organic intellectuals' rootedness in the 'latent aspirations and ... the development of the real forms of life'.[23] If this deracination infected their role with a certain abstracted elitism and idealism, in contrast to the initially 'partial' or 'specialised' character of organic intellectuals, these 'independent' intellectuals elaborated larger and universal visions of social order.

Most interpreters of Gramsci, like Carl Boggs, seem to take it more or less for granted that this implied that 'the subordinate classes might eventually produce their own revolutionary theory and consciousness without elite intervention', and that '[p]robably more than any other Marxist thinker, Gramsci sought to "democratise" theory by incorporating its traditional concerns into a new popular language, thereby concretely actualising a novel convergence of politics and philosophy'.[24] The idealist, uncommitted and deracinated traditional intellectuals are irrelevant (if not positively antithetical) to the working class struggle for hegemony. While Boggs feels compelled to register some (unspecified) reservations about the success of this enterprise, this is how Gramsci has been widely understood.

However, Gramsci's overall assessment of traditional intellectuals is more ambiguous than this suggests. In the first place, Gramsci accorded an intrinsic importance to the tradition of intellectual activity sustained by the traditional intellectuals, and their 'specialisation in the field of thought'.[25]

The professional or technical philosopher does not only 'think' with greater logical rigour, with greater coherence, with more systematic sense than do other men, but he knows the entire history of thought. In other words, he is capable of accounting for the development of thought up to his own day and he is in a position where he can take up a problem from the point which it has reached after having undergone every previous attempt at a solution. He has the same function in the field of thought that specialists have in their various scientific fields.[26]

Nor was Gramsci an advocate of a 'separate' proletarian culture; rather he insisted that the culture of the broad masses must be elevated, critically, to the level of culture achieved at any given time and beyond, 'to reintegrate the whole of society into a new superior cultural order'.[27] This was a far cry from any *proletcult*. Instead, Gramsci envisaged that the workers would critically appropriate the inherited high culture of the time. Working class organic intellectuals would strive, in effect, for a fuller, more critical, less hypocritical and less 'idealist' realisation of the latter's universal, enlightened and emancipatory tendencies. Most importantly perhaps, the society-wide scope and reach of the ideas of the traditional intellectuals, which Gramsci contrasted to the partial specialism of the organic intellectual, were necessary to a truly hegemonic politics. Traditional intellectuals, with their participation in the tradition of systematic intellectual activity, also figure centrally in any struggle for hegemony in that 'any group that is developing toward dominance ... struggle[s] to assimilate and conquer [them] "ideologically"'.[28] Competing visions of social order had to be overcome in any struggle for hegemony. For Gramsci, it would be true to say, a socialist world view, while it must ideally become organically attached and committed to the culture of the working class, was also a critical development of the existing traditional intellectual culture.[29]

It is important to recognise that Gramsci's elaborate scheme of organic and traditional intellectuals, in addition to being an attempt to reconcile the tensions of the Marxist view of intellectuals, represented an original attempt to resolve another issue: that of democracy in the age of mass politics. Whereas some contemporary thinkers despaired of the possibility of true democracy and others tended towards authoritarian solutions of one sort or another, Gramsci's mechanisms of hegemony sought to reconcile high culture and mass politics without fetish of the former nor fear of the latter. And this resolution was less *ouvriériste* than many have tended to suppose. Nevertheless, the notion of a working-class hegemony based on its own organic intellectual leadership has proved attractive enough to obscure the ambiguities involved.

And theoretical ambiguities are compounded by historical ones. While there seems to be no inherent reason why organic intellectuals of the proletariat cannot become hegemonic, and direct the struggle for hegemony (which is the closest it is possible to come, in Gramsci, to the ideal of the 'self-emancipation of the proletariat'), any candid survey of the history of European working-class movements will show that it was the traditional intellectuals who 'assimilated' and 'ideologically conquered' any organic intellectuals rather than the other way around. Joseph Schumpeter's 'bourgeois' account of the process is as persuasive as any:

> Capitalist evolution produces a labour movement which obviously is not the creation of the intellectual group. But it is not surprising that such an opportunity and the intellectual demiurge should find each other. Labour never craved intellectual leadership but intellectuals invaded labour politics. They had an important contribution to make: they verbalised the movement, supplied theories and slogans for it – class war is an excellent example – made it conscious of itself and in doing so changed its meaning ... thus, though intellectuals have not created the labour movement, they have yet worked it up into something that differs substantially from what it would be without them.[30]

One can speculate about the reasons for the difference between the actual historical scenario and the one posited by Gramsci. Firstly, the relative deprivation of the working class in terms of educational opportunity and leisure makes it extremely difficult (though hardly impossible, as seen from the history of working class self-organisation and its autodidacts) for the working class to generate enough organic intellectuals of the specialised variety – organisers of the institutions of the working class movement.

Moreover, as Gramsci himself complained, the higher education of those few from the working class who do acquire it (and their numbers have increased over time) is normally designed to create 'the most humble "administrators" and divulgators of pre-existing traditional accumulated intellectual wealth';[31] that is, traditional intellectuals of the lower ranks. Many illustrious exceptions, of course, rose further: from Raymond Williams to Ken Coates there are numerous contemporary examples. However, what such intellectuals reveal is a more powerful objection to Gramsci's scenario, namely that, as they attain prominence in their chosen intellectual arenas, they qualify more than ever as *traditional* intellectuals, even if critical ones: they absorb and elaborate the intellectual/theoretical disciplines of the established intellectual tradition rather than necessarily expressing a world-view rooted in the working class. While many continued to work for the realisation of working-class political objectives, these objectives were now formulated in terms of *theories* and are at some remove from any 'organic' working-class world-view.[32]

Thirdly – and this is perhaps the most telling criticism of any overly workerist interpretation of Gramsci's concept of organic intellectuals –

the specialised or 'organic' intellectuals of the *ruling class* have a political and directive role in society mainly *because* they operate within the systems that already structure it. The ability of an entrepreneur to be 'an organiser of masses of men ... of the confidence of the investors in his business, of the customers for his product etc.',[33] is a *consequence* rather than the cause of his or her hegemonic and ruling class position. The intellectuals of the working class, by contrast, at best organise *partial aspects* of society, in the interstices allowed by the overarching capitalist system. *Their* passage from specialised to political/directive which involves, in the first instance, the necessarily 'idealist' elaboration of a vision of social order yet to be created, can hardly be envisaged as a normal, automatic affair.

There is thus a basic contradiction between Gramsci's stipulation of the hegemonic role, with its inherently visionary and totalising require-ments, and the widespread interpretation that, in the struggle for socialism, rooted if partial organic intellectuals are the only ones that count. The problem arises, I think, because commentators have counter-poised organic and traditional intellectuals so starkly when, in fact, the real issue is one of whether the intellectuals are close to and can successfully articulate subaltern cultures and concerns, while still fulfil-ling other social-theoretical requirements of their role. And Gramsci was not wrong in his view that this was a matter of some consequence – it was, as we shall see, an issue in the case of the revisionist/social democratic intellectuals. But an exclusive concern with this question, as we shall also see, would occlude other, equally important functions which traditional intellectuals could and did perform in socialism. In fact, given the specialised character of organic intellectuals of both classes it is hard to see what the organic intellectuals would be when they have become 'political and directive' or hegemonic, if not tradition-al intellectuals. While it would be foolish to deny that shop stewards (or management executives) *could* become party philosophers, it would be equally blinkered to ignore the very different functions of the two.

Analysing Traditional Intellectuals in Politics

A working definition of (traditional) intellectuals might now be in order. Gramsci insisted that 'All men are intellectuals ... but not all men have in society the function of intellectuals'. The distinctive character of intellectuals had to be sought not in the intrinsic nature of the activity in which they are engaged – 'mental' as opposed to 'manual' labour – but rather in the 'ensemble of the system of relations in which these activities (and therefore the intellectual groups which personify them) have their place in the general complex of social relations.'[34] However, while this may have been an important caveat against the widespread inclination to fetishize intellectuals, it was hardly a definition. Indeed, definitions of intellectuals are not only notoriously difficult; they inevitably involve at least *some* specification of 'intrinsic intellectual activity'. For present purposes one may arguably say that intellectuals are those who concern themselves with the study of *social* reality: what Perry Anderson called 'culture', meaning 'the culture that is immediately central and internal to any politics ... which provides our fundamental concepts of humanity and society'. Such a definition extends mainly to the social sciences and excludes natural science (which studies nature not society) and creative art (which is not primarily conceptual).[35] Excluding both physics and poetry, such a demarcation of 'culture' has the advantage of being largely coterminous with that of ideology: namely the set of beliefs about society which informs peoples' lives and in which they 'cannot afford to be mistaken'.[36] In contemporary society, one may also say, following Regis Debray, that access to the means of mass communication is vital, 'for it involves the intellectual activity itself, the realisation or non-realisation of its concept as the action of man on man through symbolic communication, a project of influence'.[37] Clearly for Debray, as for Gramsci and many other commentators on intellectual life, true intellectual work is also distinguished by its social engagement. Philosophy is a practico-critical activity; ivory tower reflection, unless it becomes socially relevant at some stage, does not, strictly speaking, belong to the category of intellectual activity.[38]

Intellectuals are then producers of 'culture', the prevalent understandings of society and its organisation; and they are engaged, through the media, in politico-cultural public life. While they may be formally employed in a diversity of professions, they assimilate, elaborate and advance (either sympathetically or critically) the intellectual tradition to which they belong in light of what they see as the important social questions or problems of the day. They can be expected to bring a certain rigour and technical competence to their work. Their theories and visions of social order, provided they have the requisite scope and relevance, can serve as hegemonic theories/ideologies which can (re)-organise and (re)direct either the established order or a movement to replace it. The degree of elaboration and the theoretical backing and coherence of their theories become a crucial factor in determining success or failure in the ideological/intellectual contestation which usually accompanies struggles for hegemony. They also importantly determine the viability and endurance of the hegemonic order which may be established in its terms. Thus, for example, the traditional intellectuals who, in one country after another, 'invaded labour politics', shaped the character, and determined the fate of their 'socialism'.

Several factors independently influence the intellectuals' role in politics. First, the institutional and social conditions in which intellectual life is conducted can have important consequences. For example, repression and exile may impel intellectuals in radical directions while the absorption of intellectuals into the university, on the other hand, has, according to Russell Jacoby, led to a marked decline in the vitality of intellectual life as measured by their degree of engagement with society and politics outside university lecture halls and narrow specialisms.[39] Regis Debray has polemicized against the complicity of the intellectuals in the debasement of intellectual and cultural life which the mass media represents.[40] Conversely contexts of extreme political flux or constraint may also effectively prevent intellectuals from theorising social life. For instance, the left Hegelianism attacked by Marx and Engels in *The German Ideology* must be seen at least partly as a product of the constraints imposed by the German State. And in the Austro-Hungarian Empire at the close of the nineteenth century, the regime effectively prevented the emergence of sociology by censoring and exiling sociologists and patronising a facile intellectual tradition that proved unable to comprehend the conflictual reality of the Empire.[41]

Secondly, the relationship between intellectual production – theories, philosophies, strategies – and their wider politico/economic context cannot be understood by seeing each set of ideas simply as 'expressive' of 'class interests' or as a 'reflection' of social context or forces, although this may sometimes be valid. More often, theories, while more or less reflective of social realities, are more usefully seen as *creative responses* to social problems. This implies that intellectual work, while never simply an *expression* of 'material' social processes, must be *relevant* to them.[42] It is through their ability to propose resolutions to social or political problems that these theories become acceptable to social forces.

At the same time, it is also important to remember that intellectual traditions largely determine how any social problem will be formulated and its resolution attempted. That is to say, theories can be responses to their contexts, but they are formulated on a pre-given conceptual terrain and new theoretical departures are constrained by this.[43] While such philosophical traditions may offer 'greater logical rigour and greater coherence', as Gramsci pointed out, that can impart technical effectiveness to a theory as an instrument of hegemony, any given tradition has internal limits and some social and political problems may prove insoluble within its terms. Subjection to the discipline of a tradition also increases the distance of intellectuals from the social forces that are likely to be instrumental in the realisation of their prescriptions.

The practical significance of all this is that socialism in Europe was formulated by intellectuals as a critical intellectual response to the development of capitalism and the working class, and did not arise out of those developments in any 'indissoluble real process'.[44] In the case of Britain, while such a socialism proved effective in realising many of the political aims of the working class (in the Keynesian welfare state), it also remained statist and bureaucratic, and was in important ways divorced from the traditions of the same working class, to its great ultimate cost.

Finally, accounting for the political ascendancy of intellectuals (usually individuals or groups) by tracing their association with political forces in the wider context of the social problems confronted is a central concern. For example, the rise of the New Right intellectuals in the context of the crisis of social democracy in Britain in the 1970s cannot be understood apart from their links, in the initial period of their ascendancy, with certain prominent financial journalists, and soon thereafter with a particular faction of the Conservative party.[45] In the same way, while the distinctive nature of the political links that tied the social democratic and New Liberal intellectuals to the Labour Party is a central theme of the next chapter, we may now trace the parameters of the relationship of intellectuals to European socialism generally.

Traditional Intellectuals and Socialism

Contemporary 'traditional intellectuals' and their intellectual tradition have their origins in the Enlightenment, when a new stratum of secular intellectuals emerged in the context of the disintegrative social processes generated by the earliest developments of capitalism. As capitalism penetrated deeper into society, eroding its traditional social structures, the new intellectuals contested their organizing philosophies and legit-imation and set about the creation of the modern political, legal and social order. In each society the process was different, and produced nationally specific intellectual traditions. The scale of the social disloc-ations that accompanied the advent of capitalism and industry have, for example, been seen as determining something of the scope, ambition and radicalism of the intellectual responses they necessitated.[46]

The bourgeoisie and the intellectuals emerged together, with similar critical and destructive stances towards the legacy of feudalism; Mann-heim even considered the new intellectuals as a wing of the ascending bourgeoisie, 'whose only capital consisted of education'.[47] Yet while the development of capitalism created the necessary social space (in terms of a secularised intellectual life) for the development of the Enlighten-ment tradition of thought, and while for a time the thought of these new traditional intellectuals served the purposes of a revolutionary bourgeoisie, the origins and dynamic of the Enlightenment were at least as rooted in the thought of classical antiquity as in the material interests of capital.[48]

Nevertheless, the new secular intellectuals' critical stance towards traditional society, and their project for the reconstruction of society on the basis of reason, were identified at this juncture with the initial revolutionary impact of capitalism. The main force of the attack was directed at superstition and tradition-bound ways of life, which were to be replaced by a rational universal (or at least national) administrative, legal and educational order. This political project was served well by the emerging intellectual tradition whose fundamental tendency, in the words of one of its greatest historians, was

> not to observe life and portray it in terms of reflective thought. This philo-sophy believe[d] rather in an original spontaneity of thought; it attribute[d] to thought not merely an imitative function, *but the power and task of shaping life itself.* Thought consist[ed] not only in analysing and dissecting, but in actually bringing about that order of things which it conceive[d] as necessary, so that by this act of fulfilment, it [might] demonstrate its own reality and truth.[49]

To these intellectuals political power was thus not an extraneous and corrupting influence. Rather, access to political power was an integral part of the Enlightenment project, as evinced by the relationship of the *ideologues* to the French Revolution[50] – de Tocqueville saw it as 'one of the vastest and most catastrophic revolutions the world had ever known ... under the auspices of reason and by its efficacy alone'[51] – or by Bentham's assiduous epistles to various European monarchs: 'the topical relevances of their philosophy were determined solely by one motiva-tional relevance: that of societal transformation.'[52] What Michels later said of the relationship of Marxist intellectuals to the European labour movement could equally have been said of the historical relationship of these intellectuals to the ascendant bourgeoisie: '[They] intellectualised [it], endowing [its] interests with ethical aspects of a universal cultural movement, and made it conscious of a 'scientific function' – bearing the germ of a new society'.[53] But the initially emancipatory impact of Enlightenment intellectual strategies, as harnessed by the rising bour-geoisie, altered when the bourgeoisie became dominant. Whereas the early Enlightenment had represented a unity of abstract, 'scientific' positive and socially grounded critical tendencies,[54] now the two separ-ated as the positive social science inaugurated by Comte and Saint-Simon parted company with the critical legacy. (Only in Marx, the Enlightenment's truest heir, was a tension – at times uneasy – between the two retained.) And it was this largely positivist tradition, more than Marxism, that working-class movements inherited.

The relationship between traditional intellectuals and the movement of the emerging working class and socialism must be understood in the context of three factors. The first is the distinctive location of late nineteenth century intellectuals in their respective societies. By this period, wider political trends had radically changed the situation of intellectuals and divided them. The expanding absolutist-bureaucratic state began to need university graduates to run its proliferating administrative apparatus. Increasing numbers of educated people were employed by the state. However, the processes of higher education had already attained a dynamic independent of any functionally defined requirements of capitalist society and the production of graduates soon tended to outstrip their absorption into the state. Michels noted that '[f]rom the standpoint of the political state there are two main groups of intellectuals; those who have obtained [government] places and those who have unsuccessfully tried to do so.'[55] A consequence of this was the bifurcation of intellectual life in Europe into left and right wings.[56] This occurred with distinct national variations. In France, Germany and Italy conservative and progressive/socialist intellectuals seem to have been rather evenly ranged against each other. In Tsarist Russia, with its backwardness and absolutism, the intellectuals were clearly concentrated in oppositional roles. England, whose 'peculiarities' are the subject of the next chapter, 'underproduced' its intellectuals and witnessed a different, more accommodative development.[57] Here, while conservatism remained largely unintellectual, the principal intellectual tradition tended to be progressive and critical, but not radically oppositional. Historically it functioned to incorporate the working class into the existing political system.

Secondly, the distance of many intellectuals from the state, as well as their critique of the general direction of social development, led to the generation of various theories critical of it – chiefly Romanticism, both conservative and radical, and the varieties of Socialism. Socialist elements were, of course, already built into the Enlightenment vision of a transformed society – elements which undoubtedly influenced Marx. The socialism of Saint-Simon, a *déclassé* bohemian, called for a government of social 'scientists' and was an extreme-positivist variant of the Enlightenment ambition to re-cast society along rational principles. The rationalistic socialisms of many of these intellectuals did not necessarily posit the working class as socialism's political agent – that was distinctive of Marx's synthesis. More often than not, their socialism was not so much an instrument of proletarian emancipation as the intellectuals' abstractly and rationalistically conceived cure for the inhumanity and irrationality of capitalism: a rather statist/technocratic project of which Fabian Socialism in England was a notable example. On the continent, the relationship of Marxism to working-class movements tended to draw attention away from these independent intellectuals' version of socialism to which, in fact, many of Europe's most prominent intellectuals of the time adhered. Durkheim's sympathies, for example, were with a socialism which would attempt to 'combat ... the dispersive tendencies engendered by the practice of industrialisation' and where 'the industrial forces are grouped around centres of influence which regulate their cooperation'.[58] The link between such a conception of socialism and the emerging working-class movements of Europe, while firmly entrenched in certain sectors, was often tenuous.

> [T]he labour movement, though often allied with socialism, has remained distinct from it to this day and it [has] proved by no means easy for socialists to establish in the workers' world spheres of influence in which their creed is accepted as a matter of course ... the labour movement is not essentially socialist, just as socialism is not necessarily labourite or proletarian.[59]

The emergence of the organised working class constitutes the third factor. Organisations of the working class stood in need of intellectual and organisational assistance and the practical relationship to it of the traditional intellectuals helped to define their socialism. Schumpeter's account of the link between the parties of the working class and the traditional intellectuals is also corroborated by later investigations of the Marxism of the Second International;[60] and Kautsky, a self-conscious traditional intellectual, was very blunt about it, as the passage made famous by Lenin reminds us:

> Of course socialism as a doctrine has its roots in modern economic relation-ships just as the class struggle of the proletariat has, and, like the latter, emerges from the struggle against capitalist-created poverty and misery of the masses. But socialism and the class struggle arise side by side and not one out of the other; each arises under different conditions. Modern socialist consciousness can only arise on the basis of profound scientific knowledge. ... The vehicle of science is not the proletariat but the *bourgeois intelligentsia*: it was in the minds of the individual members of this stratum that modern socialism originated. ... The socialist consciousness is something introduced into the proletarian class struggle from without [*von Aussen Hineingetragenes*] and not something that arose within it spontaneously [*urwuechsig*].[61]

Eventually, after the Second World War, many European parties of the working class came to power. Their socialism now had to be put to the test in societies in need of large scale restructuring, and in such a way as to meet expectations developed by several decades of propaganda and the hopes aroused during the privations and efforts of the war: and in meeting this challenge the role of intellectuals was crucial.[62] In Britain, the recognition of the role played by intellectuals in the manage-ment of the war, and the wartime experience of planning, served both to increase the prestige of intellectuals and to give them a foretaste of the task to come.[63] Intellectuals seemed once again to have the sort of opportunity to recast whole societies that de Tocqueville had recorded with such foreboding a century and a half earlier. Their brand of socialism – technocratic, positivistic and rationalistic – though lamented by some conservative figures as 'technologico-Benthamism'[64] or by alarmist ones as even a new 'road to serfdom'[65] – was soon to become an orthodoxy. The quarter century of the immediate post-war period can fairly be characterised as the apogee of the role of the traditional intellectual, the manifestation of which in Britain was the influence on the British Labour Party, and through it on British society, of the 'revisionists'.

By the late 1960s, however, the particular economic strategy advocated by the traditional intellectuals based in the working-class movement, the 'social democrats', had become problematic. While its economic shortcomings had their own political and ideological repercussions, by then too, the inability of their strategy of social management as primarily embodied in the welfare state, conceived independently of working-class input and consequently unable to inspire its loyalty, was also seen as failing, as harming and even as victimising some of its intended beneficiaries. However, while the exhausted strategy of socialism needed to be replaced by a new more viable one, intellectuals seemed unable to respond with a new philosophy or project of progressive, if not socialist, advance. Instead they seemed in the grip of a wider, politically immobilising malaise of intellectual life.

Contemporary literature on intellectual life indicates that the symptoms of crisis pervade it. A list of these symptoms, culled from various writers, would include the institutionalisation of intellectual life in the Academy, its consequent isolation from wider social currents and its attendant disciplinary specialisation; the domination of intellectual life by the media; the substitution of market-driven decisions for any independent judgement intellectuals have had in culture and politics; and the replacement of a generally educated public, interested in social and political ideas, by a plurality of more specialised and disparate audiences.[66] Whatever the differences in emphasis, most writers speak of a general decline in the quality of intellectual life and comment on the increasing inability of intellectuals to fulfil their former social role.

Regis Debray identifies what he calls the 'media cycle' in the development of French intellectuals. By a 'cycle' he seems to mean a span of time during which a particular set of institutions, the 'physical organs' through which the 'spirit' of intellectual activity expresses itself, defines the latter's character and scope. In the two previous cycles, the university cycle and the publishing cycle, the intellectuals were able to maintain a semblance of independence (though the pressures on authors in the publishing cycle could already be seen to 'corrupt' their traditional independence). In the most recent cycle, the media cycle, however, the media impose their own logic and rhythms on intellectual life, 'atomising' its once dense social milieu and breaking down its 'evaluative norms and its scale of values'. 'This removal of constraints has two aspects: the product becomes insipid, but the producers are given a new lease of life. It is always easier for a professional to seduce amateurs than his colleagues.'[67] Given the combination of lucrative inducements and trivialising tendencies in the media, the intellectuals become complicit in the impoverishment and possibly the death of intellectual life.

No similar prominence is, of course, accorded to intellectuals by the media in the United States, but an analysis of the decline of intellectual life in that country offered by Russell Jacoby lamented the passing of the 'last' generation of public intellectuals: 'writers and thinkers who address a general and educated audience'.[68] Writing in 1987, he cast around for the 'younger intellectuals' (around forty-five years of age) and found few of them. The increased specialisation and academicisation of intellectuals and the increased bureaucratic requirement for trained professionals, while leading in some sense to an expansion of the educated public, seemed to have stunted intellectual life; instead of making wide-ranging contributions to public debate, highly intelligent people now write for specialised publics. 'This is a danger and a threat; the public culture relies on a dwindling band of older intellectuals who command the vernacular that is slipping out of reach of their successors'.[69]

Intellectual historian H. Stuart Hughes focuses on wider changes in society for his diagnosis of the malaise. Whereas for most of the century it was possible to agree on what were the dominant themes and who were leading figures in intellectual life, across its proliferating disciplines, (an enterprise at which Hughes' own energies had been fruitfully directed), any such consensus had now vanished. Canons of intellectual worth and rigour had been challenged, destroying the very notion of social thought and any possibility of an intellectual role:

> Battered by two world wars, forever collapsing and reviving, 'bourgeois' society offered the subject matter for writers who enjoyed a privileged status within it, even when they proclaimed the goal of shaking it to its foundations. Little by little the society that lent itself to majestic generalisations has fragmented. With the process of fragmentation the intellectual in the old sense has become obsolete. A society of specialists – a society defined by rigorous, often mutually incomprehensible technical competences – is mirrored in an academic world of sharply demarcated 'disciplines'; it has little room for the unattached, the free-floating, the *freischwebend* mind. We may take the death of Herbert Marcuse in 1979 and of Jean-Paul Sartre less than a year later as symptomatic. Their successors are few.[70]

If traditional intellectuals had suffered a decline, according to Hughes, they were now replaced by what he called 'sophisticated rebels', who had learned to pursue limited goals within a vast system whose capacity to absorb and defuse attacks on it became all too clear from the bitter experience of the events of 1968.

Hitherto socialism had been centrally shaped by the role of intellectuals and such a crisis of the intellectual role has implications for any democratic and therefore necessarily hegemonic left strategy for its renewal, or for another emancipatory project to replace it. As we have seen, hegemony involves direction as well as consent and the role of intellectuals is central. While, based on his complex and social understanding of the politics of knowledge and culture, Gramsci attempted to theorise a more democratic and rooted 'organic' intellectual whose relationship with her class of origin would be mutual and who would more appropriately play the intellectual role in a working-class struggle for hegemony, this organic intellectual was not the complete antithesis of the traditional. Gramsci expected organic intellectuals to perform the tasks usually performed by traditional intellectuals as well. In any case, while the question of the relationship of intellectuals to their constituency – of the politics of knowledge and culture – was important, historically, the intellectual role in European socialism tended to be played by those we would more easily recognise as traditional intellectuals. They came over to the cause of the working class in greater or smaller numbers in the late nineteenth century in Europe as intellectuals divided into conservative and critical wings. And the particular path British traditional intellectuals trod towards the politics of the working class, and the intellectual resources they brought with them, is the subject of the next chapter.

Notes

1. Stuart Hall, 'The Problem of Ideology – Marxism Without Guarantees', in Betty Matthews (ed) *Marx-100 Years On,* Lawrence and Wishart, London, 1979, p 59.

2. For example, in a recent debate on ideology, with Ernesto Laclau and Chantal Mouffe on the one side and Ellen Meiksens Wood on the other, both sides accused the other of intellectual elitism while neither party acknowledged the actual role of intellectuals in socialist strategy, however delimited and demystified. See Ernesto Laclau and Chantal Mouffe, *Hegemony and Socialist Strategy,* Verso, London, 1985; and Ellen Meiksens Wood, *The Retreat from Class,* Verso, London, 1986.

3. The most representative among them being, of course, Karl Marx and Frederick Engels, *The German Ideology* and Engels' own *Anti-Duhring.* While it is hard to dispute the complex appreciation of intellectual and cultural matters generally in the works of Marx, such routine accusations of 'idealism' and 'metaphysical thinking' were often read, by later generations of Marxists, as denying any role for intellectuals. The result was a fetishism of 'practice'.

4. Antonio Gramsci, *Selections from the Prison Notebooks,* Tr. Quintin Hoare and Geoffrey Nowell-Smith, Lawrence & Wishart, 1971, p 161.

5. *Ibid,* p 244.

6. Gwyn A. Williams, 'The Concept of "Egemonia" in the Thought of

Antonio Gramsci: Some Notes on Interpretation', *Journal of the History of Ideas*, Volune XXI, Number 4, 1960, p 587.

7. Bob Jessop, 'Accumulation Strategies, State Forms and Hegemonic Projects' in *Kapitalstate* Double Issue 10/11, 1983, pp 118–213.

8. Gramsci, *op. cit.*, p 12.

9. Louis Althusser, 'Ideology and the Ideological State Apparatuses', in *Lenin and Philosophy and Other Essays*, New Left Books, London, 1971.

10. This point cuts at least two ways: while people may reject a number of beliefs which do not accord with their experience, they will also accept many others which they cannot confirm or reject through their own experience. This, however, takes us out of the realm of ideology which must focus on the beliefs which inform people's lives and on which they 'cannot afford to be mistaken' (as Terry Eagleton puts it). Much of my initial insight on this is confirmed in Eagleton's recent book, *Ideology: An Introduction*, Verso, London, 1991.

11. Nicholas Abercrombie, Bryan Turner and Stephen Hill, *The Dominant Ideology Thesis*, London, 1981. It has been argued, for example, that given its culture of self help and dignified independence, large sections of the British working class never fully embraced the principles underlying the welfare state. Their acceptance of it was rather imputed to them by the middle class Fabians, the organisers of the 'consensus'. (David Selbourne, *Against Socialist Illusion: A Radical Argument*, Macmillan, London, 1985.)

12. Göran Therborn, *The Ideology of Power and the Power of Ideology*, New Left Books, London, 1980, p 98.

13. Gramsci, *op.cit.*, p 10.

14. Therborn also rightly differentiates between the operation of ideology upon those who are actively recruited into the organisation of a revolutionary class and upon the subaltern classes. Therborn, *op. cit.*, p 99.

15. Gramsci, *op. cit.*, p 334.

16. Alastair Davidson, *Antonio Gramsci: An Intellectual Biography*, Merlin Press, London, 1977, p 255.

17. Gramsci, *op. cit.*, p 5.

18. *Ibid*, p 6.

19. *Ibid*, p 10.

20. *Ibid*, p 334.

21. There is a strong suggestion in Gramsci that all traditional intellectuals were the organic intellectuals of a formerly dominant class; for example, the 'ecclesiastics' were formerly tied to the landed aristocracy.

22. Antonio Gramsci, *op. cit.*, p 7.

23. *Ibid*, p 6.

24. Carl Boggs, *The Two Revolutions: Antonio Gramsci and the Dilemmas of Western Marxism*, South End Press, Boston, 1984, p 17.

25. Gramsci, *op. cit.*, p 10.

26. *Ibid*, p 347.

27. Gwyn Williams, *op. cit.*, p 587. See also Antonio Gramsci, *op. cit.*, pp 344, 324–5, 345, 347 & 350.

28. Gramsci, *op. cit.*, p 10.

29. In surprising contrast to most current interpretations of Gramsci, he seems to have had a fairly non-partisan view of the established traditions of

intellectual life as evinced in the following: 'The history of philosophy as it is generally understood, that is as the history of philosophers' philosophies, is the history of attempts made and ideological initiatives undertaken by a specific class of people to change, correct or perfect the conceptions of the world that exist in any particular age and thus to change the norms of conduct that go with them; in other words, to change practical activity as a whole.' Gramsci, *op. cit.*, p 344.

30. Joseph Schumpeter, *Capitalism, Socialism and Democracy*, Harper and Row Publishers, New York, 1947, p 154. It was not only 'bourgeois' intellectuals of Schumpeter's ilk who acknowledged this crucial intervention of the intellectuals. Both Kautsky and Lenin did as well.

31. Gramsci, *op. cit.*, p 13.

32. Jonathan Ree questions histories of socialism which are blinkered by preconceived notions of proletarian purity not shared by working-class activists like those who objected the establishment of Ruskin College in 1900. They thought that 'working people ought to be admitted to the university itself, not palmed off with some inferior college up the road. "Oxford and Cambridge" they said, "and other endowed seats of learning, were the rightful inheritance of the people, and ... to attach themselves to any other educational institution would be to give their acquiescence to this deprivation of their rights."' 'Socialism and the Educated Working Class', in Carl Levy (ed), *Socialism and the Intelligentsia: 1880–1914*, Routledge and Kegan Paul, London, 1987, p 216.

33. Gramsci, *op. cit.*, p 5.

34. *Ibid*, pp 8–9.

35. Perry Anderson, 'Components of the National Culture', revised version, *English Questions*, Verso, London, 1992, p 50. First published in *New Left Review*, Number 50, July–August, 1968.

36. See footnote 10 on p 30.

37. Regis Debray, *Teachers, Writers and Celebrities: The Intellectuals of Modern France*, Verso, London, 1981, p 32.

38. This is, of course, an important implication of Gramsci's insistence that intellectual work was not defined by its intrinsic characteristics – mental labour – no matter how brilliant. More recently, Russell Jacoby (*The Last Intellectuals: American Culture in the Age of Academe*, Basic Books, New York, 1987) draws a stark contrast between intellectuals and academics – a distinction which becomes more necessary with the increasingly insular institutionalisation of so much 'mental labour' in the Academy.

39. Russell Jacoby, *op. cit.*

40. Debray, *op.cit.* In his Introduction to it Francis Mulhern traces some interesting, if at first sight unlikely, connections with Leavisite anti-industrial tendencies in Britain (pp xix–xx).

41. John Torrance, 'The Emergence of Sociology in Austria', *European Journal of Sociology*, Volume XVII, Number 2, 1976, pp 185–219.

42. Quite belying popular conceptions of intellectual activity as ivory-tower reflection, at least the prominent intellectual historian, H. Stuart Hughes would define intellectual history as 'the history of the enunciation and development of ideas that eventually inspire ... governing elites'. See his *Consciousness and Society: The Reorientation of European Social Thought, 1890–1930*, Vintage Books, New York,

1977, p 10. Gramsci also postulated a roughly similar relation between philosophy and history: 'One could say that the historical value of a philosophy can be calculated from the 'practical' efficacity it has acquired for itself, understanding 'practical' in the widest sense. If it is true that every philosophy is the expression of a society, it should react back on that society and produce certain effects, both positive and negative. The extent to which precisely it reacts back is the measure of its historical importance, of its not being individual "elucubration" but "historical fact"'. Antonio Gramsci, *op. cit.*, p 10.

43.   '[A] fact peculiar to the very existence of science: it can only pose problems on the terrain and within the horizon of a definite theoretical structure, its problematic, which constitutes its absolute and definite condition of possibility, and hence the absolute determination of *the forms in which all problems must be posed*, at any given moment in the science.' Louis Althusser, *Reading Capital*, New Left Books, London, 1970, p 25.

44.   Raymond Williams, 'Base and Superstructure', *Problems in Materialism and Culture*, Verso, London, 1980, p 81–82.

45.   On the relationship of New Right intellectuals to Thatcherism see my 'Second-Hand Dealers in Ideas: Think-tanks and Thatcherite Hegemony', *New Left Review*, Number 203, January–February 1994, pp 27–64.

46.   Such an assumption clearly underlies Perry Anderson and Tom Nairn's work on the peculiar limitations of British intellectual life.

47.   Karl Mannheim, *Ideology and Utopia*, Harcourt Brace and World Inc., New York, 1936, p 156.

48.   A work which, following Weber, stresses the importance of the classical revival represented by the Renaissance in the evolution of capitalism is Perry Anderson's *Lineages of the Absolutist State*, New Left Books, London, 1974.

49.   Ernst Cassirer, *The Philosophy of the Enlightenment*, Beacon Press, Boston, 1965, p viii.

50.   On the intellectual influence and political role of the *ideologues* in the French Revolution see Charles Van Duzer, *The Contribution of the Ideologues to French Revolutionary Thought*, Johns Hopkins Press, Baltimore, 1935.

51.   *The Old Régime and the French Revolution*, Doubleday and Co, New York, 1955, pp 143–144.

52.   Zygmunt Bauman, *Legislators and Interpreters*, Polity Press, Cambridge, 1987, p 101.

53.   Roberto Michels, *Political Parties: A Sociological Study of the Oligarchic Tendencies of Modern Democracy*, The Free Press, New York, 1960, p 123.

54.   Irving Zeitlin, *Ideology and the Development of Social Theory*, Prentice-Hall, Englewood Cliffs, N.J., 1968, p 5.

55.   Roberto Michels, 'The Intellectuals', *Encyclopaedia of the Social Sciences*, Volume III, Macmillan, London, 1932, p 120.

56.   Schumpeter, *op. cit.*, p 145.

57.   Tom Nairn, 'The English Literary Intelligentsia', in Emma Tennant (ed), *Bananas*, Quartet Books, London, 1977.

58.   Quoted in Steven Lukes, *Emile Durkheim: His Life and Work*, Penguin, Harmondsworth, 1973, p 246.

59.   Schumpeter, *op. cit.*, p 310. For an excellent historical survey and assessment of the often tenuous relationship of the working class and socialist ideas in

Britain, see James Hinton, *Labourism and Socialism*, Wheatsheaf Books, Brighton, 1983.
60. Karl Mannheim views it in not dissimilar terms. See *op. cit.*, pp 159–160.
61. Karl Kautsky on the draft programme of the Austrian Social-Democratic Party, quoted by Lenin, *op. cit.*, p 382.
62. The Americans anticipated this and made attempts to ensure the allegiance of Europe's intellectuals through the hegemony of the (CIA-financed) Congress for Cultural Freedom (on which more in Chapter Five).
63. Paul Addison, *The Road to 1945*, Jonathan Cape, London, 1975, pp 164–189.
64. F.R. Leavis, quoted in Tom Nairn, *op. cit.*, p 73.
65. Title of Friedrich Hayek's 1944 tract which sounded the alarm at the rising tide of 'collectivism'.
66. *Cf.* Jacoby, *op.cit.*; Debray *op.cit*; H. Stuart Hughes, *Sophisticated Rebels*, Harvard University Press, Cambridge, Mass., 1988; Allan Bloom, *The Closing of the American Mind*, Simon and Schuster, New York, 1983.
67. Regis Debray, *op. cit*, p 81.
68. Russell Jacoby, *op.cit.*, p 5.
69. *Ibid*, p 1–2.
70. H. Stuart Hughes, *op. cit.*, p 1–2.

3

Intellectuals and the Labour Party: An Historical Perspective

The attachment of British traditional intellectuals to the party of the world's first industrial proletariat, and the nature of the socialist theory they imparted to it, must be traced from the broader evolution of English culture or intellectual life which represents a variation on the European pattern. The most distinctive feature of modern English society – its unintellectualism – can be traced back to its founding moment: England's early bourgeois revolution had been Europe's 'most mediated and least pure'. Fought out within classes, both aristocratic and capitalist (rather than between them), and in terms of religious idioms and ideologies, its immediate result was the hegemony of aristo-cratic-agrarian-capitalist interests. The new capitalist class was the already ruling aristocracy: 'the revolution transformed the roles but not the personnel of the ruling class'.[1] Representing such a continuity of domination, rather than real social rupture, and pre-dating the mould-setting Enlightenment in Europe, the English Civil War left no signifi-cant intellectual legacy (its most radical doctrine – Puritanism – had been a religious one).

This pristine unintellectualism became, however, entrenched and self-conscious only in the process of defusing the later challenge of the only rationalist intellectual system to achieve prominence in Britain's modern evolution – Jeremy Bentham's Utilitarianism. A product of the Scottish Enlightenment, it failed to become a hegemonic ideology. Not the least reason for this was the timing and character of its chief historical agent, the industrial bourgeoisie. Its emergence under the shadow of a powerful pre-existing capitalist class coincided with the French Revolution, and rather than claiming political and cultural autonomy it cleaved to the aristocracy. As a result, Britain's ruling class evolved as an amalgam of a bourgeoisified aristocracy and a gentrified bourgeoisie. Its cultural hegemony, which was strong and tenacious, retained several markedly pre-capitalist features:

> [I]t never generated a revolutionary ideology, like that of the Enlightenment. Its thinkers were confined by the cramped horizons of their class. ... they

failed to create any general theory of society, or any philosophical synthesis of compelling dimensions ... The hegemonic ideology of this society was a much more aristocratic combination of 'traditionalism' and 'empiricism', intensely hierarchical in its emphasis, which accurately reiterated the history of the dominant agrarian class.[2]

Thus the absence of a political and social revolution in the period of capitalist industrialisation meant that in English society, in contrast to the rest of Europe, the role of intellectuals never became central. Intellectual life, which flowered in the revolutionary dislocations which accompanied the arrival of capitalism in Europe, was stifled and stunted by the staid continuities of English society. However, while the hegemonic conservative political tradition remained self-consciously unintellectual, the principal intellectual tradition was allied to successive critical tendencies in British politics – from Philosophic Radicalism to the Liberal Party and eventually the Labour Party. The character of this intellectual tradition which was thus inherited by Labour, however, was also distinctive, not to say deficient. Shorn of Benthamite theoretical ambition, it became assimilated into British political and intellectual life in a characteristically 'empirical', untheoretical and un-revolutionary manner. The ambitions of social theory, as of social action, remained modest, and 'totalising' forms of thought were eschewed. The effects of such an intellectual wherewithal were only compounded by the intellectuals' comfortable accommodation with the ruling order: as several scholars have noted, England, unlike the continental European countries, did not 'overproduce' intellectuals, and unlike the 'bifurcations' of intellectual life that occurred on the continent towards the end of the nineteenth century, the main intellectual tradition in Britain eventually became attached to the Labour Party. Moreover, its final attachment to Labour with the sudden decline of the Liberal Party after the Great War was the political incarnation of a previous intellectual shift: in the form of New Liberalism and Fabianism, it veered almost in its entirety slightly but significantly to the left. While this meant, on the one hand, that Labour's intellectual wherewithal was reformist, its empiricism, and the resulting research and documentation with which the traditional intellectuals backed their programme for the Labour Party did more than anything else to ensure its success. This distinctive trajectory reached full fruition when, after the Second World War, Labour indisputably held the credentials of the 'thinking man's party', as opposed to the then still predominantly unintellectual Conservative Party (the 'stupid party').

This chapter seeks to trace these antecedents of the traditional intellectuals of the Labour Party in the 1950s and 1960s, the revisionists – who, redefined as the 'social democrats' in the 1970s, left the Labour Party to form the Social Democratic Party. The historical continuities of this intellectual tradition are manifest not only in their thought but also in the role they aspired to play in the party, and – not least – in the conditions which governed their relationship with it. These conditions were, roughly, that the Labour Party should accept them as its sole intellectual mentors, and that it should remain essentially a 'bourgeois party of reform'.[3] Never met fully satisfactorily, from the 1970s onwards these conditions ceased to apply almost completely. And this, as we will see, was the root cause of the 1981 split which led to the formation of the SDP.

Challenge to Unintellectualism

In the context of Britain's first crisis of modernisation the upheavals of industrial development threw up political movements for the reform of archaic institutions and privileges. They never achieved political or intellectual coherence and were supported by very diverse social forces: their ideas were likewise derived from sources as disparate as the Bible, the theory of natural rights, and Anglo-Saxon institutions of customary rights. But among these Jeremy Bentham's Utilitarianism achieved the greatest critical elaboration, and best encapsulated and systematised bourgeois demands for reform.

Bentham, 'the great questioner of things established'[4], attacked the archaic nature and corruption of British state institutions, and the 'fallacies' which justified them, in the name of 'utility', a concept borrowed from Helvetius and the *Philosophes*. Bentham's highly abstract and rationalistic philosophy was reflected in systematic treatises on the reorganisation of society, its laws and institutions, on the basis of rationalism and utility – a radical Enlightenment intellectual project if ever there was one. In his own lifetime he exerted an international influence – well-known and admired in European intellectual circles and the philosopher of choice in South American essays in constitution-making. The trajectory his ideas traced in Britain, however, is worth pondering; it is widely held that the annals of nineteenth century reform legislation and administration contain few laws and initiatives which cannot be traced to Bentham's influence, yet Utilitarianism never became a hegemonic ideology.

Politically unsuccessful for most of his life, Bentham's largely posthumous influence is traced to the circle which formed around him late in his life (after he was sixty). In the pervasive reaction which followed the French Revolution, Bentham sought and found a new constituency among the Philosophic Radicals and the new intellectual element in the Whig Party drawn from the professions, especially graduates of the Scottish universities. But the Philosophic Radicals failed to become an independent third force in Parliament after the passage of the Reform

Act in 1832; the newly enfranchised middle-class electorate proved to have no appetite for further instalments of reform, especially in face of the Chartist upsurge. By 1840, the Philosophic Radicals had all but dispersed and with it scattered any hope that Utilitarianism might become a hegemonic ideology.

Perry Anderson attributes Utilitarianism's failure to gain acceptance as a hegemonic ideology to its 'intrinsic limitations: its fatally bleak materialism *ipso facto* precluded it from creating that cultural and value system which is a mark of a hegemonic ideology.'[5] Or as J.S. Mill memorably put it, 'no one, probably, who in a highly instructed age, ever attempted to give a rule to all human conduct, set out with a more limited conception of the agencies by which either human conduct *is*, or of those by which it *should* be influenced.'[6, 7] Yet what is striking, in retrospect, is how often Bentham's *system* was rejected even by his own disciples; and it seems likely that this owed as much to the unreceptive atmosphere in which both Bentham and his disciples worked, as to any intrinsic limitations of his thought. Bentham was isolated for most of his life precisely because there did not exist a significant political or intellectual constituency which would respond sympathetically to, let alone actively seek to realise, his system (or any other). Later on his circle did contain some of the greatest intellectuals and radical politicians of the time, including James and John Stuart Mill, Macaulay, John and Sarah Austin, Samuel Romilly and Francis Place. However, their intellectual link to Bentham was at best incomplete and their political aims discrete and diminutive in comparison with his systematic ones. His disciples were an instrument, but one that decisively altered the product. They rejected his system while retaining what they saw to be his method, above all his rigour and attention to detail. These were then held up as his distinctive contribution.[8]

Bentham was also unfortunate in his timing. His was an eighteenth century rationalism which came too late for England's early bourgeois revolution, but was then later harnessed to remove some of its deficiencies. This task proved awkward, however, as its rationalism struck a strange note in the age of romanticism. When the younger Mill encountered romanticism, he was overwhelmed, as were other Utilitarians. Indeed, as William Thomas points out, 'they did not put up a fight'.[9] Romanticism then served Mill and others to point up Bentham's personal and philosophical peculiarities.

Above all, Utilitarianism never became a hegemonic ideology, because the industrial bourgeoisie, its most affinal social force, never became a ruling class in its own right and name. The newly reformed Parliament of the 1830s and 40s was unresponsive to further reforming ambitions. In glorifying pastoral values primarily associated with the aristocracy and gentry, Romanticism reinforced their hegemony and subordinated the industrial bourgeoisie. The threat of the Chartist unrest from below, made more ominous by the resonance in it of continental revolutionary ambitions, became another reason for the new bourgeoisie to accept the political status quo.[10]

Thus by the close of the 1830s the independent influence of the Philosophic Radicals, as also any hope of a Utilitarian hegemony, came to an end. Bentham had died in 1832, James Mill in 1836. The effort to form a coherent party of the Philosophic Radicals was judged in retrospect by J.S. Mill, as having been 'from the first chimerical: partly because the time was unpropitious, the Reform fervour being in its period of ebb and Tory influences powerfully rallying; but still more because, as Austin so truly said, "the country did not contain the men"'.[11] The younger Mill, wavering between Utilitarianism and Romanticism, had already rejected some of Bentham's doctrines. But, more importantly, he also wanted to shed Utilitarianism's sectarian image and to bring it into the mainstream of English politics. As the new editor of the once radical *Westminster Review* he reformulated its aims:

> The review ought to represent not Radicalism but Neo-Radicalism, a Radicalism which is not democracy, not a bigoted adherence to any form of government or one kind of institution, and which is to be called Radicalism, inasmuch as it does not palter nor compromise with evils, but cuts at their roots – and a Utilitarianism which never makes a peculiar figure as such, nor would even constitute its followers a sect or a school.[12]

In this diluted, denatured, and anxiously respectable form, the ideas and method of Jeremy Bentham were thus made serviceable to the needs of English society for piecemeal social reform. Philosophic Radicalism merged with other elements such as the Peelites and Free-traders into English Liberalism during the long mid-Victorian period of prosperity that followed. This was accompanied by a marked intellectual shift. Utilitarianism, as Elie Halevy has pointed out, had contained within itself a fundamental ambiguity between an interventionist and non-interventionist aspect. Now the tension was dropped in favour of a one sided emphasis on *laissez faire*:

> [There] developed in England, twenty years after Bentham's death, a new and simplified form of the Utilitarian philosophy. Disciples of Adam Smith much more than of Bentham, the Utilitarians did not now include in their doctrine the principles of the artificial identification of interests, that is, the governmental or administrative idea; the idea of free trade and of the spontaneous identification of interests summed up the social conceptions of these doctrinaires, who were hostile to any kind of regulation and law: after the 'Westminster philosophy', as the doctrine of the parliamentary Radicals and the agitators of Charing Cross had been called, it was the 'Manchester philosophy' which triumphed.[13]

This led to a decisive narrowing of the scope of the doctrine and a corresponding diminution of its political ambition. The fabled influence of Bentham on nineteenth century legislation is usually seen as a product of pressure and advocacy by the many followers of Bentham in parliament or the administration. This, however, exaggerates its public profile. More often (as in the cases of civil service reform and the reform of the ancient universities discussed below) it took the form of a pre-emptive, piecemeal and surreptitious appropriation of Benthamite ideas and themes by an unintellectual but canny ruling class. Deprived of public recognition, Utilitarianism was sequestered, reduced almost to a style. It imparted 'a certain toughness of mind, a fearless hard-hitting logic ... it was prized by a later generation who wanted to deal with specific problems rather than construct society anew'.[14] We can see this style re-emerging later in the approach of the Fabians.

The political triumph of the ruling class over the radical forces strengthened and finally set the untheoretical, empirical mould of British intellectual life, and of the accompanying pursuit of piecemeal social reform in political life. Both were now inoculated against 'the ruinous contagion of Europe – general ideas'.[15] After its triumph over the radical agitation, British society almost seemed to defy fundamental questioning. Its intellectuals never again sought to 'put society as a whole into question'.[16] However, as Stokes noted, Utilitarianism, and such political influence as it wielded, looks, in retrospect, more impressive than anything that followed – and more impressive perhaps than later synoptic assessments such as Anderson's allowed.[17]

Institutional Consolidation of Modern British Culture

With the systematic political ambitions of Utilitarianism thus smothered, the unintellectual set of British culture and politics was institutionalised at mid-century in the recasting of two key institutions: the civil service and the universities. While Benthamite reformist pressure from without provided some of the initial impulse in both cases, the changes were actually carried out from within under the intellectual influence of Bentham's philosophical antithesis, Coleridge.

Within Britain's ruling institutions Coleridge's influence was as widespread as Bentham's was circumscribed. Bentham had questioned society and its institutions and sought to reform them according to a systematic philosophy; Coleridge sought to discover the wisdom of existing institutions and to maintain a balance between 'permanence' and 'progress'. Most of his philosophy derived from contemporary Idealist German philosophers and he gave England the equivalent of the continental Romantic reaction against the Enlightenment. J.S. Mill's contrast of Coleridge with Bentham is well-known:

the Germano-Coleridgian doctrine is, in our view of the matter, the result of
... a reaction [to Benthamite, rationalist Utilitarianism]. It expresses the revolt
of the human mind against the philosophy of the eighteenth century. It is
ontological, because that was experimental; conservative, because that was
innovative; religious, because so much of that was infidel; concrete and historical, because that was abstract and metaphysical; poetical, because that
was matter-of-fact and prosaic.[18]

The Romantics pointed to the poverty of the conception of human
nature that underlay rationalist philosophy, and focused instead on the
intangible imaginative/poetic aspects of life and society. In England, at
least, this was a key moment in the emergence of a discrete social
sphere, that of 'culture', which now housed these finer elements, and
whose contours and location on the socio-cultural terrain Raymond
Williams so intricately mapped.[19] Romanticism represented a critique
of one-sided rationalism; but instead of strengthening the latter's critical
and transformative potential it set up moral and intellectual activity as
a 'court of human appeal to be set over the processes of practical social
judgement ...'[20] thus blunting any this-worldly critical edge it may have
had. It became, as well, the champion of an idealised historical continuity and unity of a society being disrupted by industrialisation and
riven by sharp new divisions of class. In this it facilitated the continued
hegemonic domination of the aristocratic-gentry culture and its values
– an idealised organic community, pastoralism, anti-industrialism, anti-
urbanism, anti-commercialism – and cast an unflattering light on the
practical and utilitarian ones of the middle classes. In this encounter,
Benthamism was defeated and denatured.

Coleridgean Romanticism also served the continuity of hegemonic
dominance of the ruling class by adroitly shifting the weight of its
legitimacy onto a new basis – no longer birth but what came to be
known as 'cultivation'. Under the new cultural dispensation its meaning
also altered slightly: 'What in the eighteenth century had been an ideal
of personality – a personal qualification for participation in polite society
– had now, in the face of radical change, to be redefined, as a condition
on which society as a whole depended. ... Against mechanism, the
amassing of fortunes and the proposition of utility as the source of value,
it offered a different and a superior social idea.'[21] Coleridge's predictably
anti-democratic approach to the problem of modern governance lay in
the creation of a 'clerisy', a secular rather than theological National
Church, composed of 'cultivated' men who would ensure both continuity
and (limited) progress. A clerisy would be 'a morally and religiously
sound clergy and aristocracy to serve as a cultural elite that would
restore the community of England.'[22] The express purpose of the reform
of the universities was to turn out 'cultivated' members of the clerisy, and
the purpose of the reformed civil service was to receive and deploy them.

There is a still-vigorous folklore about the Northcote-Trevelyan reforms of the civil service (originating in the 1854 Report but not implemented until 1870). Lord (Noel) Annan, a leading romancer of the British intellectual tradition, celebrates them as the 'Bill of Rights' of Britain's intellectuals.[23] And indeed, they have been regarded by both admirers and critics as the founding moment of a modern civil service of scholar-bureaucrats who proved capable of adapting the institutions of government to its vastly expanded functions in the twentieth century. There is also strong agreement in tracing this to the influence of Benthamism. However, as Peter Gowan has recently shown, while there was some initial Benthamite impulse towards reform, the actual conception as well as stewardship of the reforms was the work of Coleridgeans.[24] The report's intention as well as its impact had less to do with substantial administrative issues than with re-establishing the access of the gentry (the less well-off sections of the landed ruling class which depended on Church and State for employment) to the state.[25] As a result, the reforms did not produce a new breed of efficient bureaucrats/technocrats. Rather, largely through the efforts of Coleridgeans such as Gladstone and Jowett, the hegemony of the landed ruling class was preserved in the face of their own economic (agrarian) crisis and the extension of the franchise to the propertyless.

The crux of this restoration was to harness civil service entrance exams to the curriculum of Oxford and Cambridge which actually narrowed the social range of recruitment. The principal advocates of reform were the lower ranks of the landed ruling class itself, not the industrial bourgeoisie clamouring for further avenues for material and social advancement. The centrality of Oxford and Cambridge in the education system was maintained, enabling them to furnish the state not so much with modernisers as with preservers of 'order'. And the one place in England which did produce efficient, meritocratic administrators – Haileybury College, the creation of Bentham and James Mill, founded in 1806 to train the higher echelons of Indian Civil Service – was closed.[26]

At the same time, the older universities were reformed. Here too, the initial external Utilitarian pressure was overtaken by an internal Coleridgean initiative. The establishment of the new 'red-brick' universities posed a challenge to the pre-eminence of Oxford and Cambridge in British culture. Their heavily religious curriculum, aimed at producing a clergy and governing elite on the old model, seemed increasingly outdated. The Utilitarians wanted to make the universities more useful national institutions, directly applying themselves to the needs of business and industry and of social and political progress in general. Dissenters also wanted to loosen the hold of the Church of England on the ancient universities and to end their exclusion from them. The influence and example of the Scottish universities and the newly formed University of London, through journals like *Edinburgh Review* and *Westminster Review*, combined with the demands of the Utilitarians and Dissenters, formed a powerful campaign for reform.

This campaign provoked an internal counter-movement for reform among some dons and students who, inspired by the ideas of Coleridge, wished to reform the universities before the insensitive hands of the state forced a change. The purpose of the reform at Oxford, for the Coleridgeans such as Jowett, the influential master of Balliol College (who was also involved in the Northcote-Trevelyan Report as an 'honorary insider'[27]), was to produce a 'clerisy'. Royal Commissions set up in 1850 and 1852 to recommend changes in Oxford and Cambridge respectively delivered reports much in line with these impulses, with the right balance between teaching and research, clerical and secular learning, and merit and exclusiveness. But the curriculum itself clung even more closely to the newly established but resolutely aristocratic canons of 'cultivation', rather than utility. After the reforms the ancient universities still remained small and exclusive. Moreover, their reputations soared, re-establishing their pre-eminence in British culture and consigning the newer universities, and the values they represented, to a clearly subordinate status. Established mainly by Dissenters and Utilitarians, at Manchester, Birmingham, Liverpool, Leeds, and of course, London, and representing as they did a link with industrial wealth, the newer universities never achieved the status of the older ones. There, if the aristocracy of birth was now slightly diluted by merit and talent, the aristocratic, elitist ethos and the basic structure of society would nevertheless be maintained, and even enhanced.[28]

These reforms in higher education and the civil service consolidated a distinctive pattern of English intellectual life which Lord Annan celebrated: 'the paradox of an intelligentsia which appears to conform rather than rebel against the rest of society'.[29] The dominant cultural tendency became a sort of unsystematic, self-consciously untheoretical, romantic conservatism, opposed to rationalism, to grand theory, and above all to Benthamite ideas: 'For the next hundred years, every poet, novelist and philosopher knew how to do at least one thing: to refute and deride Utilitarianism.'[30]

At the same time this hegemonic culture co-existed, in mid-Victorian Britain, with a middle-class culture which, while no longer entertaining any systematising ambitions, was nevertheless steeped in the values of practicality and utility.[31] These values, the middle classes believed, had been chiefly responsible for their industrial success. Outside the Utilitarian system, however, these ideas took the form of a positive anti-intellectualism. Even science was scorned as a theoretical pursuit. The Victorian middle class ' were of the opinion that science is speculative rubbish; that theory and practice have nothing to do with one another; and that the scientific habit of mind is an impediment rather than an aid in the conduct of ordinary affairs.'[32] Great inventors like Watt, Stephenson, Arkwright and Hargreaves shared these attitudes: their science was simply 'the art of mechanical contrivance', and their education contained no training in mathematics or science.

> When Stephenson was asked how he had invented his machines, especially the locomotive, 'he replied that it was due to a power of imagining and conceiving with the utmost precision the different parts, their forms, sizes and connections, their possible movements ... *and by dint of trying, he hit upon the practical combination*'. This method was contrasted by Taine with that of a genuine scientist like Leon Foucault: *Having one day discovered a proposition of speculative mechanics*, which Huyghens and Lagrange had overlooked, he *worked it out to its final consequences*, and this led him to the idea of his governor.[33]

Certainly there was in Britain little of the (perhaps often exaggerated) continental respect for intellectuals. In fact intellectuals as they have been defined in the last chapter – as producers of social theory – were not prominent on the cultural terrain.[34] The popular cult of practicality alongside the high cultural romanticism meant that more than any abstract treatises it was literature which emerged as the typically more influential cultural product. Indeed, Tom Nairn has argued that the quintessence of Victorian culture can be found not in abstract treatises of social theory but in its novels and essays which could 'evoke the organic continuities of English life by imaginative suggestion'.[35] These evocations worked to express and maintain the hegemony of the composite aristocratic-gentry ruling class as well as serving as the principal, anti-modern point of critique of modern industrial attitudes and culture (rather than industry or capitalism in themselves).

This trait of British culture was usually seen as connected with another: the close connection between writer and reader in Victorian literary life. The works of Victorian literary culture, 'their very lucidity, their determined preference for a common-sense mode of expression and a personalised morality, show someone conversing with other members of a family.'[36] Or as Heyck puts it:

> When Dickens denounced an antiquated part of the administrative system, when Mrs. Gaskell reported the poverty of working-class life, or when Carlyle warned of social revolution, they knew that electors, members of parliament, bureaucrats and industrial magnates would get the message.[37]

Such a cosy relationship with the established sectors of British society hardly allowed for even an illusion of intellectual independence, let alone any objective semblance of it. This close connection – which is indeed celebrated by those (including many on the left) who indulge in a romantic view of the continuity and stability that have characterized

English history – was seen by the Russian Communist Dimitri Mirsky as implying that 'the intellectuals made no attempt to think independently of their class, but rather were proud of belonging to it. In short, there were no intellectuals'.[38] While perhaps these peculiarities of English culture seem all too easy to exaggerate, it seems broadly true that, to a far greater extent than was true in France or Germany, not to mention Russia, in Britain mid-Victorian cultural figures tended to be literary or scientific thus strictly speaking falling outside the sort of intellectual category necessary for a truly hegemonic politics. Moreover, even as such they remained closely tied to the ruling class which was for the great majority their class of origin. They did not, like traditional intellectuals, form a separate social category with an independent institutional structure of its own.[39]

With the maturing of a Northcote-Trevelyan generation by the 1870s, however, this seems to have begun to change; such a social category which articulated its own role in recognisably intellectual terms had begun to emerge.[40] As against the predominantly literary mode of the mid-nineteenth century, these intellectuals now included academics, journalists, administrators, social workers and the like. They formed new institutions and forums of their own like Toynbee Hall, the Fabian Society, the Hampstead Historical Society and journals such as *The Nation*. But this new kind of intellectual nevertheless remained close to the ruling class and, more importantly perhaps, assimilated to its values. The whole point of the reforms at Oxford and Cambridge had been to reinforce at once their social exclusivity and through their pre-eminence, aristocratic-gentry cultural hegemony in English intellectual life. Indeed, in the train of the reforms the deeply ingrained caste-like impulses of British society had produced (and, as we have seen, hardly unintentionally) what Noel Annan called an 'intellectual aristocracy': a set of families, related by intermarriage, which now also produced the 'new professional civil servants'. This network included families from all parts of the now composite ruling class: Clapham Sect, Quaker and other non-conformist families; Church of England families touched with evangelicalism; and Unitarian or Philosophic Radical families, impelled by philanthropy.[41]

> They were the leaders of the new intelligentsia. Stability is not a quality usually associated with an intelligentsia, a term which, Russian in origin, suggests the shifting, shiftless members of revolutionary or literary cliques who have cut themselves adrift from the moorings of family. Yet the English intelligentsia, wedded to gradual reform of accepted institutions and able to move between the worlds of speculation and government, was stable. That it was so – that it was unexcitable and to European minds unexciting – was in part due to the influence of these academic families.[42]

While in the very long run the close ties between intellectuals and the ruling class were gradually diluted by the entrants from more modest backgrounds – more and more of them now tended to be second generation members of a growing professional class: sons and to a far smaller extent, daughters of clergymen, doctors, the lower order of bureaucrats, and the like – this expansion was not yet an 'overproduction'; it did not produce an *alienated* intelligentsia. Rather they were an emergent new stratum of comfortably-off professionals, but with a vantage point sufficiently at variance with that of the ruling class to have a world view independent of the ruling order, and possibly somewhat critical of it. According to Hobsbawm, they were

> sufficiently comfortable not to need to pursue money for material reasons, sufficiently secure in an accepted and respected social rank to be genuinely without envy of the idle rich or the business profiteers, sufficiently interested in their own work to pursue it for its own sake, and sufficiently at one with society to feel themselves to be of social use.[43]

As 'an aristocracy, secure and established like the rest of English society, accustomed to responsible and judicious utterance and sceptical of iconoclastic speculation they shied away from radical, totalising criticisms of the existing order.'[44] This was the intelligentsia which came over to the Labour Party putting the modest empiricist intellectual style at the service of the working class. This did not happen, however, without a notable radicalization of their outlook.

Liberals and Social Democrats

The new intellectuals of the late nineteenth century had inherited a political allegiance to the radical-liberal alliance which had dominated parliament from 1846 to 1874. However, the liberal legacy, a peculiar combination of high-minded principle in international affairs and social quietism at home, seemed increasingly incongruous in the face of the Great Depression. The prevailing unemployment, poverty and squalor, as well as growing working-class organisation, became new concerns. In responding to them, the intellectuals became more critical and more radical. This intellectual evolution, vividly reconstructed by Peter Clarke in his book *Liberals and Social Democrats*, led them from Liberalism to social democracy, and from the Liberal Party to Labour. Such a transition was made, however, not so much by abandoning the intellectual traditions they had inherited, as by elaborating them towards the left, in response to the social problems generated by industrial capitalism. This intellectual shift was a necessary prelude to the later political one from Liberalism to Labour.

It has been widely noted that at a time when similar social and political problems, combined with the political and intellectual challenge posed by Marxism on the continent had led, in one country after another, to the development of sociology as an alternative social theory, Britain produced no major sociology. British society faced, of course, no organised threat from Marxism, which had constituted such an impetus for continental sociology. The Marxist Social Democratic Federation led by Hyndman remained too sectarian, following a conception of class struggle that was too deterministic to allow trade union activity (including the potentially radical New Unionism of the late 1880s) to become infused with a Marxist outlook. On the other hand, the mainly literary and romantic socialism of William Morris also precluded him from playing a leading role in working-class organisation. Of course, deeply rooted forms of socialist belief did play an important role in building up the organisation of the working class: it was the work primarily of activists inspired by socialist ideals.[45] But with the decline of the militant politics of the New Unionism in the 1890s the politics of the working class remained for the time being predominantly tied to the Liberal Party. There were also specifically intellectual factors in the absence of sociology. The nascent sociological strain that could be discerned in British Idealism at this time was never adequately elaborated.[46] Not the least of the complex set of reasons for this was the occupation of the field of specifically *social* theory by an evolutionary socio-biology.

Nevertheless the 'responsible and judicious' British intellect saw the new political task and sought to harness all its native (Liberal and individualist) resources to its fulfilment. The ambiguities of J.S. Mill proved useful, of course. So, more surprisingly, did British Hegelianism. L.T. Hobhouse commended T.H. Green for his practicality and pressed him into the service, if not of a conception of socialism, at least of an empirical, practical and now politically necessary collectivism. His challenge to the theory of natural rights exemplifies the new intellectual reorientation.

> Hobhouse ... proceeded to put his own gloss upon Green's highly abstract statement of the Idealist postulate that only in a society conscious of its common interest can rights exist. 'A right', Hobhouse concluded, 'is nothing but what the good of society makes it. ... If, therefore, any right to any form of property or freedom no longer serves a good social purpose, it must go.'[47]

Such sporadic forays into the sociological realm did not lead to any overarching sociology to justify the new political course, but it did serve to loosen the hold of the deeply entrenched individualism in British culture. And a variety of arguments now emerged to serve the cause of 'collectivism' and interventionism versus individualist *laissez faire* in a series of discrete theoretical advances and interventions.

Contemporary developments in the field of economics were central to this new intellectual turn. In some respects this was even more remarkable. Although the marginalist revolution is usually credited with narrowing the scope of economics and, especially in its Austrian version (much favoured of Thatcherite intellectuals), with having profoundly conservative implications, its British variant led, in Marshall's successor Pigou, to a critique of the distributional consequences of the free market and the development of 'welfare economics'. Thus in Britain, as Elizabeth Durbin has shown, the newly founded micro-economics was used to justify state intervention so as to increase social welfare[48] and the Fabians, who constituted a distinct segment of the new intellectual stratum and who had already examined and rejected Marxism, used it in their theory of 'rents' and 'unearned incomes' to justify socialist goals.[49] This political cross-fertilisation was made possible because it was now clear to many economists that inequalities of wealth and income were larger than could be justified on economic grounds.

Such discrete, theoretically unintegrated critical impulses attacked the irrationality and inhumanity of capitalism. The common aim was to reform it piecemeal into a more rational and humane social order in which inequalities of wealth and incomes would be drastically reduced and democratic rights extended and substantiated, and in which the still marginalised and alienated working class would be integrated into the political system. In a cultural landscape dominated by *laissez-faire* Liberalism, these concerns made a shift from individualist to collectivist thought a 'necessary intellectual adjustment' on the part of the more socially conscious liberal intellectuals.[50] This was the common temper of the New Liberals as well as the Fabians.

> Since liberal theory appeared to be so fully committed to *laissez-faire*...the most obvious course seemed to be to look for alternative justifications for 'collectivism' or 'state interference'. All these would automatically tend to be regarded as 'socialist', a term which, even in 1897, in the words of an intelligent Frenchman close to the Fabians, meant no more than 'any doctrine opposed to *laissez-faire* ... *and* which concedes to society, in whatever form, the right to intervene in the production and above all in the distribution of wealth.'[51]

Despite their intellectual shortcomings and political timidity, the combined effect was the most powerful radical challenge since Chartism. Indeed, their very empiricism was turned into a great asset by the fact-collecting Fabians, who claimed that

> no reasonable person *who knows the facts* can fail to become a socialist, or, at the very least, to be converted to the Socialist policy on any subject or problem presently under discussion ... out of their own mouths, or rather out of their published material, the defenders of capitalism can be made to prove that it is inefficient, brutal and idiotic.[52]

In a culture where Marxism was absent, and where, despite the individual, often autodidactic, socialist commitments of many working-class organisers, the organised working class remained politically subordinated to Liberalism, the intellectual New Liberals and Fabians brought into British politics the only systematic socialism it had.

The new intellectuals were still by and large educated in the only mildly reformed central universities. It is perhaps significant that the only prominent intellectuals of the period who were not products of Oxford and Cambridge (apart from the Irishman, Bernard Shaw) were Sidney and Beatrice Webb (Sidney went to London University and Beatrice was the largely self-taught daughter of an eminent business-man).[53] Given their even greater distance from the gentrified intellectual culture of the time, it is not surprising that the Webbs were also among the first prominent intellectuals of their generation to call themselves socialists. The Fabians differed from the New Liberals in being avowedly inspired by Bentham's rigorous method and iconoclastic stance, and in favouring a far more comprehensive set of statist and collectivist reforms than the New Liberals. They also practised a ruthless empiricist form of critique against all forms of socialist 'cant', truly exhibiting a Benthamite 'toughness of mind', and 'fearless hard-hitting logic'.[54] They imparted to the new intellectual stratum and through it, later, to the Labour Party, a tradition of advocacy of reforms through thorough study and development of the case and the plan – the tradition of the 'Blue Books'.[55] They were also less fastidious about style, displaying substantial critical independence. Both capitalism and revolutionary socialism were targets of their pugnacious attacks. They initially also dismissed the Labour Party as a possible agent of socialism, and despite their influential studies of industrial democracy they were for a long time not committed to the labour movement either. Their original idea of the agent of socialism was a specialised and technocratic version of a 'clerisy'. What was needed, Sidney Webb contended, was a small educated elite, 'supplying ideas and principles of social reconstruction to each of the great political parties in turn, as the changing results of English politics bring them alternately to power.'[56] They largely took over the Fabian Society and through it sought to 'permeate' all parties and social institutions with Fabian ideas. In a socialism conceived independently of any mass movement, the sheer weight of evidence was expected to convince the public of the suitability of proposed reforms.

As for the New Liberals, although they were wary of the Fabians' extreme collectivism and statism, their preoccupations were not very different. The Liberal task was to win over the uneducated masses to the side of intellect. The newly established organ of the New Liberalism, the *Nation*, under the editorship of Hugh Massingham, supported the progressive Liberal government formed in 1905 while continuing to urge it towards further social reforms and even 'socialism'. As they saw it, '[t]he ideas of socialism, when translated into practical terms, coincide with the ideas to which Liberals are led when they seek to apply their principles of Liberty, Equality and the Common Good to the industrial life of our time.'[57] Socialism thus had a very loose meaning, but it also had a very wide application. The differences between the economist J.A. Hobson and the historians J.L and Barbara Hammond, who called themselves socialists, on the one hand, and political theorist Graham Wallas and the editor of the *Manchester Guardian*, C.P. Scott, who explicitly disavowed the label, on the other, were small.[58] They generally also rejected revolutionary socialism which, it was believed, would only divide society into warring classes with no guarantee of effectively delivering it from the evils of capitalism. Instead, they hoped to integrate the working class into a progressive New Liberalism.

Collectively, these intellectuals did succeed in denting the complacent façade of Victorian society. While it was the Fabians who principally imparted their spirit and style to the Labour Party, it is true to say that at this time the entire British intellectual tradition veered to the left. In this regard it is important to bear in mind that the wider culture of public life still remained largely unintellectual. No major Conservative intellectual emerged to provide an intellectual rationale for the established order (or indeed, any alternative system acceptable to the British conservatives). Conservatism was simply embodied in the deeply entrenched attitudes and practices of the British governing elite. The claim of the New Liberals and Fabians to represent the brains of the nation was to this extent fully justified.

Intellectuals Move to Labour

The New Liberals had been originally committed to fashioning a new political role for the Liberal Party, which with the extension of the franchise, would, it was widely agreed, involve giving leadership to the working class electorate. As these intellectuals saw it, the programme of the Liberal Party had to include, *in addition* to its adherence to traditional Liberal principles of extending democratic rights, free trade and a progressive foreign policy, progressive taxation, the taxation of land, a capital levy, death duties, a national minimum wage, aspects of social insurance and other measures of state intervention to protect labour. Only such a programme which was attractive to the working-class electorate could fashion a new majoritarian progressive political force and give Liberalism a new lease of life. Liberal MP John Morley's surmise that 'The extreme advanced Party is likely for the future to have on its side a great portion of the most highly cultivated intellect of the nation, and the contest will lie between brains and numbers on the one side, and wealth, rank, vested interest, possession in short, on the other',[59] was to apply to his own party. Events were to prove him right, however, only in unexpected ways.

Despite the hopeful portents of the great reforming Liberal administration of 1905-10, which incorporated important New Liberal socio-economic policies, the coalition of interests which the Liberal Party represented only grew more ramshackle in the face of the new demands before it in the period leading up to the Great War. In fact the Great War was the occasion of the break between many of the New Liberal intellectuals and the Liberal Party.[60] This political shift was the result of a complex interaction of many factors but two deserve emphasis – the impressive increase in working-class organisation during the war, and the split in the Liberal Party between the Asquithians and the followers of Lloyd George in 1916. Combined with the beginnings of an exodus of New Liberal intellectuals towards Labour, these developments encouraged the Labour Party to institutionalise its independence from Liberalism.

Paradoxically perhaps, it was above all a sense that the Liberal Party leadership had abandoned the principles of traditional Liberalism before and during the war that led so many of them to Labour.[61] The Labour Party now became a hopeful prospect precisely because of its stand on these liberal issues,[62] a fortuity which eased a possibly difficult political shift. In these circumstances the New Liberalism merely helped to bridge the social chasm that had hitherto divided middle-class intellectuals from working-class politics. Peter Clarke has assessed the complex effect of the New Liberal bridge between the Liberal and Labour parties.

> The new Liberalism, because of its insistence on the substantive compatibility of the aims of Liberalism and Labour, saved the Liberal Party from a lingering death: before 1914 by giving it hope of continued life, after 1914, by making its death sudden. If the choice between the Liberal Party and the Labour Party was only tactical, this had the effect of recruiting Liberal support from socialists before 1914 and Labour support from liberals afterwards.[63]

Thus, instead of the projected inclusion of the working class into the Liberal Party, by the 1920s the Labour Party had overtaken the Liberal Party as the principal opposition to the Conservatives. The sixty or so prominent Liberals who joined the Labour Party during and after the war, studied by C.A. Cline in *Recruits to Labour*, included such important intellectuals as Christopher Addison, Sir Norman Agnell, Noel Buxton, Hugh Dalton, Goldsworthy Lowes Dickinson, J.A. Hobson, H.W. Massingham, Sir Leo Chiozza Money, Bertrand Russell, Siegfried Sassoon, John Strachey, and H.G. Wells.[64] In general, Cline's study records the political realignment of the most prominent members of the professional middle classes from Liberalism to Labour. The Webbs also finally threw their lot in with the Labour Party. Sidney Webb had helped to draft the party's constitution of 1918, giving it the famous Clause Four and creating a new individual membership (instead of merely indirect membership through belonging to a trade union affiliated to the party) – thus incidentally creating the possibility for intellectuals to become members directly, without having to be in a trade union.

Yet although their own principles now pointed to Labour as the appropriate political vehicle for the policies they supported, many intellectuals hesitated to give their allegiance to the Labour Party and make an active political commitment to it. The Labour Party, seen as a class or a trade union party, speaking for a set of sectional interests, seemed a compromised instrument for a set of intellectuals claiming to speak for society as a whole, even though they clearly saw that it needed a 'socialist clergy such as the German social democrats had created, charged with the duty of thinking for the working class'.[65] They envisaged a distinctly Olympian role for intellect over the Labour 'interest': the former would adjudicate the justice of the latter's claims, supply it with truly radical policies (the conservatism of Labourism was already very apparent to intellectuals), and counteract the equally conservative influence of the permanent civil service in any Labour government.[66]

Thus the allegiance of the intellectuals to Labour was uneasy from the start. Hobson's decision to join Labour was typical in its misgivings. Despite his socialist inclinations, he 'never felt quite at home in a body governed by trade union members and their finances and intellectually led by full-blooded socialists'.[67] But the decline of the Liberal Party in the 1920s meant that most decided to swallow their doubts – albeit in varying degrees – and support Labour. Although Labour's new 'socialist' constitution of 1918 seemed likely further to alienate the intellectuals, MacDonald's welcome for them, based on his desire to build Labour into a truly national party, gave some reassurance.

Some, however, like Keynes, chose to remain in the Liberal Party and their reasons are very instructive. Keynes admitted in 1926 that 'the progressive forces of the country are hopelessly divided between the Liberal party and the Labour party'. But, by remaining outside the Labour Party, he said, a Liberal at least had the advantage of being able to 'work out policies without having to do lip service to trade-unionist tyrannies, to the beauties of the class war, or to doctrinaire state socialism – in none of which he believes'.[68] If Keynes' distaste for MacDonaldite rhetoric would find echoes in the intellectuals' later battles against the Labourist ethos of the party, the root of his objection to the Labour Party would prove to be of lasting and fundamental significance: 'I do not believe that the intellectual elements in the Labour Party will ever exercise adequate control'.[69] Those who joined the Labour Party differed from Keynes primarily in not sharing this belief. They too wanted intellectual influence, and hoped to get it by changing allegiances. They had despaired of the Liberal Party for this reason and, despite its obvious disadvantages, Labour seemed to them the only alternative.

The intellectuals' conditional allegiance to Labour was matched, moreover, by a conditional welcome on the part of the trade-unionist and working class Labour Party. Labour's origins had been empirical and undoctrinaire and as such, it shared the unintellectualism of the society around it. Moreover, class-ridden British society had fostered a labour movement intensely conscious of the fine gradations of class and these tended to mark out the usually middle-class intellectuals as a distinct element in the party whose relationship with its trade union element was always going to be delicate and problematic. How right Keynes was to prove in his fear that the influence of intellectuals was bound to be limited became clear to the heirs of this intellectual tradition in 1981.

For all that, it was quite an impressive intellectual influx. After the Great War, with Labour's political fortunes rising, and with its aim of proving that Labour could form a cabinet without Liberal help, its leadership could hardly ignore the ready-made pool of talent now at its disposal. MacDonald's Cabinets of 1924 and 1929–31 included many ex-Liberals (as well as two ministers who had hitherto been life-long Conservatives, Lord Chelmsford and Lord Parmoor). However, a number of factors limited the immediate impact of the newcomers on Labour's policies. The pre-war radicalisation and wartime expansion of Labour's trade union base had permitted the projection of Labour as an independent national force both politically and ideologically, and Labour's new constitution and 'socialist' ideology were expressions of this new assertion. The ex-Liberals contributed to this expansion by providing candidates, ministers, funds, and arguments. Labour's social-ism, however, at least under MacDonald's leadership, consisted in a combination of fiery rhetoric and only the most basic ameliorative policies. Accordingly, on the most urgent policy question of the 1920s, unemployment, the party saw its role as mainly defending the 'dole'. This was in line with the expectations of the trade unions: 'Their acceptance of unemployment as the price to be paid for maintaining wages made them less interested in increasing employment than in increasing unemployment benefits'.[70] Similar thinking influenced Lab-our's fiscal and monetary policies. The Webbs and Hobson, as well as Keynes, had put forward analyses favouring a public works programme, and in the context of the prevailing fiscal and economic orthodoxy the principal debates centred around the methods of financing it. But while innovative forms of deficit financing were being experimented with in the United States, Germany, France and Sweden,[71] and advocated in Britain by the Liberal Party, the Labour Party leadership, in particular its Chancellor of the Exchequer, Snowden, remained committed to 'sound finance'.

However, even while such fiscal conservatism was incongruous in a 'socialist' party and was certainly a problem, too exclusive an emphasis on it may obscure much of the genuine theoretical confusion of the time. Even Keynes' own policy prescriptions at this time, embodied in the Liberals' 1928 policy statement *Britain's Industrial Future* (otherwise known as the 'Yellow Book'), were bolder rather than more radical than those of other people – advocating *experimentation* with forms of deficit financing rather than putting forward a clearly argued and theoretically backed policy. Without an effectively counter-cyclical economic theory these remained leaps in the dark and the divisions between the expansionists and the orthodox were differences over 'political priorities rather than economic analysis'.[72]

Dowse has argued that the Independent Labour Party (ILP), which had formed an important conduit for the intellectuals' migration, in its demand for a living wage, had a viable alternative set of policies.[73] In *Socialism in Our Time*, published in 1926, the ILP had argued that capitalism could never provide a living wage and that pressure upon it to do so would only reveal its bankruptcy and create the political conditions for socialism. The demand for a living wage was a simple one which would make intuitive sense to workers, and this idea was harnessed by the leaders of the ILP, foremost among them Clifford Allen, to a policy of taking the legislative initiative, which countered the parliamentary gradualism within the Labour Party. In Dowse's view, this was a potent intellectual combination, but the ILP could never get it accepted by the trade unions or the Labour Party.[74] But it is also important to note that there were also serious doubts about the theoretical consistency and practical viability of its Hobsonian economics.[75]

A third factor contributing to the limited influence of the intellectuals in the 1920s was the fact that many of the ex-Liberal intellectuals had joined Labour primarily for its adherence to liberalism and they continued to take a greater interest in foreign affairs than in domestic policies.[76] And, lastly, after the War, many of the older generation who had been the originators of the New Liberalism tended to sink into a despairing inactivity while the younger generation, in the 1920s at least, were captured by the prevailing bohemianism of Oxford and Cambridge, inspired, not least, by the philosophy of G.E. Moore.[77]

In sum, while the influx of liberal intellectuals into Labour was spectacular, the immediate effect was limited to establishing Labour as a possible (and increasingly the only, if at the same time very problematic) political vehicle for intellectuals. Their impact on policy remained small. Only later, after 1931, did political circumstances conspire to give some of them a powerful voice in the determination of Labour policy. Their labours bore fruit in the policy documents of the early and mid 1930s such as *For Socialism and Peace* (1934) and *Labour's Immediate Programme* (1935), which formed the basis of the programme of the 1945–51 Labour governments.

This was in large part the work of some notable young intellectuals who joined the Labour Party in the 1920s. The Fabian Hugh Dalton was pre-eminent among these. Others, even younger, like Hugh Gaitskell and Evan Durbin, were converted to the cause of Labour during the 1926 General Strike which, unlike the majority of their fellow students, they worked to support.[78] Many of them were among those who were recruited by Hugh Dalton, G.D.H. Cole and others, into Labour's newly established policy-making apparatus after 1931. The evolution of their moderate but effective programme of reform must, however, be sifted out from among other more vivid, if evanescent, developments which dominated the 1930s.

British Intellectuals and the Slump

The 1930s began with dramatic events. The economic slump and the consequent unemployment and poverty generated demands for bold measures. Unable to deliver, the Labour government fell in 1931 in what was a major political crisis for the party. Among other things, it led to fundamental questioning of the parliamentary road and the possibility of 'legislating socialism'. Further, with the advent of Hitler to power in Germany, the international situation began to seem increasingly ominous and the possibility of another war became more real. Finally, an important element in the configuration of opinion at the time was the increasing popularity of the Soviet Union and socialist planning as many British intellectuals, most of them Fabians, visited the USSR and returned extremely impressed with its planning system which contrasted so sharply with the passivity of the government in the face of economic crisis at home.

Perhaps only in such an exceptionally grave atmosphere of looming catastrophe could a whole decade in the history of this distinctly unintellectual society become so completely identified in public memory with an *intellectual* phenomenon: the turn that a significant number of intellectuals (here especially encompassing literary and scientific figures) took towards communism and (to a much lesser extent) fascism. More muted but perhaps more important, in view of its more lasting significance, was the emergence of a left-of-centre 'middle opinion', a sort of consensus across parties, on the need for planning and welfare measures to better the living conditions of the working class and to overcome anarchy in the domestic economic field and in the international political arena.

The passage of so many of Britain's intellectuals known, by now, for their stability and judicious moderation, to political activism on the far left was an amazing phenomenon in its time, especially so in view of the apolitical bohemianism and aestheticism of the younger generation of intellectuals during the previous decade. Most of these newly radicalised young intellectuals were from 'good' families and educated at Oxford or Cambridge. The intensity of their new-found attachment to communism must be understood, according to Neal Wood, in the context of the politically immobilising effect of their prior ethos. The introversions of 'logical atomism' in philosophy and the irrelevance of bohemianism could lead only to nihilism; and part of their new-found political commitment was an *anti*-intellectual desire to *act*.[79][80] Predictably the flirtation with communism was brief. By the 1940s, as we shall see in the next chapter, this political commitment, which led several notable members of the emerging generation of British intellectuals to their deaths in defence of Republican Spain, was a distant, not entirely cherished memory.

Neal Wood ventures to call them a 'British radical intelligentsia',[81] alienated from society, disquieted at the first prospects of unemployment, or employment only in the lower ranks of the black-coated. He even goes on to compare them with the pre-1917 Russian intelligentsia and the German nihilists after the Great War, seeing British communism as a more limited, milder version of the continental pattern. But their much higher socio-economic status prevented them from either making a British revolution or joining British fascism. At the close of the decade they were almost all welcomed back to the establishment fold. As Wood himself points out,

> Without an intellectual aristocracy so closely tied to the middle classes the revolution of the intellectuals of Great Britain may have been of vast, even catastrophic dimensions. No doubt the traditional family relationships cushioned the impact of communism and restrained many of the nation's intellectuals from supporting the communist crusade. On the other hand, the great toleration of British society for the political 'eccentricities' of many of its young intellectuals may have resulted from their belonging to respected middle-class families so often bound together not only by ties of blood and marriage but also by those of school, university and club.[82]

If this communism of the intellectuals proved as short-lived as it was remarkable, Arthur Marwick has argued persuasively that a more lasting product of the decade was the development of what he has called a

'Middle Opinion' on the need for a more rational order in the domestic as well as in the international arena.[83] And, unlike the scientific and literary bent of the 'communist' intellectuals, this affected the primarily 'sociological' intellectuals. State ownership, planning and regulation and a measure of welfare were the principal ingredients in a widening area of agreement among intellectuals and many politicians of all parties. This constellation of 'middle opinion' notably also included some Conservative politicians, such as Harold Macmillan, Robert Boothby, John de V. Loder and Oliver Stanley.

The roots of the development of such an area of agreement are traced by Marwick to the political crisis of 1931 and the economic depression which was its proximate cause; and to the rise of a variegated peace movement whose lowest common denominator was an attempt to seek a re-ordering of international relations through international organisation; the need to respond to the militant creeds of communism and fascism and to 'rally to the defence of democracy and bring forward evidence that it too was capable of a vigorous attack on its economic and social problems';[84] and, lastly, a growing awareness of the need and possibilities of harnessing science to resolve social problems. If mechanistic Fabianism had hitherto been a distinctly small trend within the wider New Liberal and left-leaning British intellectual tradition, at least some of its 'Benthamite' impulse now pervaded British intellectual life more generally.

People from all parties as well as some notable businessmen were behind the groups that were now formed to urge the necessity of planning. The membership of the 'Next Five Years Group', for example, included Clifford Allen as Chairman, Harold Macmillan as joint treasurer, Barratt Brown as secretary, with Normal Angell, Will Arnold-Foster, John Bromley, Geoffrey Crowther, Professor Julian Huxley, Eleanor Rathbone, Sir Arthur Slater and A.E. Douglas-Smith as other Executive members.[85] Political and Economic Planning (PEP) was formed in 1931 out of many small groups already involved in propaganda of a similar sort. The peace movement against fascism also formed an important base for 'middle opinion': it drew support from notables of all parties. The National Labour Committee, made up of the National Labour MPs, was another important nucleus of like-minded people urging these policies upon the National government.

This new agreement on planning moved the middle ground of British politics significantly to the left and the membership of these groups overlapped with that of others further to the left like the Socialist League (formed to provide an intellectual outlet for members of the ILP who remained in the Labour Party after 1932). The Socialist League included intellectuals such as G.D.H. Cole, E.F. Wise, William Mellor, Sir Charles Trevelyan, J.T. Murphy, H.N. Brailsford, D.N. Pritt, Harold

Laski, Ellen Wilkinson, Aneurin Bevan and G.R. Strauss. They sought to urge the Labour Party more to the left.[86] Relying on Hobsonian redistributive theories, but suspicious of the New Deal type of reformism, they wanted a radical transformation of political conditions. This eventually pushed them outside 'middle opinion' and the League's support for the idea of a 'United Front' brought about its proscription by the Labour Party in 1937.

Emergence of Parliamentary Socialism

In the early 1930s the Labour Party was in a peculiar position. Organisationally and electorally, it had experienced a decade of growth, but the political crisis of 1931 had exposed the fact that beyond its rhetorical socialism, the party lacked viable policies which could advance the cause of socialism or even just alleviate the economic crisis. In addition to the defection of the MacDonaldite National Labour group in 1931, which led to the fall of the Labour government, the party had suffered two other splits in the previous year: on the left to the ILP led by James Maxton, and on the right to Sir Oswald Mosley's New Party. And in the General Election of 1931 most of the remaining party leaders lost their seats. This was the juncture which made it possible for a group of intellectuals, younger than most of the ex-Liberals now in the Labour Party, to make a decisive intervention whereby the party came to acquire an essentially Fabian programme – egalitarian, radical, pro-planning, and welfarist. While, of course, the new programme was the result of much collective effort, and of complex political tides, the central figure in its making, who stamped the entire process with his own energy and inclinations, was Hugh Dalton.[87] The influence he exerted over Labour's policy-making in the 1930s was accounted for not least by his exceptional position as an intellectual in the Labour Party of the 1930s.

Dalton was one of the few who fell under the influence of the Fabians while still a student. A recruit to Labour in the 1920s, he served as a junior minister at the Treasury in the second Labour government of 1929–31. The party's heavy losses in the 1931 General Election meant that a large number of prominent Labour figures, including Dalton, found themselves outside Parliament. Moreover, in a Labour Party badly battered by both the split and the electoral defeat of 1931, and deeply suspicious of outsiders, Dalton, exceptionally among the intellectuals in the party, enjoyed the trust of two of its leading figures, Ernest Bevin and Herbert Morrison. This was in large part because Dalton's allegiance to the Labour Party was distinct from that of the large phalanx of the ex-Liberal intellectuals in the party. They had joined Labour because it seemed to them it could be more reliably liberal, and they tended to concentrate on 'liberal' policies rather than specifically socialist ones. Remaining self-consciously middle-class, they also did not establish close links with the party's union and working-class leadership.[88] The renegade upper-middle class Dalton, however, took to his new anti-establishment political identity with some zest and (it seems) plausibility. After 1931 he came to be seen as a '"Transport House man", on the side of working class leaders against middle-class intellectuals'.[89] And having a lectureship at the London School of Economics with light responsibilities, as well as a private income through his wife, he was in an extremely favourable position to devote himself almost full-time to the task of policy-making. The leaders in Parliament were too preoccupied with parliamentary affairs to give much attention to long-term policy formulation. So when, in the aftermath of the debacle of 1931, the National Executive Committee (NEC) of the Labour Party set up a policy-making machinery which the party had previously lacked, Dalton, who served on the NEC, became the chair of the crucial Finance and Trade Subcommittee, as well as being one of the NEC's representatives on the TUC's Economic Committee, where he was able to persuade the General Council of the wisdom of the emerging policies. From these positions of influence he was able to direct the emerging Labour Party policy.

Over the course of the early 1930s Dalton steered the Labour Party policy process in a distinctive direction, marking a distance both from the general, if vague, extremism evident in left circles and from the 'middle opinion' on managing capitalism. The need for policy initiatives was recognised by many after the debacle of 1931, and the ex-guild socialist, G.D.H. Cole, had taken the initiative, with the blessing of Transport House, in setting up the Society for Socialist Information and Propaganda (SSIP, pronounced 'zip') and the New Fabian Research Bureau (NFRB) in 1931 to aid this process. Dalton was co-opted onto the latter (and in terms of policy-making for the party, the more influential) organisation. Throughout the 1930s the Bureau published a series of important books on policy issues, supplanting the increasingly inactive Fabian Society.[90]

Although initially enthusiastic, Dalton soon distanced himself from the 'loyal grousing' of the NFRB. The moralistic and impractical attitude which, thanks to the Coles and the generally left-wing climate of the 1930s, dominated the organisation, was uncongenial to Dalton, and there were serious disagreements which were also symptomatic of Dalton's distinctiveness. One concerned the question of 'emergency powers' which socialists such as Laski were arguing any future Labour government would have to take to forestall political opposition from 'capitalist parties'. Dalton poured ridicule on this suggestion, maintaining that it was based on an insufficiently developed understanding of the British constitution. Similarly a proposal for the nationalisation of the banking sector appeared to Dalton as being merely, and dangerously, rhetorical – 'MacDonaldite slush' – playing to the gallery without any clarity about the methods and purposes for which it was advocated.[91] In an interesting indicator of the mood of the movement, however, Dalton lost this latter political battle and the proposal was actually part of the 1934 policy document, *For Socialism and Peace*, although it was subsequently shelved.

The limitations of the NFRB meant that the real sources of party policy lay elsewhere. Dalton had begun to recruit a number of younger socialist economists into the Labour Party and to co-opt them into its policy-making machinery. Of these Hugh Gaitskell, Evan Durbin and Douglas Jay were the best known. Others included the financial journalist Nicholas Davenport, the economist Colin Clark, and the journalist Robert Fraser. Within this more or less informal intellectual grouping was another, more interesting one: the semi-secret 'XYZ Club', which was composed of a number of Labour sympathizers in the City who helped formulate much of Labour's financial policy in the 1930s, including the proposal for a national investment board that was included in *For Socialism and Peace*.[92] Through these younger economists and intellectuals the work of the wider British intellectual tradition, especially aspects of Keynesian thinking, began to enter Labour's policy thinking, although it was not until 1944 that demand management as the key to full employment became official Labour policy.

Dalton's views, and the evolving views of the Labour Party, remained distinct from 'middle opinion' on planning and intervention. Partly, no doubt, the freshness of MacDonald's betrayal constrained Dalton (and others who wished to retain the faith of the party leadership) from being seen to fraternise too much with members of other parties. But more importantly Dalton and his recruits had important political differences with 'middle opinion' as represented, say, by the Next Five Years Group. A trip to the Soviet Union in 1932 had certainly impressed Dalton tremendously, and thereafter planning became an important element in his thinking. But planning, he recognised, was not inherently Marxist or even socialist.[93] And indeed, it was not ruled out even by some Conservatives. His own goals, however, went beyond the regulation of capitalism and the amelioration of its excessively unjust effects towards a parliamentary, gradualist, egalitarian socialism. The intellectual task at hand, as he saw it, was to elaborate practicable policies for a short-term or transitional programme: 'we do better to decide the direction of advance than to debate the detail of Utopia. We must see clearly the next stretch of the journey. But we need not spend time now arguing whether, beyond the horizon, the road swerves left or right'.[94]

This was the thinking embodied in the 1934 Labour policy document, *For Socialism and Peace*, and elaborated and defended in Dalton's book,

Practical Socialism (1935). It formed the basis of subsequent Labour policy, including the manifesto of 1945. It was an intellectual direction the trade unions were willing to support and it was along these lines that the Labour Party progressed thenceforth.

Dalton, then, was the central figure in the policy-making of the 1930s. But many younger economists, for the most part encouraged and promoted in the Labour Party by Dalton himself, also worked not only at fashioning the policies Labour would pursue in office after 1945 but also at putting forward the case for a gradualist parliamentary, Keynesian socialism, in books such as Evan Durbin's *The Politics of Democratic Socialism* (1940) and Douglas Jay's *The Socialist Case* (1937). Their collective effect was such that '[b]y the outbreak of the war the Labour party had travelled light-years in the depth and sophistication of its knowledge of British financial institutions and economic policy options since the dark days of 1931'.[95] Labour's armoury now included proposals for reducing unemployment, promoting and regulating investment, nationalising industries, controlling the financial sector, and implementing progressive and redistributive taxation. The wartime acceptance of Keynesianism and the systematising of welfare as proposed in the Beveridge Plan completed the 1945 programme.

Dalton's personal influence over the post-war Labour Party would also persist through that of his protégés – intellectuals whom he had groomed for commanding positions in labour politics, including Hugh Gaitskell, Evan Durbin, Douglas Jay, Colin Clarke, Robert Fraser, John Wilmot and Nicholas Davenport, and later Anthony Crosland, Bill Rodgers and Roy Jenkins. Their fate is the subject of the rest of this study.

Notes

1. Perry Anderson, 'Origins of the Present Crisis', *New Left Review*, Number 23, January–February 1964, p 30.

2. Perry Anderson, 'Components', p 12.

3. Ralph Miliband, *Parliamentary Socialism*, Monthly Review Press, New York, 1972, pp 372–373.

4. J.S. Mill, 'Bentham' in F.R. Leavis (ed) *Mill on Bentham and Coleridge*, Chatto and Windus, London, 1950, p 41.

5. Perry Anderson, 'Origins', p 41.

6. J.S. Mill, *op.cit.*, p 63.

7. At least one of Bentham's biographers went out of his way to combat this view of Bentham as narrow, hardened, joyless rationalist. According to Charles Everett he certainly did not lack in aesthetic or emotional sympathy. If his philosophy did nevertheless exhibit the characteristics mentioned above, this was due to an unwavering commitment to rationalism rather than to a paucity of feeling or knowledge of history – a measure, surely, of radicalism rather than

limitation. Charles Everett, *The Education of Jeremy Bentham*, Columbia University Press, New York, 1931.

8. *Ibid*, p 48

9. William Thomas, *The Philosophic Radicals: Nine Studies in Theory and Practice*, Clarendon Press, Oxford, 1979, p 449.

10. Eric Stokes' classic study documents how, frustrated in England, the energies of socially radical Utilitarianism were, for a time, channelled outwards, towards the empire, especially India. If Britain was to put her stamp on India, 'Philosophic Radicalism gave it an intellectual basis and supplied it with the sciences of political economy, law and government'. *The English Utilitarians and India*, Clarendon Press, Oxford, 1950, p xiv.

11. J.S. Mill, *Autobiography*, edited by H.J. Laski, World's Classics, 1924, pp 181–2, as quoted in Stokes, *op.cit.*, p 241.

12. J.S. Mill to E. Lytton Bulwer, 23 November 1836, quoted in Stokes, *op.cit.*, p 241.

13. Elie Halévy, *The Growth of Philosophic Radicalism*, Tr. Mary Morris, Faber and Faber, London, 1972, p 514.

14. Eric Stokes, *op. cit.*, p 242.

15. Lewis Namier, quoted in Perry Anderson, 'Components', p 18.

16. Perry Anderson, 'Components', p 13.

17. 'Never again was the same height of vision to be achieved. Only in a peculiarly acute internal crisis of her history was England prepared to listen to the intellectual nostrums of Bentham and James Mill, or to be bold enough to send out [to India] as a legislator a man so inexperienced in the law as Macaulay.' Eric Stokes, *op.cit.*, p 245.

18. J.S. Mill, 'Coleridge' in F.R.Leavis (ed) *Mill on Bentham and Coleridge*, Chatto and Windus, London, 1950, p 108.

19. Raymond Williams, *Culture and Society*, Hogarth Press, London, 1958.

20. *Ibid*, p xviii.

21. *Ibid*, p 62–63.

22. T.W. Heyck, *The Transformation of Intellectual Life in Victorian England*, Croom Helm, London, 1982, p 161.

23. Noel Annan, 'The Intellectual Aristocracy', in J.H. Plumb (ed), *Studies in Social History*, Longman, London, 1955, p 247. Romance recently gave way to tragedy in *Our Age: A Portrait of a Generation*, Weidenfeld and Nicholson, London, 1990, as Annan reflected on recent Thatcherite ravages.

24. Peter Gowan, 'The Origins of the Administrative Elite', *New Left Review* Number 162, March–April 1987.

25. *Ibid*, p 17–18.

26. 'The college [was] an intellectual power-house as the directors spared no pains to attract the highest quality of teachers. Malthus taught (and wrote his famous book) there, as did Sir James Stephen and Sir James MacIntosh.' The Sanskrit Scholar Monier-Williams, subsequently a professor at Oxford, wrote that the mental training there was of such a high standard that 'nothing at all equal to it ... was to be had either at the Universities or elsewhere ... I soon discovered that if I wished to rise above the level of the average student, I should have a task before me compared to which my previous work at Oxford could only be regarded as child's play.'" Gowan, *op.cit.*, p 15.

27. *Ibid*, p 15.

28. T.W. Heyck, *op. cit.*, pp 155–189.

29. Noel Annan, 'The Intellectual Aristocracy', p 285.

30. Tom Nairn, 'The English Literary Intelligentsia', in Emma Tennant (ed), *Bananas*, Quartet, London, 1977, p 72.

31. Walter E. Houghton, *The Victorian Frame of Mind 1830–1870*, Yale University Press, New Haven, 1957, p 110.

32. *Ibid.*

33. *Ibid*, p 113.

34. See, for example, *ibid.*; Tom Nairn, *op.cit.*; T.W. Heyck, *op.cit.*

35. Tom Nairn, *op.cit.*, p 76.

36. *Ibid*, p 61.

37. Heyck, *op. cit.*, p 37.

38. *The Intelligentsia of Great Britain*, Tr. Alec Brown, Victor Gollancz, London, 1935, p 9.

39. T.W. Heyck, *op. cit.*, p 15.

40. *Ibid*, 'Introduction'.

41. Noel Annan. 'The Intellectual Aristocracy', p 285.

42. *Ibid*, p 244.

43. Eric Hobsbawm, 'The Fabians Reconsidered', in *Labouring Men*, Weidenfeld and Nicholson, London, 1964, p 267.

44. Noel Annan, 'The Intellectual Aristocracy', *op. cit.*, p 285.

45. James Cronin, 'Class and the Labour Party', *Studies in Political Economy*, Number 21, Autumn, 1986, p 124.

46. Stefan Collini, 'Sociology and Idealism in Britain, 1880–1920', *European Journal of Sociology*, Volume XIX, Number 1, 1978.

47. Peter Clarke, *Liberals and Social Democrats*, Cambridge University Press, Cambridge, 1978, p 27.

48. *New Jerusalems: The Labour Party and the Economics of Democratic Socialism*, Routledge and Kegan Paul, London, 1985, pp 32–37.

49. See A.M. McBriar, *Fabian Socialism and English Politics 1884–1918*, Cambridge University Press, Cambridge, 1966, pp 29–49.

50. Eric Hobsbawm, *op.cit.*, p 260.

51. *Ibid.*, p 261.

52. Margaret Cole quoted in Durbin, *op. cit.*, p 21.

53. All five of Clarke's principal subjects, Graham Wallas, L. T. Hobhouse, J.A. Hobson, and J.L. and Barbara (nee Bradby) Hammond, were at Oxford.

54. Eric Stokes, *op. cit.*, p 242.

55. An incident which epitomises the attitude derived from Benthamism by the Fabians is narrated by Clarke: Graham Wallas, then a Fabian, and 'nothing if not empirical, pragmatic, utilitarian', went to a lecture by William Morris where, he recalled, 'I made a rough calculation that the citizens of his commonwealth, in order to produce by the methods he advocated the quantity of beautiful and delicious things which they were to enjoy, would have to work about two hundred hours a week', Clarke, *op. cit.*, p 30.

56. Sidney Webb to Graham Wallas, 22 August 1885, Passfield Papers, quoted in Lisanne Radice, *Beatrice and Sidney Webb: Fabian Socialists*, Macmillan, London, 1984, p 61.

57. L.T. Hobhouse, quoted in Clarke, *op. cit.*, p 113.

58. Clarke, *op.cit.*

59. John Morley in *Fortnightly Review*, volume 1, p 491–2, quoted in Clarke, *op. cit.*, p 6.

60. The exhaustion of Liberalism as a vehicle for progress in the face of the mounting political demands it faced in the years leading up to the Great War has been famously analysed by George Dangerfield in *The Strange Death of Liberal England*, Capricorn Books, New York, 1961, first published, 1935.

61. Catherine Ann Cline, *Recruits to Labour*, Syracuse University Press, Syracuse, 1963, p 128.

62. See Cline, *op.cit*, pp 10–23 and Clarke, *op.cit*, p 195.

63. Clarke, *op.cit.*, p 195.

64. Cline, *op.cit*, pp 149–178.

65. Graham Wallas quoted in Clarke, *op. cit.*, p 139.

66. *Ibid.*, p 140.

67. J.A. Hobson, *Confessions of an Economic Heretic*, 1938, p 126, quoted in Clarke, *op.cit.*, p 236.

68. Quoted in Clarke, *op.cit*, p 238.

69. *Ibid.*

70. Robert Skidelsky, *Politicians and the Slump: The Labour Government of 1929–1931*, Macmillan, London, 1967, p 395.

71. *Ibid.*, p 387.

72. Donald Winch, *Economics and Policy*, Hodder and Stoughton, London, 1969, pp 121–2.

73. R.E. Dowse, *Left in the Centre: The Independent Labour Party 1843–1940*, Longman, London, 1966.

74. *Ibid.*, p 133.

75. For discussions of Hobsonian economics see Clarke, *op.cit.*, pp 226–234 and Durbin, *op.cit.*, pp 37–40.

76. Cline, *op.cit.*, pp 68–99.

77. See J.K. Johnstone, *The Bloomsbury Group: A Study of E.M. Foster, Lytton Strachey, Virginia Woolf and their Circle*, The Noonday Press, New York, 1963.

78. This group also included others such as Colin Clark, John Parker, John Dugdale, Lord Listowel, Michael Stewart, John Betjeman, and W.H. Auden. See Elizabeth Durbin, *op. cit.*, pp 94.

79. Neal Wood, *Communism and British Intellectuals*, Columbia University Press, New York, 1959, p 106.

80. In the verses of the most representative poet of that generation:

> Shut up talking, charming in the best suits to be had in town
> Lecturing on navigation while the ship is going down.
> If we really want to live, we'd better start at once to try
> If we don't, it doesn't matter, but we'd better start to die

(W.H. Auden, *Poems*, 1933 no.xxii, p 76, as quoted in Wood, *op.cit.*, p 108.)

81. *Ibid*, p 37.

82. *Ibid*, p 90

83. Arthur Marwick, 'Middle Opinion in the Thirties: Planning, Progress and Political "agreement"', in *English Historical Review*, Volume LXXIX, 1964.

84. Marwick, *op. cit.*, p 292.
85. *Ibid*, p 194.
86. Ben Pimlott, *Labour and the Left in the 1930s*, Cambridge University Press, Cambridge, 1977, p 42.
87. Ben Pimlott, *Hugh Dalton*, Jonathan Cape, London, 1988, p 206.
88. *Ibid*, pp 133–134.
89. *Ibid.*, p 204.
90. By 1939 the NFRB amalgamated with and rejuvenated the latter.
91. Pimlott, *op. cit.*, p 208.
92. *Ibid.*, p 223.
93. Pimlott, *op. cit.*, p 211. Dalton was also impressed with elements of Fascist planning in the early 1930s during a trip to Italy (pp 231–214).
94. Dalton, *Practical Socialism*, quoted in Pimlott, *op. cit.*, p 217.
95. Elizabeth Durbin, *op. cit.*, p 261.

4

Charting the Future of Post-War Socialism

The social democrats who left the Labour Party in 1981 were the legatees of the intellectuals who had joined the Labour Party in the inter-war period, and whose efforts gave Labour the memorable programme of 1945–51. These intellectuals had represented Britain's principal intellectual tradition and the formation of the Social Democratic Party (SDP) marked the historic end of its relationship to the Labour Party. Given this intellectual descent which the SDP's creators could claim, however, the new party suffered from an ironic flaw: it was a party without a clear programme. The technologically advanced media management amid which the SDP was launched did not prevent many from noting this. The fashionable 'democratic' (and technological) expedient of polling its growing membership to arrive at policies only reinforced the aura of opportunism that hung around the fledgling party. The appeal to abstract 'moderation' seemed to many, not only on the left, empty and artless. The few policies the party did have (such as support for the European Economic Community [EEC], and an incomes policy – which in themselves could hardly be said to add up to a new approach to politics) could not support its claim to represent 'brave new beginnings' – or to be 'breaking the mould'.

This philosophical paucity, whose later determinants will become clear in succeeding chapters, certainly contrasted with their own relative intellectual vitality in the 1950s and 1960s. Even a member of the new Labour left, opposed to these 'right-wing intellectuals', now invoked this past vitality, if only to score the SDP's current vacuity.[1] But by and large such tributes from the left for the work of the representatives of what was, as late as the 1950s, Britain's principal intellectual tradition, even when given for obviously rhetorical effect, were rare. For although, as the recognised heirs of the interwar generation of intellectuals, they had fashioned the only coherent new programme for further socialist advance to be tabled in the Labour Party at the time (or, for that matter, since), this programme has only invited disdain from the rest of the socialist left. Perhaps this was because, unlike the intellectuals of the

1930s, who had backed Labour's existing aims with concrete and well-researched programmes for their practical achievement, this younger generation attempted a bold revision of the aims and methods of socialism thus earning themselves the label 'revisionists'.[2] Not surprisingly this drew the ire of those in the left who espoused some unrevised, and unrevisable, socialism.

Both as phrase and phenomenon, 'revisionism' has always carried an aura of infamy, at least among more 'orthodox' socialist intellectuals: it was a retreat from socialist goals and ambitions, a comfortable compromise with the *status quo* within capitalism and an acceptance of the limits of parliamentary democracy.[3] Despite obvious differences between the Marxism of continental social democracy and British Labour's unintellectual Labourism, there were certainly interesting parallels with the classical revisionism of Eduard Bernstein in the Second International. Both arose at a time of relative prosperity, when dire predictions of inevitable immiseration were hard to sustain. Significant headway had also been made by the respective working-class movements in securing better material conditions and political reforms. In such a context, revisionism was based on the successes of reformism and on faith in the political pliability of the liberal state for socialist purposes.[4] And in both cases the revisionists were accused of renouncing socialism by narrowing its vision. The later British revisionists achieved this through a sort of pincer movement; on the one hand they emphasised the extent to which the achievements of the Attlee governments had attained their immediate goals, and on the other how, in the light of the changes thus wrought, traditional socialist goals were significantly reduced in their urgency. By the same token, however, they also attempted to put socialism on a new basis in keeping with changed circumstances. As such, revisionism has no successor. For this reason, and because the revisionist programme was the only coherent programme to be tabled in the Labour Party (the Bevanite left, as we shall see in the next chapter, having notably refrained even from the attempt), it surely deserves to be critically appreciated on its own terms rather than disdained and thus ignored further.

Having said that, it is nevertheless true that the eventual fate of revisionism, intended as the 'second instalment' of socialism in Britain, when tested in government in 1964–70, bore no comparison to the first. In the labour movement, the Labour governments of 1964–70 (and, later, 1974–79) are more memorable for their failures and betrayals than any achievements. And certainly, as the intellectual architects of the programme which, implicitly at least, underlay these governments, the revisionists must shoulder the responsibility for at least the failures, if not the betrayals. And it is equally undeniable that at the root of these failures lay a fundamental and fatal complacency in revisionism about the economic and political possibilities offered by the British state and capitalism.

For the revisionists, like previous generations of Labour's intellectuals, who, paradoxically for a 'socialist' intelligentsia, have largely conformed to the prevailing political and cultural trends, were themselves products of a particular milieu and politico-cultural conjuncture – one even more deradicalising than others in recent experience. It is to the distinctive position of the revisionists in post-war British culture and politics that we must now turn. The intellectual and political resources it afforded them, and the nature of the intellectual task they sought to accomplish with them are essential preludes to a discussion of revisionism as a philosophy and political strategy – its characteristic ideals, theoretical claims and principal assumptions.

British Culture and Politics at Mid-Century

In the 1950s and early 1960s the Labour Party appeared to firmly consolidate its position as the 'thinking man's party'. There was a remarkable increase of intellectuals in the Labour Party and, in a reflection of the importance accorded to them in British state and society generally during wartime and post-war reconstruction, there seemed to be a greater welcome and far less suspicion of them in the Labour Party too.[5] The intellectuals, for their part, also seemed to overcome the sort of misgivings they tended to have about the Labour Party – its class basis or its potential for extremism – as Labour's position in British politics was no longer so much at the left of British politics as at its centre as the chief architect of its post-war political framework. In fact, in a shift of which the evolution of a 'middle-opinion' among intellectuals in the 1930s seemed in retrospect a portent, the political centre of gravity of post-war British society more generally also moved to the left during the war: wartime mobilization had required rhetorical, ideological and material concessions to the working class, 'equal sacrifices' being exchanged for 'fair shares'. It was an idea which, it seemed at the time, would remain the basis of British political culture for generations to come,[6] and which created the remarkable consensual support for the socialist achievements of the post-war Labour governments in building the welfare state, in accepting responsibility for the performance of the economy and for important measures of nationalization. Later Conservative governments testified to the strength of this ideological shift by accepting its main elements in a new political settlement. At the same time, the continuing decline of the Liberal Party after the Second World War only contributed to Labour's cultural consolidation. Given the centrality of intellectuals to the successes of 1945–51, this greater intellectual presence in the post-war Labour Party

may appear hopeful, but the full implications of this cultural consolidation were more ambiguous for the Labour Party than appears at first
sight – it occurred at a time when Britain's already unrevolutionary
tradition underwent a further serious deradicalisation.

The Cultural Restoration

Over the course of the 1940s British culture underwent a complex
reconfiguration whose content amounted, in contrast to the electoral
'revolution' of 1945, to a restoration: the intellectual polarization so
apparent in the 1930s was, by the late 1940s and early 1950s, con-
spicuously absent. In comparison with most other states in the advanced
capitalist world, the domestic political climate in Britain appeared both
harmonious and progressive. It seemed as though with radical achievements like the victory against fascism, the reforming achievements of
the Labour government and decolonisation came the apotheosis of the
dissident intellectual – the many 'communist', bohemian, modernist
and post-impressionist intellectuals of the 1920s and 1930s were now
reconciled with the former targets of their vociferous criticism: 'Did the
fifties have anything to match the refusal of a peerage by one of the
greatest intellectuals of the twenties and thirties, R.H.Tawney, reported
in Dr.Thomas Jones' correspondence? On the contrary, it could show
an avowed anarchist [Herbert Read] and an ardent exponent of the
avant-garde in art and literature accepting a knighthood [J.M. Keynes
accepted a peerage].'[7]

This restoration was admittedly most marked among artistic or
literary intellectuals who began to distance themselves from progressive
politics generally: they had led the radicalisation of the 1930s amid talk
of commitment and action, and now led the return to the nation,
affecting a sophisticated disdain for the dreary materialism of working-
class politics. While the reforms of the post-war Labour governments
had to be acknowledged as genuinely progressive, they also, it seemed,
deprived the pursuit of the working-class cause of any urgency and
inspiration, as Kingsley Amis, for one, argued. It was not just that the
Labour Party had become divorced from its former utopian elements,
but that this very utopianism appeared stale, mere 'clichés'.[8]

> [I]t is worth noticing that the issues which will attract our contemporary
> romantic [literary intellectual] are non-political ones, or ones that are not in
> the first place political: the colour bar, horror-comics, juvenile delinquency,
> the abolition of capital punishment, the reform of the laws relating to divorce
> and homosexuality. ... One feels that a progressive party should have this
> reform on its programme, but to adopt it in an election campaign, which
> would undoubtedly attract many romantics, would be likely to have the
> opposite effect on the rank and file. I cannot see myself explaining, to an

audience of dockers, say, just why homosexual relations between consenting adults should be freed from legal penalty.[9]

But literary intellectuals had never been crucial to Labour's ascendancy and their apathy was distinguished by Amis himself from the centrality to the Labour Party of the 'sociological' intellectuals – 'economists, social scientists, statisticians and the like and I detect somewhere in the background the sinister hand of the London School of Economics'.[10] The expansion of the universities had indeed provided room for a more sizeable ('sociological' – and therefore necessarily pro-Labour) intellectual contingent to emerge. The political wing of this new generation of intellectuals found smooth paths to the top echelons of the Labour Party, principally in the Parliamentary Labour Party. However, while not exemplary of the restoration, they could not entirely escape its wider cultural influences.

One of these, which is less paradoxical than it seems, was the reassertion of the 'aristocratic-gentry' culture of the British ruling classes after the war. This, Edward Shils claims, happened all the more easily in that the rebellion of the literary intellectuals in the inter-war period had been directed more against *bourgeois* culture than against its historically more powerful aristocratic-gentry counterpart. Already, then, the former had appeared 'mean and paltry'. Now the hegemonic aristocratic-gentry culture cultivated in the central universities and the higher civil service shared in the general vindication of British society which came with victory in the war; and its indolent style of self-conscious impracticality and amateurism seemed even more invulnerable.

> Continental vacations, the connoisseurship of wine and food, the knowledge of wild flowers and birds, an acquaintance with the writings of Jane Austen, a knowing indulgence of the worthies of the English past, an appreciation of 'more leisurely epochs', doing one's job dutifully and reliably, the cultivation of personal relations – these were the elements in the ethos of the newly emerging British intellectual class after the Second World War. It was around an ethos of this sort that the new attachment to Great Britain was formed. It was in its attachment to symbols of a culture which have always been associated with a 'stake in the country' that the British intellectual class was finding its way home.[11]

In such a cultural shift, the utilitarian and practical values of the middle class which, while never in the vanguard of British culture had enjoyed a certain contained vigour, became more consciously subordinate than ever. Even as the Butler Education Act of 1944 opened up the possibility, for the first time in British history, of the production of vast numbers of the classless educated – a social category viewed with great apprehension by the guardians of British culture – their assimilation into the dominant culture was being carried out with considerably greater ease. Oxford, Cambridge and London Universities expanded substantially with state support granted under the 1944 Act, and, through the institution of scholarships, took in a socially more diverse student population. In the post-war period the new and expanding 'intellectual bureaucracies' of the BBC, the universities, institutions of state-supported arts, Fleet Street, and other fields, not to mention the state itself, for a time at least, absorbed the new graduates faster than they could be trained. The 'young meteors' ('the phrase suggests both their rapid trajectory and their inherent evanescence'),[12] were a 'new talent class': a source of much social optimism as they seemed to integrate themselves smoothly into existing and expanding cultural institutions rather than leading any new social revolution. The new centrality of intellectuals in state and politics, and the substantial expansion in the number of the educated did not, even now, imply an 'overproduction' of intellectuals on the Continental pattern.

Eventually, however, the contradiction between the reassertion of the elite intellectual ethos and the more popular origins of the educated bore fruit in the shape of the 'angry' generation of the late 1950s, in the development of the New Left after 1956, and in the popular cultural movements of the 1960s. And these developments perhaps finally signalled a belated 'overproduction' of intellectuals in Britain.[13] But until then, the noted decline in the power of the traditional aristocracy was matched by a rise in that of an upper middle class, including intellectuals and professionals, carefully assimilated to the ruling culture. Despite their expansion, cultural institutions were controlled by a decreasing number of directors and governors drawn from these classes. The leadership of the major parties (now including Labour), formerly the province of the leisured gentry, had been taken over by the educated professional upper middle class.[14] (The Conservatives, however, continued to distinguish themselves with their unintellectualism: as Annan noted in his chronicle, 'Conservatives impressed the unimpressionable [at Oxford and Cambridge] who disliked being fooled or taken in by theories'.)[15]

The Socialist Impasse

The political climate of the early 1950s when, with the Labour Party in opposition, revisionism began to take shape was dominated by relative affluence and the Cold War. While they generally combined to consign most socialist politics to a historical doldrums, revisionism, as a particularly truncated form of socialist politics, represented an adaptation to these circumstances.

The 'Age of Affluence' was largely a creation of the post-war 'long boom' – an upswing in the world economy which lasted almost twenty years from the early 1950s till the late 1960s. Victory in the war had worked to conceal the underlying weakness and decline of British industry and special factors favoured the British economy in the early part of this period – lack of competition from a Europe still recovering from the devastation of the war, and continued access to export markets in the colonies and recent ex-colonies. Restrictions on the convertibility of sterling until 1958 kept its holders' trade largely within the 'Sterling Area'. Annual growth rates for the British economy were high by historical standards and the bargaining power of unions in a fully employed economy (which at times went through manpower shortages) meant that wages continued to rise at historically unprecedented rates even under Tory rule. Such a robust capitalism belied traditional socialist gloom about its fate only recently underlined by the Great Depression. Moreover, supported by the Welfare State, post-war mass-consumption-based capitalism revolutionised the lifestyles of an increasingly better-paid working class. It enjoyed not only acceptable housing, education, paid holidays and a variety of social services designed to increase security, but also travel, television and other consumer durables. While on the whole these developments were unquestionably for the better, they had a corrosive influence on working-class culture – breaking down the solidarities of common privation and hardship which marked out working class communities and sustained their culture. This culture now gave way to a more materialistic, atomised and media-dominated one.[16]

The Cold War, to which the Labour Party was committed, actually gave 'socialism' (as well as Communism from which it was never fully distinguishable) a negative connotation. The content of *that* socialism had to be changed, and it was this that the revisionists set about to achieve. Thus together 'affluence' and the Cold War inflicted a 'double taboo' on socialism: 'Full employment and rising incomes rendered the classical socialist solutions – in particular social ownership of the means of production – redundant; the spectre of Russian 'totalitarianism' rendered them menacing'.[17] The terrain of the left had changed radically. The enthusiasm of a section of British intellectuals for communism in the 1930s was now a distant memory and served only as an inoculation against its temptations.

An important feature of this impasse of socialist politics was that no more radical force, within the Labour Party or outside it, could effectively unsettle or gainsay revisionism's conformity with the reinforced, if diffuse, conservatism in post-war Britain. Despite its shortcomings it was the only major attempt on the left to chart a new course for socialism in the altered circumstances of post-war Britain. The New Left, which emerged in the anti-Stalinist and anti-imperialist conjuncture of 1956, represented important impulses which attempted to transcend the pervasive political apathy and depoliticisation. In the words of the cultural symbol of the age, Jimmy Porter, 'people of our generation aren't able to die for good causes any longer. ... There aren't any good, brave causes left. If the big bang does come, and we'll all get killed off, it won't be in the aid of the old-fashioned grand design. It'll just be for the Brave New-nothing-very-much-thank-you.'[18] The New Left's failure to score any major victories inside the Labour Party, or in British society at large, cannot be attributed only to the political weight of the Labour Party on the British left and of the revisionists inside it. More importantly perhaps it failed to adjust intellectually to the vast changes in British society. While the New Left pitted itself against a number of worthwhile targets – nuclear war, the Cold War, racism, continuing poverty and squalor, conditions in hospitals, schools and prisons, archaic attitudes and laws, the trivialising media and the hold of the Establishment, to name only a few – both the problems themselves and their causes, remained too diverse, numerous and diffuse. As Perry Anderson pointed out, the New Left failed completely

> to offer any structural analysis of British society. ... Instead of a systematic sociology of British capitalism, it tended to rely on a simplistic rhetoric in which the 'common people', 'ordinary men and women' were opposed to the 'interests', the 'establishment', etc. Described as 'humanist', the idiom was, in fact, populist and pre-socialist. It represented a major failure of nerve and intelligence, an inability to name things as they were, which constantly yielded the initiative to the Labour Right in the polemics between it and the New Left in this period.[19]

The left of the Labour Party, which shared this intellectual failure, compounded it further by remaining parliamentarian in its outlook. Unlike the Campaign for Nuclear Disarmament (CND), which captured so much youthful disillusion outside the Labour Party, it offered no novel approach to politics, and unlike the revisionists inside it, displayed no intellectual vitality within the parliamentary mode.

The Revisionist Generation

If in the inter-war period intellectuals had wavered at the prospect of joining the Labour Party, in the 1950s and 1960s new generations of intellectuals streamed into the Labour Party as though completing a natural journey.

With the virtual rout of the Liberal Party, combined with its right-ward shift in the 1950s, three prominent Liberals brought up the straggling rear of the Liberal exodus to Labour which had begun more than four decades before. The reasons for their defection underlined Labour's inheritance of Britain's main 'thinking' traditions.

Before the war and indeed up to 1945, Liberals accepted the necessity for a considerable degree of economic planning. This point of view has been completely abandoned by nearly all their official spokesmen. ... Thirty years ago Mr.Maynard Keynes (as he then was) wrote: the political problem of mankind is to combine three things: economic efficiency, social justice and individual liberty. The problem has become far more urgent than it was in 1926, but the objective remains the same. Today it seems to us that the only effective instrument for achieving it is the Labour Party.[20]

And inside the party too, they smoothly took their place as the heirs of the previous generation of intellectuals, with the added advantage of being able to reflect their glory as the chief authors of its 'first instalment of socialism'. An accommodation between the intellectual middle class and trade union elements now replaced the tensions of the 1930s. Political possibilities for the intellectuals were further enhanced as the Labour left became reconciled to the 'responsible radicalism' of the new government both because of the consensus in British politics and because of the participation of many of its leaders in the 1945–51 governments. Prime examples of the former trend were John Strachey and Sir Stafford Cripps (leading 'communists' of the 1930s), while Aneurin Bevan represented the latter.

The social range of intellectual recruitment to Labour widened, but within limits: middle or upper middle class families predominated, if now with notable exceptions like Roy Jenkins and Bill Rodgers, who came from a comfortable trade union and a working-class background respectively. While the centrality of public schools gave way to an increasing grammar school component, the central universities continued their tenacious hold on the intellectual stratum. A prominent Labour intellectual of this generation who had not been to Oxford, Cambridge or London universities was rare. And, perhaps more than their class of origin, these narrow and rarefied milieux, and the even closer circles of their Fabian and Labour clubs, fostered friendships, affinities and political allegiances in each generation of intellectual recruits, and the revisionists were no exception.

With unintellectualism still central to the 'stupid party', the principal competition to Labour, among the intellectually inclined students, was further to its left. While in Cambridge a communist-controlled Socialist Club had combined the whole left until 1939, according to Raymond Williams,[21] in the post-war period, these left networks and circles, although stronger than ever, were divided clearly into those which accepted or would work with Communists and those who did not and would not. The intellectuals' relationship to the Labour Party had also been cultivated in informal circles around those dons who participated in Labour activities – the 'Cole group' around G.D.H. Cole in Oxford being a prominent case in point.[22] After the war, Labour's recruitment was especially brisk among the large number of returning soldiers at Oxford and Cambridge. By 1951 the Labour Party had drawn many young graduates into its parliamentary party: Anthony Wedgewood Benn, George Chetwynd, Anthony Crosland, Denis Healey, Roy Jenkins, Christopher Mayhew, George Thomson, Harold Wilson, and Michael Young. These university circles naturally extended to academics and intellectuals (not to say higher civil servants) outside the Labour Party. Jenkins, Crosland, Philip Williams and Denis Healey were part of the post-war generation of 'de-mobbed' officers. The generation of Bill Rodgers and Shirley Williams was taught by Crosland.

In addition to Labour Clubs and fairly frequent speeches and discussions by Labour's intellectuals, like Richard Crossman and Hugh Dalton, at the central universities, there was at least one, more purposive, agency of intellectual recruitment to Labour. In the 1950s, renouncing governmental ambition, Hugh Dalton had focused his attention on the party's 'inner counsels', to wit, the National Executive Committee (NEC). He also renewed his talent-scouting much more enthusiastically, devoting more time than ever to cultivating the political careers of the younger generation through his contact with the university Labour Clubs and the Fabian Society. He met many intellectually-inclined aspiring politicians and, if impressed, he would apply himself to 'booking seats' for them (as he called it),[23] that is, finding them parliamentary seats. After fighting a hopeless seat, or perhaps two, they would graduate to a marginal or safe one. Labour's electoral ascendancy from 1945 to 1955 greatly aided this process. As long as Labour had the largest share of the votes, it meant that there were more safe or winnable seats into with these young protégés could be 'parachuted'.[24] Dalton's activities probably also meant that the influx, which otherwise might have been less coordinated, led to the creation of a self-conscious and close-knit intellectual circle among those whom he called, with characteristically brutal candour, his 'poodles'.[25] However, Dalton's activities only accelerated and directed what was already a secular trend.

This much larger group of intellectuals changed the composition of the Parliamentary Labour Party (PLP) significantly. Until the Second World War, despite the crucial input of intellectuals into its politics and platform, the PLP largely reflected Labour's trade union roots in the overwhelmingly working-class and trade union origins of its MPs. However, in the post-war period a greater tolerance, indeed welcome, for a sizeable intellectual or professional middle class element was apparent. In 1918–35 working-class MPs in the PLP constituted 72 per cent, while the professions were 24 per cent. In 1951 these figures were 45 per cent and 45.5 per cent respectively.[26] And in the Attlee governments just under half the cabinet ministers came from intellectual or professional backgrounds. The reasons behind this included Labour's successful wartime invasion of significant sectors of the middle-class electoral territory,[27] wariness of certain types of working-class representatives susceptible to the 'aristocratic embrace' (the 'treachery' of Ramsay MacDonald, however unjustifiably, was still strong in Labour memory), and the success of the intellectuals attached to the party in the wartime and post-war governments. In a working-class party this intellectual element was also set apart, and as Ben Pimlott notes, post-war electoral circumstances gave rise to a clear group solidarity among them:

> So large was the post-war [Parliamentary] Party that there emerged identifiable social groupings within the ranks of the non-union middle-class MPs. The most dominant was a kind of public school and Oxbridge club: the nucleus of the so-called Hampstead set. Within this unacknowledged society's social walls, close friendships were forged and inevitable rivalries developed.[28]

In their still largely middle-class origins, their training at the central universities, and in their attachment to the principal British intellectual tradition, the revisionist generation thus fit the mould of British traditional intellectuals. As such they also cultivated interests outside politics whether professional (many had careers independent of Labour Party politics), intellectual, or literary, and by training and inclination they identified with the pre-existing intellectual element in the party. There were also, however, important differences in their ethos and political role when compared with the previous generation.

The very ease of their insertion into Labour politics marked them out. The revisionist generation entered parliament having spent very foreshortened periods of apprenticeship on the lower rungs of the party. Some served the party in a strictly intellectual capacity before entering parliament – the International Department (e.g. Denis Healey, 1945–52) and the Fabian Society (e.g. Bill Rodgers, 1951–60). Partly as a consequence, the nature of the intellectuals' relationship to the Labour Party was significantly different from those of the pre-war days when the relative weakness of the Labour Party, and its jealously maintained working-class identity, had meant that intellectuals became more involved with the labour movement than they had reason or opportunity for later. Ben Pimlott put his finger on the difference between a Dalton and a Gaitskell:

> Dalton had been shaped by the passions of Webbian Fabianism at its most evangelical, by the scramble for a seat in the anarchic early 1920s, by the traumas of 1931, by wheeler-dealing on the NEC – all before he became a senior minister. Gaitskell's public service career, by contrast, had a smooth upward trajectory, without any background in the rough and tumble of Labour political life.[29]

The contrast with other revisionists, even younger than Gaitskell, was, if anything, sharper. A precondition of any influence previous generations of intellectuals could exert in the party in the 1930s was a long and diverse involvement with the labour movement and its institutions, *first-hand*. In the 1950s and 1960s, by contrast, the Labour Party had become, as one of the two main parties which together dominated the political system, a 'normalised' component of the party system. Within it, Labour distinguished itself from the Conservative Party in providing a political platform for intellectuals. The revisionists thus saw themselves as performing, mainly if not exclusively, an intellectual function: of giving ideas to (and thus ultimately leading) the Labour Party. Their swift movement into the stratosphere of parliamentary politics left little time or opportunity for tarrying in the dense underbrush of the labour movement where they might have imbibed more strongly its traditions of solidarity and loyalty. Theirs was a world of parliamentary affairs (and, by aspiration, of government), constituency cultivation, and, for some, literary and other professional endeavours; of the Fabian Society and journals like *Encounter*, *Political Quarterly*, and *Socialist Commentary*. Any lack of what Pimlott called 'party feeling'[30] became both cause and consequence of the distance of these intellectuals from the lower reaches of the trade unions and the Labour Party which Labour's electoral strength in this period did nothing to minimise. It also made for a certain political naïveté, exhibited paradigmatically, as will be discussed in Chapter Five, by Gaitskell in his attempt to excise Clause 4 from the party's constitution.

Another major difference derived from Labour's new centrality to post-war British politics. The Labour Party was no longer a place for the marginal. Rather, as the consensus prevailed, it became ideologically and intellectually the *centre*. The price of this centrality was paid in the increased moderation of the younger more numerous generation of intellectuals compared with the older. While Dalton was unquestionably a Fabian socialist, the revisionist generation was more expressive of the liberal-Keynesian collectivism of the civil service, which had always been cultivated at Oxford and Cambridge. If their predecessors had rendered crucial service to Labour, by tempering the discordance between the almost other-worldly utopianism and this-worldly paralysis, by injecting a well-measured dose of realism and theoretical sophistication, the revisionist generation while still dedicated to 'facts', 'expertise' and undogmatic sensitivity to altered political, social and (sometimes) economic circumstances, also represented a dwindling of radicalism. This imparted to their strategy its fatal complacency.

This moderation was apparent, for example, in revisionists' unquestioned allegiance to the British constitution. Doubts about it, entertained in the 1930s by some of their intellectual predecessors,[31] were regarded as buried once and for all. The reformist successes of the Attlee governments, combined with the general climate of cultural restoration, meant that they became deeply committed to the existing parliamentary system. Their political style was in the main 'responsible' – 'government' rather than 'opposition'-minded – as Crossman was to point out,[32] and their aim was a Labour Party under their direction as the 'natural party of government'. When the incongruity of such a posture on the part of a 'socialist' party was pointed out, Crosland rationalised it by characteristically raising settled pragmatism to the level of principle:

> Those who follow the ethic of responsibility … hold themselves accountable for the consequences of their actions. Lacking the moral pride which enables them to say that one single end transcends all others and justifies a total sacrifice, they accept the limitations of political action. They grapple with pragmatic questions of choice and priorities, and perceive the need for reconciliation and compromise. They behave like a Church, which recognises that the world is wicked and imperfect but still believes that they can help a majority of the people some way along the road: and not like a sect, concerned only with its exclusive membership and with the one millennial choice between salvation and damnation. They, too, have ethical standards, of equal value to those of the dedicated purists. But, their aim is different – the best that can be achieved, consistently with their principles under given circumstances. Unlike the chiliasts, therefore, they are concerned with political power.[33]

But the sociological and cultural determinants of the revisionists' outlook are just as important as their alleged lack of moral pride.

Finally, *modernisation* rather than traditional socialism became central to their vision. In the wake of the socialist successes of the Attlee governments, Britain's principal problem, it appeared – especially when compared to the dynamism of American society and later the modernity of reconstructed Europe – was that it was drab, class-ridden and weighed down with tradition. Like so many other intellectuals of their generation, many if not most of the new Labour intellectuals had visited the US (and several married Americans)[34] and been impressed by its apparent classlessness and dynamism. Unable to proclaim the ultra-capitalist society as the model for Labour, it was Sweden which Crosland increasingly named as worthy of emulation. Modern and welfarist, it had the additional advantage of a hegemonic Social Democratic party with a long and creditable governing record. In Fabianism they had also inherited the native modernising intellectual tradition, such as it was. But the already contained modernising impulse of this tradition tended to be compromised by the self-consciously leisured and cultivated amateurism of the cultural restoration which in the 1950s cast its shadow on the 'sociological' intellectuals just as much as on literary ones. Crosland, for example, while acknowledging the Fabians' achievement, wanted to repudiate their unseemly, even *gauche*, zeal.

But now we surely need a different set of values. Permeation has more than
done its job. To-day we are all incipient bureaucrats and practical administrators. We have all, so to speak, been trained at the LSE, are familiar with
Blue Books and White Papers, and know our way around Whitehall. We
realise that we must guard against romantic or Utopian notions: that hard
work and research are virtues: that we must do nothing foolish or impulsive:
and that Fabian pamphlets must be diligently studied. We know these things
too well. Posthumously the Webbs have won their battle, and converted a
generation to their standards. Now the time has come for a reaction: for a
greater emphasis on private life, on freedom and dissent, on culture, beauty,
leisure and even frivolity. Total abstinence and a good filing system are not
now the right sign-posts to the socialist Utopia: or at least, if they are, some
of us will fall by the wayside.[35]

Without its non-conformist zeal, however, Fabianism risked being denatured. The revisionists may have been attracted by the results of
modernisation, but it is less clear that they were whole-hearted about
what had so far proved the necessary intellectual stance for achieving
it in British conditions.

The Development of Revisionism: 1951–1956

The successful completion of the 1945 Labour programme, *Let Us Face
the Future* by 1948, and the directionlessness that had afflicted the Labour
government thereafter, had led many of its members to face the 1951
defeat with immense relief. Public acrimony between the advocates of
consolidation (including Attlee and most of the moderate leadership)
and the advocates of 'more socialism' (who had recently precipitated
themselves as the Bevanites) contributed to the less than glorious end
of an historic government. It was clearly time to chart, and strike out
in, new directions. Older Labour intellectuals actively pressed the
younger generation into service for the task of fashioning a new programme for Labour. A new project of restating socialism and its goals
initiated in 1949 principally by G.D.H. Cole, with the help of Margaret
Cole, Richard Crossman, and John Strachey, resulted in the 1952
publication of *New Fabian Essays* under the editorship of Richard
Crossman.[36] The group who initiated this project initially contained a
wide assortment of political opinion and included the Bevanites Richard
Crossman, Ian Mikardo and Harold Wilson. Indeed, except for a brief
period of Bevanite upsurge in the mid-1950s, left and right in the
Labour Party were not so sharply distinguished. *New Fabian Essays* thus
contained articles by John Strachey, Anthony Crosland, Roy Jenkins,
Auten Albu, Margaret Cole and Denis Healey, all identified with the
revisionist tendency, as well as essays by the Bevanites, Richard Crossman and Ian Mikardo. This was the beginning of revisionism. With
William Rodgers starting, initially part-time, as General Secretary of

the Fabian Society in 1951, the project of programmatic and philosophical rethinking, no doubt initiated in a more catholic spirit, was soon inherited by the young revisionists.

There was wide agreement on the need for some reformulation of party policy and philosophy in view of the 'symptoms of a ... serious ailment, a failure of the sense of direction which alone can unify and sustain a great political party.'[37] While the title of the collection revealed the younger intellectuals' consciousness of their intellectual heritage, Crossman also clearly marked out the distinctiveness of their new task from the one the original Fabian had set themselves:

> Most of the early Fabians ... repudiated socialist theory as dangerous Teutonic verbiage. They assumed that everyone knew the difference between justice and injustice, happiness and unhappiness, and that it was the job of the Fabian Society to show the British trade unionist – and any politician who cared to listen – the way to make Britain an efficient example of socially planned happiness. This Benthamite approach to socialism, in contrast to the Marxist theories of the Continent, had considerable advantages. It suited the anti-intellectual bias of the Labour Movement, and it faithfully reflected the conscientious objection to dogma, whether theological or political, on which our British conception of personal freedom rests.[38]

In diagnosing the programmatic exhaustion which plagued the last years of the Attlee government, Crossman pointed to the inability of cabinet ministers to take part in 'freewheeling discussions of socialist policy' while in office. However, there was also something more fundamental. Given that Labour's 1945 programme had been essentially a set of discrete proposals for reform only held together by a diffuse ethical yearning for socialist utopia, this exhaustion was inevitable. The crux of the problem, as Crossman clearly saw it, was a lack of theory.

> [The] absence of a theoretical basis for practical programmes of action is the main reason why the post-war Labour Government marked the end of a century of social reform and not, as its socialist supporters had hoped, the beginning of a new epoch. ... Philosophy begins where pragmatism fails. When the common-sense socialist has come to the end of his programme and there are no longer a number of obvious reforms which men of goodwill broadly agree should be carried out, it is time to sit back and reflect.[39]

Despite their immensely successful programme, intellectuals in the Labour Party had hitherto only serviced labourism. According theory such centrality in the formulation of Labour's new socialism (a truer socialism, moreover, than the common sense social reform of the recent past) surely marked the new security and ascendance which intellectuals now enjoyed in the Labour Party. However, there was also another, more systematic, reason for the centrality of theory. In the 1930s Fabianism had been able to provide the necessary bureaucratic/

intellectual element for the achievement of the already established and immediate goals of the labour movement for greater equality, material advancement and security. But any further steps in the 1950s needed a new input. However, the working-class movement of the 1950s seemed in no condition to generate fresh perspectives or demands. The trade union leadership of the 1950s, comfortable with leaving politics to the politicians, seemed to have turned their entire attention to the goal of ever better wage settlements for their members and the secondary problem of eradicating the 'Communist menace' from the movement. Under the control of this right-wing leadership the movement paid less and less attention to the tasks of political mobilisation and education for socialism which had formerly occupied at least a significant minority in the movement. The labour movement was thus unable, on its own, to provide a new set of 'obvious' reforms for the party to take up. The onus of providing a new programme, necessarily therefore, lay on theory.

Revisionism's Intellectual Resources

This early recognition of the need for an overarching *theoretical* basis on which any reliable future programme for socialist politics had to be built was one thing and the ability of the empiricist, untheoretical British intellectual tradition to supply such theory, quite another.

Indeed, during the inter-war period the native empiricist and narrow bent of British culture, averse to larger social theorization, had received strong reinforcement – a paradoxically theoretical and philosophical one – by what Perry Anderson, in his 1969 survey of post-war British culture, dubbed the 'White Emigration': the arrival in Britain from Europe of significant numbers of conservative and even counter-revolutionary intellectuals fleeing the social upheavals of their own societies. There operated, according to Anderson, a process of elective affinity in their choice of destination. Britain's social tranquillity and lack of revolutionary history attracted a definite type of European intellectual – one who was fleeing 'the ruinous contagion of Europe – general ideas'. Many Austrians came, including Karl Popper and F.A. von Hayek – which was hardly surprising given that the dominant intellectual tradition of the former Austro-Hungarian empire had self-consciously aspired to the empiricism and singular conservatism of its British counterpart. Anderson argued that this ironically had the effect of imparting a highly theoretical, indeed dogmatic, shape to previous doxic verities – '[i]n effect the émigrés for the first time systematized the refusal of system. They codified the slovenly empiricism of the past, and thereby narrowed and hardened it.'

The émigré intellectuals dominated in all fields except economics (which was dominated by the 'retotalisation' of the field by the most prominent native intellectual of his time, Keynes) and literary criticism ('for obvious reasons'). The émigrés' main intellectual conversation was conducted with British conservatism, making it theoretical: its chickens would not come to roost until the rise of the New Right in the 1970s. Their immediate impact on the style and orientation of the revisionists was more general and diffuse. As the already narrow English philosophy moved into the precise but rarefied realms of linguistic philosophy under the momentous impact of Wittgenstein, on the one hand it even more dogmatically exempted itself from the requirement of theorising and articulating the wider social experience and, on the other, it legitimised a widened scope for empirically based, scientific or expert, technical decisions in social inquiry and administration. This had a debilitating effect on socialist thought as Iris Murdoch pointed out. More than conservatism, socialism needed a social and political theory. But philosophy seemed to have become a logical, technical and empirical matter and more generally, theorising had come to be regarded as inherently illiberal: 'liberal-minded persons [it was felt] should surround their choices with a minimum of theory, relying rather on open above-board references to facts or to principles'.[40] (This mania for precision and factual grounding, and hostility to theory, was also, as we know, a valuable weapon against communism in the atmosphere of the Cold War.) In a philosophical environment where 'imprecision' was elevated to the status of a grave misdemeanour, speculation in ethics and politics was marginalised even more effectively than before. Thus re-inforced, the empiricism of the Fabian tradition led, in revisionism, to an approach to the problems of post-war Britain that attempted to attack social problems on the basis of empirical knowledge but did not challenge the wider intellectual and political framework in which the solutions were proposed.

With the sociological deficiency of British culture thus reinforced, on questions of wider social theory the revisionists resorted to the combination of imported American behaviouralist political science and the native empirical traditions in social administration which stood in for a proper sociology in British culture.[41] However, American political sociology only seemed to impoverish further what passed for social thought. Its 'value-freedom', its devotion to 'facts', and its general restriction of its field of vision to the level of symptoms proved eminently compatible with native empiricist inclinations. Political scientists like the Canadian Robert Mackenzie, the American Richard Rose, David Butler and the pollster Mark Abrams directly and indirectly influenced the thinking of the revisionists. Crosland, among others, took their work very seriously, regarding it as 'proper and appropriate study for the politician'.[42] Its findings, such as the 'embourgeoisement' of the working class and the politically harmful nature of Labour's 'class image', became central to their understanding of the changes in post-war British society. Even the most reactionary conclusion of this political sociology eventually found its way into revisionism: that democracy could only be sustained by limiting the amount of political participation. In the late 1960s Crosland argued against proposals for increased political participation: A 'continuous political activism by the great bulk of the population would ... pose a great threat to the stability of our democracy.'[43] Crosland also saw the increased influence of the media in the political process as reducing the need for activism.

> The elan of the rank and file is less essential to winning elections. With the growing penetration of the mass media, political campaigning has become increasingly centralised; and the traditional local activists, and door to door canvassing and the rest, are now largely a ritual.[44]

Given the narrow perspectives of such a social theory, even modest attempts at theorising the state in British politics, such as those made by the new converts to Marxism in the 1930s, were now no longer made at least outside the confines of British Trotskyism.[45] For their part the revisionists adopted a domesticated, empirical, technically fastidious, if also politically unthreatening intellectual style.

The 'end of ideology' thesis, central to both American political sociology and, through the work, most notably of Karl Popper and Isaiah Berlin, to the White Emigration in British culture, was also part of the revisionist world view. First put forward by Edward Shils at a Congress for Cultural Freedom meeting in 1954, it was later popularised and elaborated by others, most notably Daniel Bell, in his collection of essays of the same name.[46] Although not published until 1960, the views expressed in *The End of Ideology* incubated in the 1950s in interaction with other prominent western centre-left intellectuals, including revisionists such as Crosland – an interaction which was facilitated by the activities of the Congress for Cultural Freedom. The basic argument was that in the western democracies at least, politics no longer revolved around ideologies. Indeed, ideology, unable to deal with the complexities of the modern world, had itself become the object of social scientific analysis. Political issues in western democracies in the post-war, welfarist, Keynesian, affluent era were now largely technical ones which would be resolved by experts and intellectuals in progressive directions without the need for mass participation, or any political polarisation of opinion, around them. This demise of ideology was hardly lamentable, even if a few talented but misguided intellectuals on the emerging 'new left' insisted on thinking otherwise: 'Ideology makes it unnecessary for people to confront individual issues on their individual merits'.[47] This obviously appealed to the revisionists.

As traditional intellectuals, claiming to speak for society as a whole, the revisionists still retained a certain squeamishness about their allegiance to a class-based political party. The centrality of the Labour Party to the new consensus politics and the wider range of its political recruitment and electoral support, which meant that it was less of a *partisan* or sectional position, had already eased matters somewhat. Now the end of ideology thesis seemed to imply that with the abolition of the most stark inequities of pre-war capitalism, the issues that so passionately divided societies had lost their urgency. Moreover, it encouraged a cult of 'expertise' which was also not unpalatable to the revisionists. Politics could now be managed by professional parliamentary politicians and a few intellectuals with a social conscience in progressive, humane, socially generous and tolerant directions.

It was within this imported 'sociological' understanding that the revisionists now placed their inherited intellectual wherewithal. The practical core of their outlook continued to be dominated by the native intellectual resources of Fabian gradualism and research and Keynesianism. Through this, they underscored their membership in the native intellectual tradition which, by thus providing the basis for the hegemonic ideology still retained its prominence in British politics.

Given revisionism's conformity with the dominant cultural trends of its time, Crosland's *The Future of Socialism*, which was and remains the principal statement of the revisionist world-view, was a book which, in a sense, had been widely read before it was written. Its distinctive achievement was to have synthesised and distilled much available social scientific research and the overall drift of popular opinion. In doing this Crosland also fashioned an overarching political and theoretical perspective. This was the basis of its popularity. Its following was huge and in the 1950s, many who had read the book (and probably many others who hadn't) found their way to socialism through its ideas.

Journals and Institutions of Revisionism

The Labour Party policy documents of the late 1950s and early 1960s which reflected the influence of revisionism were only the culmination of a longer endeavour which was played out in other, intellectual, arenas.

Revisionism originated as mentioned earlier, under the auspices of the Fabian Society, which, refurbished and rejuvenated in the post-war period, accommodated the new intellectual generation. By 1951, with the recent deaths of many long-standing officers, its executive included many of Labour's younger intellectuals such as Anthony Crosland, Richard Crossman, Hugh Gaitskell, Roy Jenkins, Ian Mikardo, Shirley Williams, Bill Rodgers and Harold Wilson. And, as we have seen, a process of rethinking Labour's programme had been initiated within it in 1949, directed in the first instance at 'the keen minority of thinking people'.[48] The Fabian Society had an air of an exclusive club and it became one of the hothouses of revisionism. It became an important focus for the intellectuals who contributed actively to its organisation, publication and other activities, like summer schools and university lectures. In the years which followed, the development of revisionism could also be witnessed in the journal *Socialist Commentary* and frequent articles in *Encounter*, the high-brow, predominantly cultural, magazine, as well as in Fabian pamphlets.

Socialist Commentary brought a continental influence to revisionism. Although it did not become famous as the house journal of the revisionists until almost a decade later, when the latter emerged as an identifiable intellectual tendency, one can trace in its pages the themes and preoccupations of the revisionists beginning in the late 1940s. The journal which became so intimately identified with British revisionism actually originated in the quite obscure activities of German socialist (SPD) émigrés during and immediately after the war. Its earlier incarnation, *Militant Vanguard*, was a tiny journal whose duplicated copies began circulation during the war. Owing to the continued rationing of paper after it, *Socialist Commentary* was only able to start regular publication as a monthly magazine in 1949. Like the paper, its publishers were also rechristened: Militant Vanguard International became the Socialist Union. The core of émigrés in the Socialist Union saw themselves as 'Nelsonites' – followers of a little-known German Kantian philosopher called Leonard Nelson. Originally members of the *Unabhaengige Sozialdemokratische Partei der Deutschlands* (USPD), the break-away caused by the SPD's support for the First World War, they had rejoined the SPD after the war (while the majority of the USPD joined the *Kommunistiche Partei der Deutschlands*). The Nelsonites retained, however, their identity in the *Internationaler Jugendbund* (IJB) and, after 1926, the *Internationaler Sozialisticher Kampfbund* (ISK). In the words of Mary Saran, founder editor of *Socialist Commentary*, the journal 'stressed the ethical foundations of socialism, anchored in the philosophical concepts of Kant, Fries and Nelson. … The group saw in ideals and the education of those willing to serve them a 'better security' (the title of one of Nelson's pamphlets) for the achievement of socialism, meaning a classless and just society, than in the 'scientific' analysis of the trends of development in society which, according to Marxian teaching, showed that socialism was the necessary historical outcome'.[49] This group was later expelled from the German SPD for attempting, like Bernstein earlier, to get it to shelve its revolutionary Marxist (Erfurt) programme (which it eventually did in 1959). Essentially revisionist socialists in the classical sense, they imparted some of their spirit to the young British revisionists of whom Tony Crosland was an early recruit.

These values of an ethical, gradualist socialism were the basis of *Socialist Commentary*. Apart from the link to the classical revisionism of German social democracy, there was at least one other notable international cross-current: Willi Eichler and Erich Ollenhauer were members of this émigré group who, upon returning to Germany after the war, were to play central roles in the reorientation of the SPD in the revisionist Bad Godesberg programme of 1959.[50] The British members of the Socialist Union included the industrial relations expert Allan Flanders, Rita Hinden of the Fabian Colonial Bureau (and much-loved figure in the Labour Party), Margaret Cole and others, all of whom also sat on the editorial board of *Socialist Commentary*. The rather younger revisionists were mainly contributors to the journal and during the 1950s Hugh Gaitskell was the treasurer of a supporting organisation, Friends of *Socialist Commentary*. From the early 1950s Gaitskell, Crosland, Jenkins, Healey, Michael Young, Patrick Gordon-Walker and other notable revisionists all appeared in the pages of *Socialist Commentary*.

But, while *Socialist Commentary* and the Socialist Union may have aided the revisionist project, their views remained, for the British revisionists, a little eccentric. This eccentricity had more to do with tone and style than with content – they tended to have a more old-fashioned mind-set, revealed in their language which eschewed that of modern social science.[51] In an interesting contrast with revisionism, the Socialist Union held 'managerialism', which established ever more remote centres of power and alienated individuals from communities to be one of the principal dangers of the contemporary era. Crosland, on the other hand (as we shall see), celebrated these same developments as representing the diffusion of the power structure in private industry.

The magazine *Encounter* was set up in 1953 by the Congress for Cultural Freedom (CCF), a US-based organisation.[52] Edited by a number of prominent cultural luminaries including Stephen Spender, Melvyn Lasky and Irving Kristol, from the very start it hit an ultra-sophisticated cultural key. It provided Britain, for the first time, with a fashionable and popular cultural magazine of a sort which had been characteristic of continental intellectual life. And it was widely read and contributed to by leading socialists and liberals. In the late 1960s it was discovered that the CCF, and through it *Encounter* magazine, had been in receipt of CIA funds between 1953–64, and that the CCF had been part of a larger cultural Cold War campaign conducted by the CIA. Following these disclosures *Encounter* capitulated to the evidence while still making protestations as to its editorial independence. It was, however, widely seen to have been compromised, especially in the area of foreign affairs where it had consistently forsworn any criticism of US foreign policy. Suspicions continue to hang about the revisionists' liaison with this periodical, and it may be pertinent to clarify that many leading British intellectuals (including some to the left of the revisionists) wrote for it: as a prestigious forum with a wide and sophisticated audience, it was a valued medium for intellectual exchange. The revelations of the late 1960s made many of its former contributors and patrons feel duped and many publicly dissociated themselves from it. The revisionists, however, were more sanguine. They felt their association with it to have been of a purely instrumental sort.[53]

Revisionism in the Affluent Society

In addressing the question of the future direction and policies of the Labour Party as it went into opposition in 1951, revisionism was inevitably shaped by its interpretation of Labour's experience of 1945–51. The reforming achievements of these years were principally based on Labour's programme of the 1930s. The war years had added to it the recommendations of the 1942 Beveridge Report on welfare and the 1944 White Paper on Employment Policy which confirmed the acceptance of Keynesianism in government fiscal and monetary policy.

Between 1945 and 1948 a welfare state infrastructure, with the National Health Service as its proudest show-piece, had been laid down; redistributive taxation and planning for the maintenance of full employment became the basis of fiscal policy; and a number of key industries were nationalised, bringing much needed rationalization and economies of scale and purportedly increasing the government's ability to influence the economy as a whole. In retrospect it is clear that these achievements fell far short of what might have been hoped.[54] Nationalisation did not amount to socialisation. Nor were nationalised industries used to influence the overall direction of the economy. Apart from subsidising the private sector, they seemed no different from private sector firms. The pioneering reforms in the area of welfare turned out to be less egalitarian than had been expected and their bureaucratic nature failed to generate public participation and loyalty. Despite progressive taxation, except for significant 'once off' redistributions of incomes between the highest and lowest income brackets which had tended to take place in the exceptional circumstance of the world wars, other reductions in income disparities were only marginal.[55] In the face of balance of payments constraints, overall economic policy remained orthodox and after the convertibility crisis of 1947 austerity, a wage freeze and a devaluation (in 1949) were the highlights.

However, an appreciation of revisionism – its strengths *and* limitations – is easier if one also looks at the revisionist's own assessment of the record of the Attlee governments: wartime efforts at the amelioration of 'primary poverty' had been successful and were augmented thereafter by transfers through family allowances and national insurance. There had also just been a significant redistribution of incomes and the revisionists expected the trend to continue, albeit more moderately, in the future. A fully employed buoyant economy, strong trade unions, and the beginnings of a structure of public expenditure directed towards the creation of a host of common amenities such as education and health, all contributed to a bias for optimism. Nationalisation of key industries had brought rationalisation and efficiency in previously un-economic units. In short the principal pledges accumulated since the 1930s seemed to have been honourably redeemed.

Now, however, the Labour Party did not have a clear socialist way forward. While certainly effective and popular, the synthesis of the late 1930s had produced only a short term programme for Labour, reflected in the title of the 1937 party document, *Labour's Immediate Programme*. But the new task also differed qualitatively from that which the preceding generation of traditional intellectuals had performed for the party in the 1930s. Then the intellectual tasks had consisted in synthesising working-class demands accumulated over at least forty years, into a programme that also took into account the technical realities of the capitalist economy. While it had been no mean task, and was crucial to the achievements the Attlee governments could claim to their credit, it did not amount to a definitive socialism. As the young Roy Jenkins put it:

> In fact, the domestic measures which found their way into the Labour Pro-grammes leading up to 1945 and which were implemented in the succeeding years largely chose themselves. They did this not because they flowed auto-matically from the vision of a fully socialist society towards which their advocates were looking (although once chosen, they certainly became steps in that direction), but because they were designed to deal with specific and keenly felt grievances. They were the answer to the most obvious and the most irksome flaws in the old system. ... So far as the motives of those who gave their support were concerned, the five years following 1945 were, as Mr. Crossman has remarked, the end of a century of social reform rather than the beginning of a new era of socialism.[56]

As the revisionists saw it, what was required was a fundamental re-examination of the party's aims and methods in an accompanying re-theorisation of society. This had, in any case, never been done by Labour's intellectuals and it became even more urgent given the changes wrought by the Attlee governments, and the changes occurring in the wider economic environment in which any future socialism would have to operate.

Recent changes in British society required, in the first instance, some corresponding changes in the socialist aims: the revisionists reassessed their urgency and reordered their priorities. As the Conservatives accepted the terms of the post-war settlement, the achievements of the Attlee period were seen as irreversible. This meant, moreover, that the revisionists had to go about the business of 'asking for support for change from an already largely tolerable state of affairs'.[57] The urgency of basic material improvement was now lost. This reassessment also informed revisionism's reordering of conventional socialist aims in a structure of priorities: in the revisionist world-view, equality stood above all other aims. Its achievement provided the ordering principle in all other areas of policy: these were now accorded the status of means and not independent goals in themselves. They would be judged by their utility in approximating more closely the supreme aim of equality. If the formerly strident march towards the socialist utopia acquired, in revisionist's hands, a more leisured, indeed gentlemanly gait, the revisionist utopia remained a recognisably socialist one. Roy Jenkins's early list of revisionist objectives would have found few socialist dissenters: '[W]hat we want is more equality, more democratic participation in the work of running society as a whole, but particularly in industry, more effective community control over the shape of the economy, and at the same time the greatest possible dissemination of power and decision to individuals so far as consumption is considered, and to smaller units so far as production is considered.'[58]

Equality was, primarily if not exclusively, material equality and the revisionists' principal criticism of the Attlee record was its less than fulsome achievement in this important area. While creditable redistributions had occurred, it had

> stopped short at a point at which 1% of the population still ha[d] nearly 50% of the nation's capital wealth; at which there [were] 400 persons owning more than a million pounds' worth of property; at which there [were] still about 2,100 persons with gross incomes of more than 20,000 pounds a year (60% of these incomes being less than a half earned, and nearly 40% of them wholly unearned); and at which, even after the present heavy rates of direct taxation, the largest net incomes [were] still more than thirty times the smallest adult wage.[59]

Equality could not, of course, be considered any sort of levelling and, in its diminished material urgency, could afford to be generous – to be breached in the interests of variety, experimentation and economic growth. Nor was it a mean, meritocratic 'equality of opportunity'.

> [I]n Britain equality of opportunity and social mobility, though they lead to the most admirable distribution of intelligence are not enough. They need, not to be played down, as some sociologists would have us do, but to be combined with measures, above all in the educational field, to equalise the distribution of rewards and privileges so as to diminish the degree of class stratification, the injustice of large inequalities, and the collective discontents which come from too great a dispersion of rewards. The limited goal is not, from a socialist point of view, sufficient.[60]

Laying proportionally greater emphasis on non-material aspects of equality in an attack on the centrality of economics reminiscent of classical Bernsteinian revisionism, revisionism's non-material ambitions included fostering a dynamic and ideologically classless society like America, combined with a greater realisation of material equality than obtained there. To equality of incomes and wealth had to be added that of opportunity and reward, and also social respect and status. These were justified by Crosland not only on the basis of social justice but, going beyond 'metaphysical' speculation and into the precise realm of sociology, also on the basis of the social advantages of eliminating social waste (of talent), social snobbery, collective resentments and elitism.

The methods by which equality was to be progressively attained were diverse. If the recent redistribution of earned incomes was now a parameter of social debate, the next problem of economic equality was to attack the still wide disparities of wealth and hence of unearned incomes through the imposition of large death duties, a tax on gifts *inter vivos* to pre-empt evasion of the former, and stiffer corporate profits taxes and individual taxation. But this material redistribution between classes had its limits as a means of improving the standards of living of the bulk of the population. Indeed, in terms of incomes, by 1956 Crosland could declare that 'if we are considering vertical redistribution *between entire social classes*, there are too few pounds. When the pound taken from the millionaire has to be spread in farthings amongst 960 beneficiaries, the welfare criterion inevitably gives an ambiguous answer; and few people would judge that a clear gain would result.'[61] And while in the interests of equality and justice a further redistribution of wealth should be carried out, equality was not now primarily a question of further redistribution, but rather one of seeing to it that the proceeds of further economic growth were distributed in a way that enhanced rather than diminished the standards of equality achieved in Britain. While on the one hand this emphasis on growth as the basis of (future) equality represented a commonsensical recognition of the less than unlimited prospects of the other route, it also underlined their reliance on the dynamics of a capitalist economy.

Equality was also to be served through the expansion and improvement of state services and social infrastructure – increasing *common* social and civic amenities. Such schemes included the expansion of municipal ownership of housing, a qualitatively better state secondary education system able to match the standards of public and grammar schools, state support for the arts, the extension of social security through a National Superannuation Scheme, and so on. This was to be done, not by expanding state expenditure relative to GNP (which, in the interests of personal liberty, could only be increased marginally), but would surely require the expansion of state revenues in absolute terms, which could only come through a fast-growing economy. Economic growth was also central in that an indiscriminate expansion of government services in a stagnant economy would eventually begin to eat into working-class incomes without a corresponding significant redistribution.

The principal avenue of advance toward equality in its non-material (social and cultural) aspects lay in dealing with the highly stratified, elitist system of education in Britain – the source of its class-ridden culture. The revisionists proposed a closer integration of grammar and public schools within a comprehensive state school system on the basis of a more equitable entrance system than one based on the ability to pay.

Clearly, in this affably generous revisionist scheme of things there was little room for the divisive and jarring methods of the past. The most important and contentious aspect of revisionism was the displacement of public ownership from its status as an important goal of Labour governments to one below even that of a worthy instrument for equality. The revisionists were certainly committed to the principle of a mixed economy. This meant in practice that they accepted the nationalisations that had already been carried out by the previous Labour governments. But, they pointed out, nationalisations had hitherto been carried through for a motley collection of reasons, each specific to the industry nationalised, and that they did not add up to a unified theory of the aims and place of nationalisation in socialism.[62] If equality was to be the primary aim of socialism now, nationalisation could no longer be regarded as the goal of socialism as it was in some quarters of the left. On revisionist principles it had to be treated as a means, to be justified on the basis of the merits of each case, on its ability to promote the clearly articulated aims of socialism. As far as the aim of equality was concerned, in contemporary capitalism, Crosland asserted, 'it is perfectly possible, even in a rapidly growing economy, to limit net rewards to shareholders by methods other than nationalisation'.[63] And, furthermore, public ownership in this scenario might take such diverse forms as cooperative enterprise, municipalisation and the nationalisation of individual firms, as well as the traditional centralised, industry-wide form principally used by Labour governments. To the extent that nationalisation provided the government with additional leverage on the pace of the economy, the leverage it had already acquired by the early 1950s was sufficient, by revisionist estimates.

Rather than nationalisation, governmental control over the economy was now to be exerted by planning. This was especially feasible since the disjunction between ownership and control and the consequent decline in power of the individual capitalist magnate and the rise of corporate technocracy greatly increased the potential for effective planning. And the revisionists had included quite an array of planning instruments in their directive arsenal. On the side of production they included public ownership, regional policy, fiscal incentives and measures against monopoly. On the side of incomes, as we have seen, taxation and transfers were meant to ensure greater equality over time. However, these only supplemented, and marginally aided, the Keynesian manipulation of macro-economic aggregates on the demand side which was now economic orthodoxy. This would serve to maintain economic growth and full employment which were to be the primary factors in future equality. For the revisionists, the possibility of Keynesian intervention had resolved any problems of the trade cycle with its propensity to boom and bust:

> Traditionally, or at least since Marx, socialist thought has been dominated by the economic problems posed by capitalism: poverty, mass unemployment, squalor, instability, and even the possibility of the imminent collapse of the whole system. These were problems of the most severe and urgent character, and it was correct to argue that major economic changes must precede the execution of socialist policy in other fields. But, it is gradually ceasing to be correct today. Capitalism has been reformed almost out of recognition. Despite occasional minor recessions and balance of payments crises, full employment and at least a tolerable degree of stability are likely to be maintained.[64]

Keynesianism was, however, only the keystone of revisionism's deep faith in the basic progressiveness and rationality of capitalism to which governments only needed to apply small correctives. Given the generally satisfactory functioning of the market in allocating productive resources efficiently, and the ability of governments to easily correct its less than satisfactory (unequal) allocation of incomes, Crosland could see no reason for more detailed planning. There was, of course, the possibility, clearly foreseen by Keynesians, that full employment and the consequent strengthening of the industrial bargaining power of the unions, would lead to wage-push inflation. Such a situation would necessitate more detailed control over incomes and prices but, this eventuality was regarded as remote and Crosland, at least, did not consider its implications in detail.[65]

Post-war capitalism in its current high-growth mass-production phase (whose longevity it hardly occurred to the revisionists to question in the 1950s) also embodied a more secular equalising logic. Its virtuous circle, in which high wages in productive jobs led to larger markets for mass-produced cheap consumer goods, itself brought material prosperity to the working class without expanding upper-class consumables to the same extent. Increased working-class access to products formerly the province of upper-class consumption also encouraged an ideological de-classing of British society. Indeed it is very interesting to see how Crosland consistently resisted most suggestions that capitalism could be inefficient, unjust or irrational in spheres other than the distribution of wealth and incomes.[66] The latter problems could and should be dealt with through a combination of redistributive fiscal measures, state and common services and economic growth. Pointing to any other foibles of capitalism amounted to petty quibbling: the capitalism of Crosland's imagination was eminently plannable, reformable. Crosland provided an acerbic defence of rising material standards as a socialist objective against paternalist objections to the vulgarity and acquisitiveness this might generate.

> I should ... regard a sustained rise in material standards as wholly desirable – probably because it will increase personal contentment, but certainly on grounds of personal freedom, since rising standards inevitably widen the area of choice and opportunity: on grounds of social justice, which surely requires that the masses, for so long deprived of luxuries which others have enjoyed, should now also be admitted to the world of material ease, if only to see whether they do in fact enjoy it: on strict egalitarian grounds, since rising consumption increases the fact and consciousness of social equality and so contributes to the fundamental aims of socialism: and on grounds of democratic anti-paternalism, since this is clearly what the workers want. And anyone who tells them they are wrong, and that in fact they are simply becoming vulgarised, or Americanised, will be given rather short shrift, especially if he himself appears to have a good deal of material fat which might be melted off.[67]

Thus shorn of its less comfortable edges, the egalitarianism of the revisionists seemed almost mainstream, while the atmosphere of buoyant economic expectations made the prospect of the achieving such goals seem concretely near.

While these gradual advances toward greater equality were seen as further steps in the social revolution set in motion by the previous Labour government, there were also important socialist goals beyond them. With the achievement of the aim of greater substantial equality, Crosland affirmed, 'we shall turn our attention increasingly to other, and in the long run more important, spheres – of personal freedom, happiness, and cultural endeavour: the cultivation of leisure, beauty, grace, gaiety, excitement, and of all the proper pursuits, whether elevated, vulgar, or eccentric, which contribute to the varied fabric of a full private and family life'.[68] Personal freedom from any intolerable and archaic restrictions in the social and cultural spheres had to be championed by a 'party of advance', as Roy Jenkins called it. The targets of this drive for social and cultural modernization included 'the divorce laws, licensing laws, prehistoric (and flagrantly unfair) abortion laws, obsolete penalties for sexual abnormality, the illiterate censorship of books and plays, and the remaining restrictions on the equal rights of women.'[69] The revisionists' goal then was a prosperous, urbane, civilised, equal, free and tolerant society – one in their own self-image.

The Underlying Assumptions

This light and breezy revisionist utopia was, however, underwritten by key but problematic political and economic assumptions.

From the start the revisionists had been immune to the fear that the return of Conservative government would mean a return to the pre-war style of confrontational crisis-prone capitalism complete with rising poverty, unemployment, insecurity and distress. They recognised that the Attlee governments had maintained but not created full employment and fully expected that a Conservative government would continue to do likewise, as they indeed did. In these circumstances the 'inevitability of gradualism' principle could reassert itself and the achievement of Labour's socialist goals would take place through periods of Labour reforms necessarily interrupted by periods of Conservative rule (seen as stemming not necessarily from any class interests, but rather from the natural conservatism of the people). Roy Jenkins saw direct parallels between the fates of the two great reforming administrations of twentieth century Britain, whose reforms had survived long periods of Tory rule by and large intact. The Conservatives in the twentieth century, faced on the one hand with the need to compete for the working-class vote and on the other with the loss of nerve of the class it had traditionally represented, had, as Jenkins saw it, taken to habitually stealing Liberal and Labour clothes. He was also keenly aware that the 1945 landslide had crucially rested on a substantial middle-class support and this could not but be rather fickle. The plain result would be electoral oscillation between the two great parties in the land – and, as far as Jenkins was concerned, there was much to be said for this amicable arrangement. This pattern, he felt, would continue in the foreseeable future.

The improbability of uninterrupted power for Labour was no threat to socialism. Indeed, it was positively necessary in that, as the experience of the past had shown, the achievement of a reforming government's programme in office led to a programmatic exhaustion which could be remedied only in the comparative leisure of opposition. This elaborately comfortable scenario revealed the revisionists' faith in existing con-stitutional and administrative arrangements.

Perhaps the most important assumptions related to economic growth. It was critical to the achievement of revisionism's defining aim of greater equality through progressive redistribution, through the expansion of state services it could afford, and given the particular regime of ac-cumulation based on mass production, through the equalisation of

consumption patterns it spontaneously seemed to generate. Since the
revisionists looked upon any drastic increase in the government's share
in the GNP with disfavour, vast areas of social investment, designed to
promote better and more equal conditions of life in British society, also
depended on continued growth at least of the magnitudes enjoyed by
the British economy in the 1950s.

Substantial slowdown in growth would reveal a central gap in the
revisionist strategy for which the revisionists, while being well aware of
it, had no adequate resolution. It was about the kind of planning any
revisionist government would be required to undertake in such conditions. As we have seen, Croslandite revisionist planning was essentially
macro-economic. The manipulation of fiscal and (albeit to a lesser
extent) monetary levers was supposed to ensure, among other things,
full employment and stable economic growth. However, even assuming
that economic growth sustained its post-war rates (which it did not),
many Keynesians had pointed to the possibility that the combination of
full employment and strong trade unions engaged in free collective
bargaining was likely to have inflationary consequences.[70] The only
solution would be a national coordination of wage increases in an
incomes policy. As David Marquand has recently pointed out, this
potentially implicated the government in a much more 'hands on' form
of planning than anything seriously contemplated or planned for by the
revisionists.[71] Moreover, the possibility that Labour's trade union base,
traditionally jealous of its independence from legal and political regulation, would oppose this could never be ruled out. But if the unions
would not concede the principle, they had in the past demonstrated
their willingness to support statutory wage limits under Labour government as in the Crippsian wage freeze of 1948. And as we shall see,
Crosland, perhaps uniquely among the leading revisionists, seemed to
have understood the need to leave it at that, and the futility of opposing
these deep reflexes of the labour movement, and he, at least, explicitly
ruled out any statutory incomes policy.[72] Revisionism did not produce
a theoretical or systematic solution to this problem and relied, instead,
on the stock panacea of economic growth (and accompanying productivity increases) to dampen down inflation. Indeed, the unions' sectional
economism was accommodated within revisionism such that the central
but weighty principle of equality was laced with the effervescence of
higher living standards for all.

By the 1964–70 Wilson governments it became apparent that these
assumptions no longer held and that the revisionism of the 1950s was
overtaken by events. The survival of social democracy in the 1970s
came to depend on the ability of the revisionists to revise Croslandite
revisionism to produce a viable strategy for socialism. No such attempt
was, however, forthcoming from revisionist quarters. On the contrary,

the preoccupation of most of the revisionists with the European issue, and the resulting political marginalization they suffered, sapped any intellectual initiative. And there is also room for doubt whether they could, given their theoretical wherewithal, rise to the occasion in the vastly more difficult circumstances of the 1970s and 1980s. The long term result of this was, of course, the intellectual vacuity of the intellectuals' party, the SDP; and its eventual absorption into political Liberalism, which had itself, by the early twentieth century, become bereft of any distinctive perspective on society and politics. But this is to invade the territory of later chapters.

Notes

1. Ken Coates, *The Social Democrats: Those Who Went and Those Who Stayed*, Spokesman, Nottingham, 1983.

2. In 1940, the young Private Crosland of the Royal Welsh Fusiliers who, with the publication of *The Future of Socialism* in 1956, emerged as the most substantial revisionist intellectual in the Labour Party had written, 'I am revising Marxism & will emerge as the modern Bernstein'. Quoted in Susan Crosland, *Tony Crosland*, Jonathan Cape, London, 1982, p 13.

3. This, however, surely says more about socialist dogmatism than about the specific 'heresy' being condemned. When it first made its appearance, in the debates over strategy in the Second International, revisionism represented an attempt to re-theorise *existing political practice* in a theory which would no longer, like the revolutionary theory of the Erfurt Programme, be at odds with it. See Peter Gay, *The Dilemma of Democratic Socialism: Eduard Bernstein's Challenge to Marx*, Columbia University Press, New York, 1952, p 270.

4. Carl Schorske, *German Social Democracy: The Development of the Great Schism 1905–1917*, Harvard University Press, Cambridge, 1955.

5. Noel Annan records in this connection that during the Second World War, '[r]emembering the battle of skilled minds [of the First World War], the authorities treated intellectuals as a species to be preserved to do the jobs intellectuals can do'. (*Our Age*, Wiedenfeld and Nicholson, London, 1990, p 205). Such an outlook on the uses of intellectuals had also, it would seem, infused the Labour Party.

6. The story of this experience and the emergence from it of the post-war consensus has been vividly reconstructed by Paul Addison in his *The Road to 1945*, Jonathan Cape, London, 1975.

7. Edward Shils, 'British Intellectuals in the Mid-Twentieth Century', in *The Intellectuals and the Powers and Other Essays*, University of Chicago Press, Chicago and London, 1972, p 135, p 138–9.

8. Kingsley Amis, *Socialism and the Intellectuals*, Fabian Tract 304, The Fabian Society, London, 1957, p 12.

9. *Ibid*, p 10.

10. *Ibid*, p 2.

11. Shils, *op.cit.*, p 147–8.

12. Robert Hewison, *Too Much: Art and Society in the Sixties*, Macmillan, London, 1986, p73.

13. Tom Nairn, 'The English Literary Intelligentsia', in Emma Tennant (ed), *Bananas*, Quartet, London, 1977, pp 82–3.

14. W.L. Guttsman, *The British Political Elite*, Macgibbon and Kee, London, 1968.

15. Annan, *op. cit.*, p 175.

16. For an analysis of the disappearing Northern working-class culture and the emergent popular culture of the 1950s see especially Richard Hoggart, *The Uses of Literacy*, Chatto and Windus, London, 1957.

17. Perry Anderson, 'The Left in the Fifties', *New Left Review*, Number 29, January–February 1965, p 4.

18. John Osborne, *Look Back in Anger*, S.G. Phillips, Inc., New York, 1957, p 84.

19. Perry Anderson, 'The Left in the Fifties', p 18.

20. *Keesings Contemporary Archives* July 28–August 4 1956, p 15007. Statement issued by Mr. Dingle Foot, QC, Mr. Wilfred Roberts and Mr. Philip Hopkins.

21. Raymond Williams, *Politics and Letters*, Verso, London, 1979, p 41.

22. Norman Mackenzie, 'After the Stalemate State', in Mackenzie (ed), *Conviction*, MacGibbon and Kee, London, 1958, p. 11.

23. Ben Pimlott, *Hugh Dalton*, Jonathan Cape, London, 1988, p 630.

24. By contrast, in the 1970s there was far less room for such 'seat reservations' which resulted in a completely different path of entry for the intellectuals of the new Labour left. As fewer and fewer seats remained safe, candidate selection inevitably became more contested, and party credentials more important.

25. Dalton's 'poodles' included practically all of the members of the revisionist tendency of that generation: Brian Abel-Smith, Michael Barnes, George Chetwynd, Tony Crosland, Nicholas Davenport, Desmond Donnolley, Geoffrey de Freitas, Hugh Gaitskell, Patrick Gordon-Walker, Denis Healey, Denis Howell, Douglas Jay, Roy Jenkins, Christopher Mayhew, William Rodgers, Dick Taverne, John Wilmot, Woodrow Wyatt. There were others, trade-unionists, who were also encouraged by Dalton, including Barbara Castle and James Callaghan. This list is compiled from Ben Pimlott, *op.cit*, which provides an entertaining account of this aspect of Dalton's activities.

26. See Guttsman, *op. cit*, p 105.

27. This trend led Arthur Greenwood to claim in 1945 that 'we are a really national party. We are a cross-section of national life and this is something that has never happened before'. (Quoted in Paul Addison, *op.cit.*, 1975, p 268.)

28. Pimlott, *op. cit.*, p 602.

29. *Ibid*, p 586.

30. *Ibid*.

31. In the general 'communist' atmosphere of the 1930s that emblem of the age, Harold Laski, probably went farther than most when he declaimed, 'Socialist measures ... are not obtainable by constitutional means ... if socialists wish to secure a State built with the principles of their faith, they can only do so by revolutionary means' (quoted in Kingsley Martin, *Harold Laski: A Biographical Memoir*, Gollancz, London, 1953, pp 83–83) – even if he could not imbue this radicalism with any plausible consistency.

32. R.H.S. Crossman, *Labour and the Affluent Society*, Fabian Tract 325, Fabian Society, London, 1959, pp 4–6.

33. Anthony Crosland, *Can Labour Win?*, Fabian Tract 324, The Fabian Society, London, 1960, p 2.

34. A process finding a late manifestation in the marriage of Shirley Williams, after the defeat of the Social Democrats in 1987, to a liberal American political scientist.

35. Anthony Crosland, *The Future of Socialism*, Jonathan Cape, London, 1956, p 524.

36. Richard Crossman (ed) *New Fabian Essays*, J.M. Dent and Sons, London, 1970, first published 1952.

37. R.H.S. Crossman, 'Towards a Philosophy of Socialism', in *New Fabian Essays*, pp 1–2.

38. *Ibid*, p 4.

39. R.H.S. Crossman, 'Towards a Philosophy of Socialism', p 6. See A.H. Halsey, 'Provincials and Professionals: The British Post-War Sociologists', *European Journal of Sociology*, Volume XXIII, 1982.

40. Iris Murdoch, 'A House of Theory', in Norman MacKenzie (ed), *op. cit.*, p 226.

41. From a toe-hold at the LSE, sociology as a discipline, though still retaining a strongly empirical and untheoretical cast, did develop from the 1950s onwards, especially outside the still more or less disdainful central universities.

42. C.A.R. Crosland, *Can Labour Win?*, Fabian Tract Number 324, Fabian Society, London, 1960, p 2.

43. Anthony Crosland, 'Socialists in a Dangerous World' supplement to *Socialist Commentary*, November 1968, p 6. By the late 1950s, however, there was emerging a more widespread concern with the closed and archaic character of British state and society. (See for example Hugh Thomas (ed), *The Establishment*, Anthony Blond, London, 1959.) The concerns which underlay the notion of the 'Establishment', and which gained increasing currency, could not be theorised through the current political sociology and required a more sophisticated theoretical framework. From the early 1960s onwards, the work of Perry Anderson and Tom Nairn brought the insights of Continental Marxism to bear on British society in an essentially Gramscian theorisation of the development of the modern British state, its class character and its political reflexes.

44. Alasdair MacIntyre, 'The End of Ideology and the End of the End of Ideology' in *Against the Self-Images of the Age*, Schocken Books, New York, p. 3. On the Congress for Cultural Freedom see pp 85–6 below. Daniel Bell's work is *The End of Ideology: On the Exhaustion of Political Ideas in the Fifties*, The Free Press, New York, 1960.

45. One attempt to theorise the British State from a Marxist point of view did appear in 1958, *The British State* by James Harvey and Katherine Hood, Lawrence & Wishart, London.

46. Daniel Bell, *op. cit.*

47. *Ibid*, p 405.

48. See G.D.H. Cole, 'An Open Letter to Members', *Fabian Journal*, Number 1, May 1950.

49. Mary Saran, *Never Give Up: Memoirs*, Oswald Wolff, London, 1976, pp 47–

48. *The Liberal Conspiracy: The Congress for Cultural Freedom and the Struggle for the Mind of Postwar Europe*, The Free Press, New York, 1989, pp. 59–80 and 219–34 by Peter Coleman is a sympathetic account.

50. There is no detailed account of the SPD exiles in London. Mary Saran's memoirs have been helpful but see also, Anthony Glees, 'The SPD in Emigration and Resistance, 1933–1945', in Roger Fletcher (ed), *Bernstein to Brandt: A Short History of German Social Democracy*, Edward Arnold, London, 1987, pp 183–192.

51. For example, contrary to the revisionist goal of equality above all others, members of the Socialist Union tended to regard equality as a carry-over from the bygone materialist days and not quite in tune with the ethical socialism they sought to propound. They sought instead more intangible values like human fulfilment.

52. The following paragraph is based largely on Christopher Lasch's critical account 'The Cultural Cold War: A Short History of the Congress for Cultural Freedom', in his *The Agony of the American Left*, Alfred A. Knopf, New York, 1969.

53. Interview with David Marquand, 30 August 1989.

54. See Colin Leys' synoptic discussion of the fate of the principal elements of Labour's programme in this period in *Politics in Britain*, Verso, London, 1989, pp 64–68.

55. An important critical analysis on the trends of income redistribution in Britain is John Westergaard and Henrietta Resler, *Class in Capitalist Society: A Study of Contemporary Britain*, Heinemann, London, 1975.

56. Roy Jenkins, *Pursuit of Progress: A critical analysis of the achievement and prospect of the Labour Party*, William Heinemann, London, 1953, p 169.

57. *Ibid*, p 171.

58. *Ibid*, p 172.

59. Roy Jenkins, 'Equality', in R.H.S. Crossman (ed), *op.cit.*, p 73.

60. C.A.R. Crosland, *The Future of Socialism*, p 237.

61. *Ibid* p 191.

62. *Ibid*, p 84–107 and Hugh Gaitskell, *Socialism and Nationalisation*, Fabian Tract Number 300, The Fabian Society, London, 1956.

63. C.A.R. Crosland, *The Future of Socialism*, p 485.

64. *Ibid*, p 517.

65. *Ibid*, p 504.

66. See for example his discussion of advertising and the Galbraith thesis of private affluence/public squalor in 'Production in an Age of Affluence', *The Listener*, 25 September 1958.

67. Crosland, *The Future of Socialism*, p 292.

68. *Ibid*, p 520.

69. *Ibid*, p 522.

70. William Beveridge in his *Full Employment in a Free Society*, Allen and Unwin, London, 1944, had pointed this out, p 199.

71. David Marquand, *The Unprincipled Society: New Demands and Old Politics*, Jonathan Cape, London, 1988, pp 50–62.

72. C.A.R. Crosland, *The Future of Socialism*, pp 444–6.

5

The Revisionist Struggle
for Hegemony

The revisionists in the Labour Party spanned several political generations: beginning with that of Gaitskell, Durbin and Jay who, as we have seen, were inducted into Labour's policy-making in the 1930s and became MPs in 1945, and ending with that of David Owen, John Mackintosh and David Marquand, revisionism's last notable recruits, who were first elected to parliament in 1964. They were united by their common adherence to revisionism, but, more than its intrinsic qualities, their fate as a group of intellectuals in the Labour Party was tied up with the specifically *political* project which also distinguished them: for the first time in Labour's history they sought to establish the main tenets of an intellectual outlook, namely revisionism, as an official doctrinal basis for the party's policies and strategy. The revisionists were in many ways well-placed to perform this task: the welcome which they received in the post-war Labour Party, their increased numbers, the patronage they enjoyed from the veteran leadership of the party, their intellectual ascendancy as the *only* group of intellectuals in the Labour Party to articulate a new programme in the 1950s and, lastly, the close alliance between the party leadership and major trade union leaders constituted major advantages. The election of Hugh Gaitskell, himself a revisionist, as the leader of the party in 1956 seemed to secure revisionist control over the party. And for a time it appeared to some, like Stephen Haseler, that revisionism now formed the basis of party policy and that this demonstrated that the revisionists had 'won the battle for the soul of the Labour Party'.[1] However, Haseler, it seems, spoke too soon. Events, beginning with the resurgence of left wing and trade union militancy in the late 1960s and 1970s, definitively demonstrated how shallow Labour's putative conversion to revisionism had been. Instead, it became clear, Labour continued to be governed not by revisionism, nor by any other clearly elaborated philosophy or ideology but by the more diffuse set of impulses deeply rooted in the culture of the labour movement which had been branded as 'Labourism'. A large component of this almost genetic defect was an unintellectualism. While the term 'Labourism' was coined to provide a powerful, explanation of Labour's congenital imperviousness to socialist philosophy and the practices which would derive from it, it has, surprisingly perhaps, not been used to illuminate the fate of the only set of intellectuals to attempt to effectively hegemonise the Labour Party and who, moreover, had been historically the most well placed to do so. This chapter seeks to trace the failure of the revisionist struggle for hegemony over the Labour Party, a political project upon which, with their considerable advantages, the revisionists embarked in relative innocence of its difficulties.

The Apparent Opposition to Revisionism: Bevanism

The difficulties did not lie in any well-elaborated philosophical opposition. The revisionists were the heirs to Britain's principal intellectual tradition which was now linked to the Labour Party. It is true that not all intellectuals joined the Labour Party. Some were communists, but the Cold War and increased popular distrust of the Soviet Union had rendered the CPGB increasingly marginal. Only from the late 1950s onwards, with the emergence of CND and, later, of the New Left, did the intellectual left outside the Labour Party increase in size and general cultural significance. There was, however, apparently at least, a more important source of intellectual opposition to the revisionists. In the Labour Party itself, the Bevanites, the product of the regrouping of the left around the figure of Aneurin Bevan after his resignation from cabinet in 1951, clashed with the moderate leadership of Attlee, dominating the first period of opposition from 1951–1955. However, despite the prominence of the Bevanites in the 1950s, the intellectual as well as political challenge they presented to the revisionists was largely illusory.

In the first place, the intellectuals of the Bevanite/Tribunite left were generally exceptions who proved the rule that intellectuals in the party in this period were generally revisionist. Most Bevanites had their roots in the trade union movement. Frustrated ambition, as with Bevan and Wilson, was also part of the energy behind Bevanism. Michael Foot, from a prominent Liberal family, was at his best pursuing moral causes in distant lands in the best traditions of English Liberalism, with his brilliant pamphleteering, involvement in the Campaign for Nuclear Disarmament, and polemical journalism. Richard Crossman, whose intellectual vitality often outshone that of the revisionists, was an independent maverick intellectual whose allegiance to Bevanism was, at best, spasmodic and issue-based. He was also committed to a broadly revisionist programme. Bevan himself, a working-class autodidact, also eventually came down on the side of a broadly social democratic programme.

Indeed, if throughout the 1950s Bevanism constituted the principal ideological challenge to revisionism in the Labour Party, it was a particularly stunted one. If the revisionists had picked up the theoretical gauntlet, and started a major process of policy and philosophical reformulation, what of the left? Although politically very vocal and significant, the Labour left, whether as the *Keep Left* group of the late 1940s or under the post-1951 rubric of Bevanism, never represented any major theoretical departures.[2] Revisionism had taken its impetus from the admission of intellectual bankruptcy following the accomplishment of the programme of the post-war Labour government, and from the quite obvious fact that its achievement had significantly changed the playing field for socialist politics. Bevan and his followers, in contrast, by adopting an accusatory stance of 'not enough socialism', remained, as an ironic but logical consequence, tied to the old programme whose true fulfilment they seemed to be calling for.

The Bevanite lack of concrete proposals for domestic reform was matched by its emphasis on questions of foreign policy. This pre-occupation was reflected in Bevan's choice (when he finally entered the shadow cabinet in 1958) of the office of shadow Foreign Secretary, where he felt he had something distinctive to contribute, over the shadow chancellorship. However, whether this was indeed the case even in this, his chosen field, is open to question. Chasing the chimera of a socialist foreign policy or flying the banner of high-minded English liberalism in foreign affairs did not constitute an alternative. Further, the Labour left's anti-Americanism and anti-Cold War ideology, mani-fested in their determined opposition to German rearmament and their more benevolent attitude towards the Soviet Union and the eastern bloc, prevented any major rethinking about the nature of 'actually existing socialism'. This was, according to their chronicler, the Bevanites' 'greatest single deficiency'.[3] What was more, in the shadow cabinet Bevan was satisfied that he could provide the 'will to implement the party's [revisionist] programme' and could therefore concentrate on achieving a Labour victory. Whether this was a *volte face* or an ac-ceptance of the limitations of the possible, it strongly suggests that the Bevanites lacked a coherent alternative.

Bevan had never attempted to organise the Bevanites and thought that this was even less necessary after entering the shadow cabinet. His following of around thirty MPs had hitherto consisted of many who supported him without necessarily understanding his positions, while others had supported him for their own tactical, political or even careerist reasons. Bevanism was principally a parliamentary movement; this was to prove one of the main differences between the Bevanites and the new Labour left of the 1970s, the former remaining wedded to ideas of parliamentary independence in contrast to the latter's enthusiasm for extra-parliamentary politics. This was an especially serious limitation in that, despite its sensitivity to the working-class unrest visible in the late 1940s and early 1950s, Bevanism was unable to gain support from the loyalist unions. This was graphically illustrated in Bevan's devastating defeat in the contests for the party treasurership against Gaitskell in 1954 and 1955. While he was right in his assumption of a wide support among the union rank and file, in the prevailing loyalism 'Bevan's reliance on spontaneous union democracy was clearly optimistic'.[4]

The only issue on which the Bevanites had made a strong showing at a Labour Party Conference was on German rearmament (in 1954) where their vote included a heterogeneous coalition of opponents of German militarism (notably Dalton), pacifists, and Bevanites. On the other hand, Bevanism caught the mood of the restive constituency rank and file and it dominated the constituency section of the National Executive Committees consistently in the period. Outside the reach of loyalist trade union politics, by 1952 all but one of the seats on the NEC's Constituency Section were held by Bevanites.[5] The vote of the constituency section reflected disillusionment with the Labour government and the party's loss of socialist momentum after 1948. However, those impatient for further signs of radicalism and new departures ironically fixed their aspirations on a Labour left which was intellectually rather conservative, if not actually bankrupt. Nor were there any organizational links. Perhaps, in the context of a more vigorous (and theoretical) working-class movement, a hegemonic politics on the left of the Labour Party, for which Bevanism was such a poor excuse, might have emerged to contest revisionism more strongly. As things were, the new departures were produced by the revisionists.

In the early 1950s there were those, like Strachey and Cripps, who wished to reconcile with the left. This wish had then appeared naïve, for at no time did either side indicate that they would be willing to surrender their doctrinal positions in order to do so. But the capitulation of Bevan in 1957 and the ensuing disorganisation of the Labour left suggests that they had a better understanding than most of the narrowness of the doctrinal, as opposed to the rhetorical, gap which separated Bevanism from revisionism.

The Real Opposition to Revisionism: Labourism

Revisionism's principal opposition in the Labour Party lay not in any opposing philosophy but in 'Labourism' – Labour's imperviousness to philosophies or ideas in general. The term was coined in 1961 by

Ralph Miliband, and it soon came to denote the remarkable 'similarity of problems which have beset the [Labour Party] throughout its history'.[6] Many on the left used it more widely to refer to the untheorised reflexes embodied in the labour movement – its culture and institutions which made it incapable of professing or practising a genuinely theoretical socialism. As such, however, it was criticised as unhistorical: a 'set of enduring reflexes, partially embodied in a set of institutions', often used as a 'stand-in for a history of the Labour Party'.[7]

However, Tom Nairn used it in a more limited sense to denote the Labour Party's *genetic* imperviousness to ideas and explicit doctrines[8] – its unintellectualism – acquired from its roots in the unintellectual English society. In that socialism depends crucially for its strength on ideas and theories, it was this, rather than any other aspect of Labour's constitution that was the most important obstacle to making Labour a socialist (or even a reliably progressive) party. In this sense, originating in the intellectuals' (including, as we shall see in Chapter Seven, the social democrats') critique of the intractability of the Labour Party to their projects, Labourism as an explanation is symptomatically valid.

Labour's relative success in achieving many of its more urgent economistic goals (though not without crucial intervention by intellectuals) only reinforced this unintellectual attachment to traditions and symbols which resides principally in the unintellectual 'centre' of the party which includes the trade union and constituency rank and file, and the bulk of the MPs. It works to ensure the unity of the party against potentially or actually divisive intellectuals and their doctrines. But, in the absence of a theoretical guide with a greater elaboration and broader scope than the impulses of trade unionist economism, the wider purposes for which governmental power is to be gained tend to remain vague, and at worst, null. This pragmatic Labourist centre holds the ultimate power through the party conference and determines its direction.

The mechanisms of Labourism functioned, initially at least, to promote the power of the revisionists. The revisionists inherited the alliance between Attlee's moderate leadership and major trade union leaders which from 1949 onwards 'organised and coordinated every major vote at Conference'.[9] It was largely the outcome of the successful co-optation of the trade unions into the programme of the Attlee governments despite the remarkably low participation of trade union leaders in them.[10] The trade union loyalism of the 1950s was further enhanced when the earlier, more independent trade union leadership, wary of the potential for leadership betrayal, was replaced by a new one, led by Arthur Deakin of the Transport and General Workers Union, Tom Williamson of the National Union of General and Municipal Workers and Will Lawther of the Mineworkers, which tended to be more uncritical of the leadership. Furthermore, the logistics of this loyalism were eased by the emergence in the 1950s of a cluster of large trade unions which together determined the majority of votes at Conference. During the 1950s Labourist loyalism and trade union discipline were deployed to sustain the power of the leadership, initially the moderate leadership of Attlee and later the revisionist leadership of Gaitskell.

Union leaders justified union non-interference in party and government by means of the long-standing parliamentalist division of Labour between political and industrial wings, particularly appropriate in an era of full employment as the unions travelled down the path of a complacent economism. Indeed, they even sought to employ the prestige of the government and party leadership in their vigorous campaign against communism. However, proscription by the Labour Party meant that the communist presence, while important in the 1940s, was, in fact, limited to the Trades Union Congress and within the party it was the Bevanite left which constituted the principal target. This loyalist relationship, between the party and union leaderships, established under Attlee, was, initially at least, strengthened under Gaitskell. Gaitskell had been a major advocate of the anti-communist enterprise, and had assiduously cultivated links with the leaders of the large trade unions dating back to his days as Minister of Fuel and Power in the Attlee governments. For their part, the new union leaders, '[d]istrusting Attlee's "soft" handling of the Bevanites ... threw [their] weight behind the younger middle-class intellectuals in the Parliamentary Party whose leading personality, Hugh Gaitskell, [as Chancellor] had precipitated the confrontation with Bevan in 1951.'[11] Indeed common hostility towards the communists and the Labour left drew the trade union leadership and the revisionist intellectuals together.

However, while it seemed favourable to the revisionists, this alliance contained important contradictions. Firstly, by exploiting the loyalism of the trade unions in this way, the revisionists were also reinforcing the idea of Conference sovereignty. This had its dangers for the independent influence of the revisionist element, lacking an independent grass roots base of its own. It was at Conference, eventually, that the revisionist struggle for hegemony foundered – both when Gaitskell failed in his bid to excise Clause 4 from the party constitution and effect a doctrinal revolution in the party, and when he was able to win Conference back to his position on nuclear disarmament only at the cost of renouncing what had become a central tenet of the revisionist strategy – British entry into the Common Market.

Secondly, while revisionism seemed perfectly suited to the new trade unionism of 'affluence' and the optimistic economism it seemed to engender, the doctrine was not based on it. True, their basic empiricism meant that their view of the changes in British society tended to be intuitive and superficial – well within the categories of common sense – and there was, consequently, a congruence between their analysis and the views of other sections of society, such as the trade unions. This enabled them to combine arguments about doctrine with others (seemingly populist) about giving the people what they wanted. For example, for Crosland, steadily rising living standards were justified by their actual and ideological egalitarian effects; he argued that greater affluence would enable greater equality through redistribution and also independently create an American-style ideological de-classing of British society. Whatever the intellectual justification, the aim itself was certainly in line with the aspirations of the trade unions.[12] But, especially in non-economic areas, the support of the trade unions could not always be assumed. On cultural issues, for example, the revisionists succumbed to the authority of traditional English romantic-literary elitism, deploring what they saw as the debasement of culture through its commercialisation. (The more 'with-it' Crosland may seem to be an exception to this. He was able to rationalise contemporary trends in popular culture with his 'each to his own' dedication to 'freedom' and enjoyment of frivolity.) Their liberalism on many social issues like the abolition of capital punishment, legalisation of abortion, and homosexuality could also run against the grain of Labourist attitudes.

Thirdly, the relationship of the intellectuals with the predominating and overwhelmingly Labourist trade union element in the Labour Party was always a potentially difficult one. The 1931 split, for example, was felt by leaders of the trade unions to be a 'betrayal of the intellectuals'. Following that, having seen to it that the trade-unions were given a greater formal part in policy-making in the shape of the National Joint Council of the party's NEC and the TUC General Council, they were willing to allow for a wider role for the intellectuals. If the 1930s and 1940s had seen an increasing tolerance and even welcome for intellectuals, this was for most part explained by the convergence between the intellectuals' Fabian project and traditional economistic goals of the trade-union movement. In the Attlee governments, there was always a bare majority in cabinet for working-class, if not trade unionist, MPs and the cabinet was always mindful of the sovereignty of Conference, in effect of the trade unions in the party. The trade unions who embodied Labourism also paid for and, to a significant extent, controlled it. As such, there were limits to which intellectuals could assert hegemony against their inclinations.

This was especially problematic in that the revisionists hardly played any significant mobilising or pedagogic role in the labour movement. Apart from links at the top level between the leaderships of the party and the unions, which generally characterised the post-war Labour

Party, most of the revisionist intellectuals cultivated few links with the grass roots of the labour movement. Their existence revolved around the parliamentary party – they elected the leader and determined and justified policy, and many of them saw themselves as based more in the electorate than in the party or the unions. This is not surprising when one sees that their main extra-parliamentary activities were constituency surgeries and election campaigns. They were more at home addressing student and other by-and-large educated middle-class audiences. While during the Campaign for Democratic Socialism (see below) they did work with trade union leaders to bring about a vote for multilateralism and NATO at the party Conference, this contact was largely confined to union leaders, and the urgency of the initial effort was ultimately eased by the decline of the Campaign for Nuclear Disarmament and the left after 1960. The mainly middle-class intellectuals always remained foreign to the culture of Labourism, even in its loyalist phase. Moreover, with the death of Arthur Deakin in 1956, this alliance began to show cracks at the moment of Gaitskell's succession to the leadership. Thus, even in that period of revisionist ascendancy, a temperamentally uncompromising leader like Gaitskell was forced to follow the practice of other Labour leaders who looked for compromising and often contradictory formulae. These undermined the integrity of the revisionist outlook to preserve party unity through obeisance to Labour's traditions and symbols. In view of this, it was at least an exaggeration, to say, as Tom Nairn did, that

> in the Labour Party they have always, in fact, maintained in power a clique of intellectuals, through their agency one particular stratum of the intelligentsia has been able to achieve an extraordinary unity and continuity of domination over the British working class movement.[13]

While there was an almost unique confluence of aims between the intellectuals and the trade union leaders which had obtained since the 1930s, Nairn's account, to which Labourist unintellectualism is otherwise central, ignores both the difficulties of the intellectual element in the party in the pre-war period, and its post-war inability to achieve hegemony over the Labour Party, despite its increased status and numbers. The revisionist advance in the Labour Party did not end in their hegemonic (because doctrinal) control over the Labour Party but soon became a long struggle in which Labourism stalled and denatured the revisionist doctrine as the price of their continued leadership.

The Fortunes of the Revisionists

Every major milestone in the path the revisionists traced in the Labour Party in the 1950s and 1960s bespoke the limits of their intellectual ascendancy. The election of Gaitskell as leader of the party in 1956 was a result not of their intellectual pre-eminence in the party but of political manoeuvring among Labour's top leadership. While revisionist policies began to be adopted by the party, when after the 1959 election defeat Gaitskell attempted to excise Clause Four from the party constitution in a bolder attempt to make revisionism Labour's strategic perspective, he was defeated, not by a rival doctrine or even political tendency (in a final demonstration of Bevanism's doctrinal nullity, Bevan had capitulated to the revisionist leadership in 1957) but by a groundswell of Labourist sentimentality. And under Gaitskell the revisionists came as close to a hegemonic position in the party as they were going to. His death in 1963, and the election of Harold Wilson as leader, marked the beginning of the decline of the revisionists' position in the party. While the 1961 party document, *Signposts for the Sixties*, remained the basis of the *New Britain* manifesto of 1964, the revisionists' political position was eroded, not least due to Wilson's deeply ingrained hostility towards them.

The Mantle of the Moderates: 1951–1955

Attlee's continuing leadership after Labour's 1951 General Election defeat turned out to be a holding operation against the possibility of Herbert Morrison's succession to the leadership. While rooted in his unexplained dislike for Morrison,[14] this course of action cost the Labour Party heavily in terms of the internal divisions between the moderate (and programmatically exhausted) leadership and the Bevanites (caused mainly by the frustrated ambitions of Bevan and some important Bevanites)[15] which plagued the first period of opposition, 1951–55. While the intellectual processes which resulted, by the mid-1950s, in revisionism were already under way, little in the way of doctrinal development was manifest in Party documents of this period. The 1953 party document, *Challenge to Britain*, contained minimal proposals for renationalisation of the steel industry, nationalisation of road transport and conditional promises for the selective nationalisations in medium and light industry like engineering and chemicals. Its language was also vague enough to allow many Bevanites to support it so that there was no full scale debate on public ownership nor on the general philosophical orientation of the Party. This was partly also a consequence of the complacency with which Labour still viewed its electoral prospects. The possibility that Labour might lose the next election seems not to have been seriously contemplated and, as a result, there was no impulse at the level of the leadership to change the main lines of the party's programme under electoral, let alone theoretical and programmatic, pressures.

In the aftermath of the General Election of 1955, Morrison's support inside the party had waned enough to ensure Gaitskell's success in the leadership election of that year. Morrison secured only forty votes and, with Bevan's support confined to the standard left wing seventy votes, Gaitskell won handsomely with 157. The election of Gaitskell as leader, however, being in one part the product of manoeuvring by Attlee, and in another, substantial, part the result of the trust which Gaitskell had cultivated among the loyalist triumvirate of trade union bosses, by no means signified the doctrinal triumph of the revisionists. Less than a year later the large trade unions' loyalty to the Labour Party leadership, which had sustained the power of the moderates and was expected to do the same for a revisionist leadership, began to show some cracks. In 1956, with the death of Deakin and the retirement of Lawther, two of the 'big three' loyalist union leaders were gone. While the exact nature of the trade union leadership which was to replace old-style loyalism was yet to become clearly defined (see Chapter Six), the task of securing the all-important trade union consent was faced by Gaitskell and the revisionists in a way that it had not recently been faced by Attlee and the moderates.

Gaitskell's Struggles 1956–63: Revisionism as Party Philosophy?

After the 1955 defeat the party could no longer ignore the need for a more purposeful and attractive programme that would appeal to a vastly changed electorate. In 1956 Crosland published *The Future of Socialism* and it was followed within a year by Gaitskell's Fabian pamphlet, *Socialism and Nationalisation*.[16] The development of revisionism had begun largely outside the Labour Party machinery and in the early years (1951–1954) the revisionists were conspicuous by their absence in the policy making machinery of the party. Under Gaitskell's leadership many revisionists were co-opted onto the study groups and policy subcommittees of the party. Gaitskell himself drafted important philosophical documents like *Towards Equality* in 1956 and *Labour's Aims* in 1960. By the time revisionism entered the complex process of policy making in the Labour Party, where any view would be subject to compromise with others, the revisionists' case had already been made outside, and prior to, the policy process.

The year 1957 brought major gains for the revisionists. That year's party policy document on public ownership, *Industry and Society*, fully reflected revisionist views. And *Industry and Society* won approval at the 1957 Party Conference. In confining its nationalisation proposals to steel and road transport, it did not differ sharply from the inclinations of the previous moderate leadership. The difference lay, however, in the revisionist arguments through which the case was made. *Industry and Society* argued for a mixed economy, rejecting traditional forms of public ownership on the basis that they had become redundant in promoting further advances towards equality or social control of industry and specified that any further state participation in the economy would take the form of state purchase of shares in large firms.[17]

The 1957 Conference also saw a final reversal for the left as Bevan, now Shadow Foreign Minister, made a dramatic gesture of his reconciliation with the new party leadership. And he chose to do this on an issue of foreign and defence policy, appealing to delegates to endorse the platform's position on defence which renounced unilateral nuclear disarmament. Using the words of Sam Watson, the miners' leader, Bevan asked Conference not to send a British Foreign Secretary 'naked into the international conference chamber'. And in what seemed to be a doctrinal about-turn he added:

> What you are saying is that a British Foreign Secretary gets up in the United Nations without consultation – mark this; this is a responsible attitude! – without telling any of the members of the Commonwealth, without concerting with them, that the British labour movement decides unilaterally that this country contracts out of all its commitments and obligations entered into with other countries and members of the Commonwealth – without consultation at all. And you call that statesmanship. I call it an emotional spasm.[18]

Bevan's admiring biographer, Michael Foot, recorded the event and its significance: as Bevan spoke the language of 'responsibility' and 'statesmanship' and Hugh Gaitskell and the revisionists rejoiced 'demurely', '[t]he Left of the Party looked for a moment as if it had exterminated itself. Without its incomparable leader it was unlikely to gather strength for years.'[19] The personification of the Labour left in the charismatic persona of Aneurin Bevan, whose working-class background and fiery rhetoric had lent a certain authenticity to its calls for more socialism, and the absence of an alternative second-level leadership meant that the movement lost more than a leader with Bevan's capitulation. After that, although the Bevanites remained organised around *Tribune*, they engaged in few debates with the leadership on questions of either domestic or foreign policy. The left which gathered strength in the subsequent phase of activism, both outside and later within the Labour Party, was a completely different socio-political phenomenon from the parliamentary rump of the 1930s Left which Bevanism had been.

However, neither *Industry and Society*, nor the capitulation of Bevan and the party unity it now afforded, were able to carry the Labour Party to power in 1959. There was a deep flaw in their electoral appeal. The revisionist case, based in large part on a claim to be able to manage the economy more efficiently, was a puny challenge to seeming Tory competence in the 'Age of Affluence'. Labour's third successive defeat and its worst electoral performance since 1935 was clearly un-anticipated in all quarters of the party. While such a defeat was naturally the occasion for a major reappraisal of party philosophy and strategy, the interpretation of this experience also finally resolved the revisionists on their road to confrontation with Labourism. However, the events which followed only disclosed the limits of their power in the party.

While the left predictably inferred that the drift toward revisionism was electorally costly, it had no alternative. The revisionists, gathered at Hugh Gaitskell's house in Hampstead, adopted a diametrically opposed approach. They were all agreed that there had to be a more open demonstration of the party's changed directions, but it was less clear how far they could or should go in this enterprise. The example of the German SPD, which had just then (in 1959) dropped Marxism as the official view of the party, was attractive to their (already) Euro-peanist and revisionist counterparts in the Labour Party. The revision-ists' in-house monthly, *Socialist Commentary*, also promoted such a change of direction. Douglas Jay went further than most when he proposed '1) to drop nationalisation, 2) drop the Trade Unions, 3) drop the name 'Labour Party', 4) drop the principle of political independence, & make agreements, even up to merger, with the Liberals'.[20] In publishing these proposals in *Forward*[21] without consulting Gaitskell or any of the other revisionists, Jay also set off rumours in the Labour Party of a plot by the 'Hampstead Set' to deradicalise the party. Most revisionists were, however, far from contemplating anything so drastic. But they equally felt it was necessary to finally deal with the ambiguities which still surrounded Labour's purpose and methods as well as its public image. The best way to do this was to bring Labour's constitution in line with revisionism's most contentious as well as most fundamental departure from traditional socialist methods – nationalization and Clause 4 of the party constitution inevitably became the bone of contention.

The only prominent revisionist to take seriously the consideration that Clause 4 was central to the inspiration that brought to the party its army of socialist constituency activists was Crosland. In a portent of his later parting of ways with the rest of the revisionists, Crosland doubted the value of a battle over Clause 4: it would be more trouble than it was worth. However, Gaitskell, whose style of leadership was 'positive, open and uncompromising on fundamentals',[22] not to say obstinate, went against Crosland's advice and against that of his closest friends among the union leaders, to present the 1959 Conference with a thorough review of the revisionist case against nationalisation.

The revisionist case against nationalization was, as we have seen, mainly economic. But, in the aftermath of the 1959 general election defeat, part of the rationale for the revisionists' case also came in the guise of a political sociology of the electorate of 1959. Mark Abrams' study of the 1959 General Election attempted to demonstrate what was already being said by many mainstream political sociologists, that in the eyes of the changing electorate nationalisation was an anachronism – redundant at best. Rita Hinden, editor of *Socialist Commentary* drew the moral for public ownership.

> Public ownership has not become a handicap because it is reckoned to have failed in all cases. One of the most interesting features of the survey is the extent to which the *success* of many of the nationalised industries is recognised. But, the two cases considered to be failures, coal and railways, have been notably unsuccessful, and even in the others where success is admitted, it does not seem to have been of a character to whet a desire for more. The results have, apparently, not been sufficiently distinctive, in kind or degree, from the achievements of successful private enterprise, to stir popular enthusiasm for public ownership as a political principle.[23]

The only intellectual critique of the revisionist position from within the Labour Party came from Richard Crossman in his *Labour in the Affluent Society*. However, while coming from one of the most brilliant intellectuals in the Labour Party, and one uncaptured by revisionism as a political tendency, it displayed the serious flaws of the Labour left's stance. Arguing that the creeping crisis of western capitalism (now apparent not through its internal contradictions, but through the demonstrated productive superiority of Soviet or state managed societies) required Labour to hold itself in reserve, unsullied, ready for the coming crash, the many internal contradictions of this approach were easily exposed by the revisionists.[24] Crossman's argument also permitted the revisionists, devoted to the (albeit) gradual amelioration of the living conditions and life prospects of the common people in the present, to focus on its political implication: 'Under these circumstances the Labour Party must play the role of Cassandra. It had no immediate hope of winning power, since Left-wing parties in Britain can win elections only at moments of crisis; and the crisis is not yet upon us.'[25]

In his speech at the 1959 Conference Gaitskell argued that the long-term economic and social changes that British society had been undergoing since the war – the decline of traditional industries, the absence of any fear of unemployment in a situation of near-full employment, and changes in consumption patterns meant that there was an inevitable decline in the Labour vote. In this situation, the Labour Party needed to modernise itself, rid itself of shibboleths, 'to avoid becoming [like] small cliques of isolated doctrine ridden fanatics, out of touch with the main stream of social life in our time.'[26] While public ownership would continue to have a role, a state-controlled economy was no longer the goal the Labour Party ought to strive for. He ended by appealing to the party to bring Clause 4 'up to date' since by itself 'it cannot possibly be regarded as adequate'. It was now up to the Labour Party policy machinery to bring an appropriate form of words to the next conference. This, if anything, was the revisionists' ultimate bid for formal hegemony in the party. Given this, Gaitskell was particularly well-equipped to lead this charge. As leader of the revisionists, the traditional intellectuals in the Labour Party, he epitomised their philosophy and style: clear thinking, plain talking and 'responsible'. His lack of intimacy with all but the top echelons of the labour movement, a trait he shared with other revisionist intellectuals, gave him an image and reputation of coldness and aloofness, though more than once he had occasion to display a capacity for emotional advocacy which proved all the more effective for sounding as if it was wrung out of him. At Blackpool, as elsewhere, he saw his role as a moderniser, educating the party into a clarity as to its fundamentals, ridding it of archaic and ill-defined attitudes and longings.

However, despite the revisionists' intellectual high ground, and Gaitskell's strength as leader, in this very bid for hegemony they were taught a lesson (which Gaitskell, at least, learned very well, as he was to demonstrate in 1962 over the issue of British entry into the European Economic Community). The Labour Party, right and left, had a great emotional investment in its constitution and traditions, and Clause 4, printed on every party membership card, lay, for many members and activists, at their heart. The reaction was massive and completely unforeseen. Gaitskell was defeated. Instead of a revision of Clause 4, he was forced to accept a compromise – the attachment of a new declaration of aims alongside the disputed clause, which represented no doctrinal break whatsoever. Crosland, who from the start had opposed what he regarded as a quixotic political misadventure, put his finger on the problem: The sacred deities of Labourism were not lightly questioned.

> The older party stalwart, brought up in the inter-war years to equate socialism with the nationalisation of the means of production, feels lost and bewildered if deprived of this familiar sheet-anchor. The dogma of nationalisation informed and symbolised his early years of struggle; if he is asked to give it up, he feels he is being asked to say that his whole political life, to which he sacrificed so much, was pointless and wasted. This feeling is wrong but natural. Again, some middle-class socialists, to whom (as to converts in other fields) militancy and attachment to dogma are psychologically necessary, react to any suggestion of heterodoxy in a highly emotional and over-determined manner.[27]

Revisionism, by questioning these verities, destroyed the simplicity and conviction of the faith.

If this was a largely symbolic defeat, hardly fatal for the revisionists whose intellectual ascendancy remained uncontested (for what competing doctrine *could* contest it?), worse was to follow. Over the next two years, under the pressure of a widespread anti-nuclear movement gathering force outside the Labour Party, Gaitskell and his fellow revisionists suffered a defeat at conference on a major policy issue – nuclear defence policy. It was also seen, moreover, as a challenge to Gaitskell's leadership.

In 1960, the defeat of the platform had become a *fait accompli* over the previous summer when four large unions, USDAW, T&GWU, AEU and the NUR had all become committed to unilateral nuclear disarmament, reflecting the rising fear of nuclear war after the production of the hydrogen bomb in 1957. The Campaign for Nuclear Disarmament manifested its strength in the first Aldermaston March in 1958. It mobilised large numbers of people, both middle and working class, and inevitably infected not only the Labour left but also large sections of the trade union movement.

Fully anticipating defeat at the 1960 Conference, Gaitskell nevertheless made a surprisingly bold stand. Instead of accepting the decision of Conference which he knew was coming, or attempting, as leader of the party, to use any of a number of methods of evading or otherwise circumventing it, Gaitskell chose to confront its decision head on. He laid out lucidly and coherently the case for multilateralism, vehemently attacking the unilateralists and exploiting every inconsistency in their argument. He appealed to the delegates to think again (while knowing full well that there was no chance of it). And in closing his speech, he vowed to 'fight, fight and fight again' against the impending unilateralist decision of Conference. In doing this he was also confronting the constitutional issue of the authority of Conference in relation to the parliamentary party.

> It is not in dispute that the vast majority of Labour Members of Parliament are utterly opposed to unilateralism and neutralism. So what do you expect them to do? Change their minds overnight? ... Supposing all of us, like well-behaved sheep, were to follow the policies of unilateralism and neutralism, what kind of impression would that make on the British people? ... I do not believe that Labour Members of Parliament are prepared to act as time-servers ... because they are men of conscience and honour ... honest men, loyal men, steadfast men, experienced men, with a lifetime of service to the Labour Movement.

> There are other people too ... who share our convictions. What sort of people do you think they are? What sort of people do you think we are? Do you think we can simply accept a decision of this kind? Do you think we can become overnight the pacifists, unilateralists and fellow travellers that other people are?[28]

That the speech was stirring and effective was witnessed by the fact that it swayed the majority of uncommitted votes over to opposing the unilateralist resolution. However most votes which belonged to the unions had been predetermined at the previous summer's trade union conferences and could not now be altered. 1960 was however, a 'pyrrhic defeat',[29] overturned a year later, thus enhancing the prestige of the leader.

A number of factors contributed to the eventual revisionist triumph. CND's inability to synthesise an integrated view of the Cold War – and the consequent limitation of its power to the moral and practical, as opposed to the theoretical, realm – meant, inevitably, that it was somewhat overtaken by events (even if also vindicated by them) upon the 1960 cancellation of the Blue Streak delivery system. In effect, Britain had, at least in the short run, become unilateralist, lacking an effective delivery system to replace the outdated one, and now depending on the NATO 'nuclear umbrella'. This seemed to make the unilateralist case for Britain irrelevant and led to the dissipation of unilateralism as a force both in the Labour Party and the wider CND movement. Further, on the eve of the 1960 conference, in the aftermath of the defeat over Clause Four and the impending one over unilateralism, a movement on the right of the party was launched by two revisionists (Bill Rodgers and Tony Crosland) to rally support for the leader. The Campaign for Democratic Socialism (CDS) aimed to integrate the right of the party at the leadership and constituency and trade union levels in order to oppose unilateralism effectively. Left organisation in Victory for Socialism, *Tribune*, and CND, had to be countered. While CDS's policy manifesto reiterated the main tenets of the revisionist philosophy without adding anything new, it was far more than an organisation of revisionists. The CDS campaigned for support in the PLP, in various Constituency Labour Parties (CLPs), and in the trade unions. What aided their efforts was the shifting of the ground of the debate (principally by Gaitskell) from unilateralism to neutralism. A document entitled *Policy for Peace*, taking a stand in support for NATO on the grounds that 'Britain could not opt out of the world power political system without damaging itself and the world in the process',[30] was adopted by the TUC General Council and the Labour Party National Executive Committee, and it was the basis on which the Campaign for Democratic Socialism campaigned for support in the trade unions and the CLPs.

These battles facilitated a further bond among the revisionists. CDS became an important recruiting ground for them and many young parliamentary candidates were recruited in the period, including Bill Rodgers, Philip Williams, Dick Taverne and David Marquand. The committee to draft its manifesto had included Alfred Robens (MP),

Denis Howell (former MP), Bill Rodgers, Ivan Yates (political journalist), Dick Taverne (barrister and ex-candidate for Putney), Patrick Gordon-Walker (Shadow Foreign Secretary), Philip Williams (Fellow of Nuffield College, Oxford), Frank Pickstock (Oxford local councillor) and Tony Crosland (MP).

The Campaign for Democratic Socialism operated (partly covertly) to recruit to its cause local opinion leaders, leading members of the General Management Committees of CLPs, and key officers of trade unions who could argue persuasively in favour of the leadership's policy. It also issued a monthly newsletter, *Campaign*. Many of the techniques of these intellectuals prefigured those of the new Labour left in the mid-1970s, including that of sending 'model resolutions' to local parties, designed to survive with their main content intact through the complicated (and highly political) process of 'compositing' the many resolutions into a few before Conference. The effectiveness of CDS is difficult to judge, especially in a context where other factors mentioned above, as well as the growing stature of Gaitskell as leader after his stand in 1960, also influenced the Conference vote. What can be said with some confidence is that they managed to organise and inform 'moderate', as opposed to revisionist, opinion in the party.

> C.D.S. offered [the moderates] the advantages of a group of reputable party members working inside and not outside the party framework. They had secured the goodwill of many party and union leaders, and they made clear that they were supporting Mr. Gaitskell because of the policies he represented and not because he was a personal friend of theirs. In the field the C.D.S. supplied facts and arguments to help give confidence to their supporters.[31]

At the 1961 Conference there was another factor which aided the Gaitskellite victory – the desire for party unity. Ex-Bevanites like Crossman and Wilson joined forces with the Gaitskellites to demonstrate unity on the defence issue as well as on domestic ones. The process of building a Gaitskellite ascendancy which had begun with Bevan's 1957 capitulation was now completed. Gaitskell had been able to eclipse his defeat over Clause 4 by his victory on defence. The Labour left was also in a more conciliatory mood than ever, and furthermore the question of conference sovereignty was apparently settled honourably with the leadership of Gaitskell and the unity of the party both paradoxically underscored.

> [T]he manner of Gaitskell's defeat was full of paradox. As was subsequently pointed out, to fight against a conference decision in order to reverse it implied an acceptance of the very authority which was being challenged. The roots of the paradox lay to some extent in the fact that even some supporters of Gaitskell's challenge in 1960 were affected by the belief that the conference was the arena where the final decision would be settled. The

logic of the Party's procedures as well as the residue of the traditional belief in Conference sovereignty determined that this should be so. Thus, explicit in the editorial of *Socialist Commentary* in November 1960 was the understanding that Gaitskell and his supporters had a year to show that the 1960 Conference decision did not represent majority opinion in the Party. In 1961 the votes would be counted and this would be decisive.[32]

This vindication of Gaitskell's leadership seemed to compensate for the trials the revisionist leadership had undergone in the previous two years. They could perhaps be seen merely as rude shocks to the party, at least occasioned in part by tactical errors on Gaitskell's part such as the confrontation over Clause 4. However, the confrontation was probably as necessary as it was revealing: the revisionists learned that although their views could be officially endorsed, piecemeal, this did not mean that they could easily penetrate and counter the long-standing and diffuse hegemony of the venerated institutions, unquestioned practices and sacred symbols of the labour movement. Whatever Labour's need for a properly theoretical programme, revisionism would not be official party policy. And Gaitskell, at least, learned this lesson well enough and his triumph in 1961 came at a price for revisionism. Having fought to rally the party, Gaitskell, now unwilling to squander the hard-won unity chose in the following year to persue a cause which over recent years became an important part of their policy/philosophy – British entry into the Common Market.

Gaitskell claimed that to take an abstract stand for entry would only open rifts in the party again. He explained his anxiety to avoid another open split to Roy Jenkins who, like most of the revisionists, wished him to take a clearer stand.

> [I]t is not really a matter of what I think; it is a question of carrying the Party ... if I were to do what you want, we should be more likely to lose control altogether. Certainly the Union Conferences have only gone the way they have because of these conditions which, you say, I am continually stressing.[33]

Thus in October 1962 he deployed his full rhetorical capacities, as well as the entire repertoire of Labour symbolism – appealing to the greatness of British civilisation, the Commonwealth and so on – in order to rally the party. In a flourish, to be bitterly remembered by his revisionist colleagues for a long time, he declared, 'We must be clear about this: it [the Common Market] does mean if [political federation] is the idea, the end of Britain as an independent European state. ... It means an end of a thousand years of history.'[34] The contrast between the 'unparalleled ovation'[35] this speech received on the floor of the conference and the grim sense of betrayal with which the Europeanist revisionists faced it can not be overemphasised. But if it was a betrayal, it was also, at the same time, a necessary obeisance before the logic of the Labour Party as a political creature. And it was a fair demonstration of the limits that 'Labourism' set before any group of intellectuals and their projects in the Labour Party.

In denying the revisionists an intellectual hegemony the Labour Party had also postponed indefinitely any consideration of the need for an intellectually articulated and justified strategy. While the revisionism may be condemned as right-wing, it certainly reflected a large swathe of opinion inside the Labour Party – at least as it was, stripped of Labourist traditionalism and sentimentality. And it would, for the first time in Labour's history, have brought doctrine and theory at the heart of socialist politics: all sections of the party would be compelled to articulate their conflicts and fight them out – the precondition of an effectively hegemonic form of politics on the left.

Gaitskell's untimely death in 1963 delivered the costly prize of party unity into the hands of Harold Wilson, only months after the revisionists paid the price for it. Wilson's leadership further weakened the party's commitment to a fully revisionist programme. But by default revisionism remained the at least tacit basis of the programme of the next Labour government and its experience clearly revealed revisionism's shaky foundations.

Revisionism in the 1964–70 Labour Governments

In fact, the decline of specifically revisionist influence on party policy, which was already revealed in the abandonment of the revisionist position in favour of Common Market entry in Gaitskell's own drive for party unity, was also apparent in the major party policy document, *Signposts for the Sixties*, prepared for the 1961 Blackpool conference. It also formed the basis of the 1964 General Election manifesto and was drawn up by a committee consisting of revisionists and left-wing reconcilers and was a truly joint effort. If the revisionism of the 1950s had been sanguine about the prospects of growth and the performance of the British economy, in a more troubled economic climate *Signposts for the Sixties* advocated a major overhaul of the economy. Instead of further nationalisation, which was still considered redundant, it proposed to build up the public sector alongside an intact private sector, creating new public enterprises in the science- and growth-based industries in which government already financed most of the research. This helped to make the Tory arguments about the sanctity of the private sector appear ridiculous. Galbraith's 'private affluence/public squalor' thesis had also been accepted into the revisionist canon although Crosland had important reservations about its arguments against the importance of further economic growth, at least in the special conditions of Britain.[36]

Signposts thus advocated greater housing and road building and other public infrastructure expenditures in a redirection of resources from excessive private consumption into badly needed public and common uses.

The left also brought on board a general thrust toward capitalist modernization which reflected the growing concern about the closed, archaic and inefficient institutions of British state and economy and society.[37] These were symptomatic of the growing mood in Britain which saw its problems as being institutional in a manner far more radical than Crosland's identification of the ideology of class and the need to eradicate it through a reform of the system of education. *Signposts* argued that a 'symptom of Britain's declining vigour is the growth of new forms of privilege and the rapid concentration of economic power. ... The economy is still dominated by a small ruling caste.'[38] Labour advocated a 'major shake-up at the top' to make way for 'the keen young executives, production engineers and scientists who are at present denied their legitimate prospects for promotion'.[39] The rhetoric of science, technology, modernization and opportunity was also meant to outdo the jaded consumerist appeal of Tory affluence, especially among young voters.

Electorally at least, this proved an attractive mix of policies and appeals and the 1964 election victory brought Labour to office with a programme whose distinctive radicalism consisted in schemes for economic and technological modernization. While rhetorically grand and obviously appealing, these remained far less well-thought-out than the basically revisionist programme upon which they had been grafted.

Moreover, Labour's default revisionism had never amounted to revisionist control over the party and its overall direction and, under Wilson, ambiguities about the party's purposes ran even deeper:

> [I]nternal debate in opposition about the long-term objectives of the Labour Party had never been satisfactorily resolved. Wilson did not see this as a problem. He turned the party towards the simple goal of gaining power through a series of essentially non-ideological appeals. This left a large question mark over the purpose for which power had been gained which was to underlie much of the internal debate in the government.[40]

While Gaitskell had been forced to rally the centre of the party to remain leader, Wilson did so enthusiastically. Further, Wilson, famous for his long political memory, never forgave the revisionists for not voting for him in the first ballot in the 1963 leadership election and did what he could to minimise their influence in his Cabinet. Out of a total of, on average, twenty-three cabinet members, revisionists never numbered more than between three and five. Revisionists in cabinet in this period were: Roy Jenkins, George Brown, Tony Crosland, Patrick

Gordon-Walker, Denis Healey, George Thomson and Douglas Jay. Their collective influence was further undermined by placing them in competing departments. Furthermore, Wilson's constant suspicions that his colleagues were plotting to unseat him led him to practice a policy of 'divide and rule' amongst those whom he saw as his chief rivals in cabinet. Thus revisionists remained but one part of the destructively managed cabinet with no scope for carrying out a coordinated policy.

The crisis-ridden history of the 1964–70 Labour governments has been recorded in detail.[41] The title of one such record, 'Breach of Promise', encapsulates the general verdict on its performance. Whether judged on the basis of the ideals of the revisionist programme, the even more flamboyant promises contained in the 1964 election manifesto, or the hopes that a Labour government, after thirteen years of Conservative rule, naturally aroused, its performance, despite a few notable achievements, was an historic disappointment. Only in the sphere of material equality could the government be said to have made some small advance. This, however, came mainly through long pending increases in transfer payments to the lowest paid, the unemployed and the retired. The much talked-about schemes for capital gains taxation and a National Superannuation Scheme came to nothing. Nor did the government succeed in its promised modernisation of the British economy, its overhaul from top to bottom to reverse the trends of sluggish economic growth and declining international competitiveness. Instead, almost immediately it assumed office, the government was confronted with a huge balance of payments deficit and the inadequacy of its response to it was a portent for the short-term pragmatism, reflecting little of the larger vision of the revisionist, or indeed any other socialist programme, which dominated the Wilson governments.

The balance of payments deficit to the tune of £750–800 million was the combined result of the long pre-election boom engineered by the Conservative Chancellor of the Exchequer, Reginald Maudling, and a pound overvalued in the interests of its role as an international reserve currency. The logical, albeit only initial, step of devaluation was ruled out, principally by Wilson, acting, as Ponting would have it, under American pressure combined with his own native reluctance to diminish the international role of sterling which the British economy, for its part, had not been strong enough to sustain. The revisionists in cabinet had favoured an early devaluation, especially after the 1966 election victory converted a meagre majority of three into a hefty one of one hundred, only to be overruled time and again by Wilson. An early devaluation, combined with active measures to deal with the deflation it would necessarily entail, might have allowed the Labour government time to reap some of the benefits that were expected after the initial period of difficulties. As things turned out, with Wilson refusing to countenance devaluation until it was practically forced upon them in 1967, the government only ended up delivering a healthy balance of payments position to the Conservatives who took office in 1970.

While on the question of devaluation, the revisionists' judgement was sound, most of their most important economic assumptions came unstuck during government. While devaluation might have created an early breathing space for the government, the scale and depth of Britain's economic problems that had begun to reveal themselves clearly required analysis of a penetration and strength the revisionists' were ill-equipped to provide. The balance of payments problems and associated 'stop-go' cycles were already the symptoms of Britain's century-long relative economic decline, rooted in the structure of British industry and its diminishing international competitiveness. It was also clear that an economy externalised on such a scale as Britain's could not assume an ability to stabilize the macro-economic environment without coming to terms with the international nature of financial and capital flows. However, the revisionists were wedded to a 'national' Keynesianism which assumed that the territorial boundaries of the state were just as real in the financial realm as in the political. Nor, on the other hand, did they have a more active interventionist policy concerned with regenerating British industry.

For growth was *assumed*, rather than problematised by the revisionists. They did not spend much time worrying about the problems of fostering it – only about redistributing it equitably. Indeed, this had been the principal thrust of progressive thought beginning with the New Liberals. Revisionist economic management, in the aftermath of the 'bonfire' of wartime physical controls, consisted in tinkering with macro-economic aggregates on the demand side to produce slight adjustments in the pace of growth and various fiscal incentives to produce the small correctives needed in its direction. The revisionists were so sanguine in their projections of economic growth that Crosland could assert in *The Future of Socialism* that while growth was key to the achievement of socialist objectives,

> I no longer regard questions of growth and efficiency as being, on the long view, of primary importance to socialism. We stand, in Britain, on the threshold of mass abundance; and within a decade the average family will enjoy a standard of living which, whether or not it fully satisfies their aspirations, will certainly convince the reformer that he should turn his main attention elsewhere.[42]

Their economic outlook, formed in the early 1950s, did not reflect the seriousness of the problems of industrial decline whose symptoms began to resurface in the 1960s, nor of more general unreliability of capitalist growth.

Already, in the early 1960s, it could be doubted if the revisionists had any more a viable economic strategy. With the evaporation of optimistic growth expectations, the Macmillan government was already forced into greater interventionism in the management of the economy (in the shape of the National Economic Development Council) than the revisionists were normally willing to contemplate or were practically prepared to implement. Having rejected the old model of national-isation, their proposals took the form of 'competitive public enterprise' wherein the government could buy existing firms (not take over entire industries), or set up new ones and attempt to set the standards in profitability, productivity, investment, labour relations and other areas in the industry as a whole. In this way not only would aggregate public ownership expand, but the problems of British competitiveness would also be surmounted. As Crosland envisaged it, 'the ultimate socialist aim ... is not an unending chain of public monopolies, but a diverse, diffused, pluralist, heterogeneous pattern of ownership.'[43] While this was an innovative approach, it hardly constituted the sort of tactile and thoroughgoing industrial policy that the economic problems they purported to deal with would seem to have required. Most of the instruments of economic planning and management were still those of the old macro-economic manipulation of the demand side. And even these could hardly be used to reflate the economy in the context of a perpetual state of crisis in the balance of payments that plagued most of the 1964–70 government's life.

These crises killed the five-year 'National Plan', the centrepiece of the wider Wilsonite modernization programme, billed in the early days of the government as 'covering all aspects of the country's economic development for the next five years ... a major advance in economic policy making in the United Kingdom.'[44] Its grandiose projections of an average annual growth rate of 4.5 per cent were shelved by July 1966 in the face of another dose of cuts and deflation. The story of the Department of Economic Affairs (DEA) also revealed the limits of the Wilsonite strategy for modernization. The National Plan and the new DEA which went with it were meant to counter 'the dead hand of the Treasury' in economic policy-making. It was becoming widely accepted that the Treasury, which concerned itself excessively with the balance of payments and the value of Sterling, was not necessarily the right agent for a policy for promoting growth and competitiveness in Britain.

But, once set up, the DEA and the National Plan suffered from Wilson's inability to provide sufficient attention and support for them, and to his political machinations against his rivals. Equally responsible for their failure was the ability of various government departments, and especially the Treasury, to keep a tight grip on their spheres of policy, not ceding to the DEA the powers it would have needed to direct the economic fate of Britain. They were also able to consciously obstruct its path. Other modernising reforms, in the law, and the civil service, which had been parts of the Wilsonite modernisation programme, remained superficial, both in intent and impact. Any change on this front would have required a major restructuring and overhaul of the structures and attitudes at Whitehall. Indeed, the importance of the attitudes of the predominantly conservative civil service was another symptom of the looseness and informality of a set-up which could never be called to account for its actions – an inefficient, at worst dangerous, attribute in a state structure. Clearly, this institutional inertia of British society had been underestimated as an obstacle to modernising reforms. This also had implications for revisionist assumptions about the pliability of the British state to the purposes of a socialist government. The political scenario in which the revisionists saw themselves as acting assumed that the governmental structure that obtained in Britain would be largely adequate to the vast expansion of its powers and responsibilities envisaged by the revisionists, and that it would be an efficient tool for the management of society along revisionist social democratic lines.

And the Labour government, most memorably perhaps, also came up against the chief economic limitation of revisionism – its inability to deal with the potentially inflationary consequences of a combination of full employment and free collective bargaining. To the constant economic troubles of the government in the late 1960s was added the problem of high and competitive wage settlements. In fact there were at least two problems here. According to the revisionists, the trade unions' commitment to free collective bargaining, in addition to being inflationary in a fully employed economy, potentially also worked against equality. And most of them argued for the elaboration of some form of statutory incomes policy. But the possibility of an incomes policy implied that the structure of the labour movement could be used to enforce it. In fact, the loose agglomeration of industry-wide national unions combined with the power of shop-floor wage bargaining meant that it was almost impossible to co-ordinate an incomes policy. Even if they had wanted to, the national trade union leaders who signed this agreement would have been powerless to enforce it, given the tradition of shop-floor wage bargaining. Already well before the elections of 1964, the trade unions' opposition to 'any form of wage restraint'[45] had become evident. The British trade union movement, built up over more than a century of defensive action against the encroaching powers of employers and governments, could not, given its long established culture, lend itself to the kind of control that a national policy on wages required (and the revisionists had never been involved in any grassroots attempt to change it in accordance with their own objectives). While a wider incomes policy, which also included the control of profits and dividends, had gained intermittent and not very convincing approval at party conferences, this was also more problematic for revisionism than it seemed. It involved a viable strategy for economic growth and an apparatus for economic planning which lay, effectively at least, beyond the revisionists' line of vision. The attempt at a voluntary policy of wage restraint, arrived at in April 1965, seemed powerless to stem the increasingly inflationary process of disorganised shop-floor wage-bargaining. The government's (and the revisionists') response to these economic problems was to look away from the limitations of their own strategy and focus on those of the trade union structure. The problem, as it came to be seen, was to shield British industry from the wage pressures of full employment and the solution was thus to regulate industrial relations.

By the late 1960s, there was a serious disjunction between the Government's felt need to regulate industrial relations, and the refusal of the unions to countenance any state interference in this area. The uproar over the proposals in the government White Paper *In Place of Strife* was the single most important factor in the Government's loss of office in 1970. In retrospect the failure to obtain the trade unions' compliance in a national economic policy, a problem which was to recur in the 1974–79 period of office, was judged, from a revisionist point of view as probably the Government's greatest failure – even greater than the badly handled currency situation:

> It can be argued that had not the exchange rate of the currency for so long been given absolute priority the Government would have turned in a better performance in promoting growth. Even so, at any given rate of exchange, the tendency for wages and costs to be pushed up faster than the increase in national productivity is a problem which no government can ignore.[46]

The one unambiguous success in this period of government was the 'permissive society legislation': a wide-ranging programme of social reform which included the abolition of capital punishment, divorce law reform, easier abortions, the legalisation of adult male homosexuality and the abolition of theatre censorship. The granting of permission to appeal to the European Court of Human Rights for the first time 'was to have a major long-term impact, bringing major changes in British law and practices in a number of areas from prisoners' rights to corporal punishment in schools. By the late 1980s Britain had lost more cases at the court than any other country.'[47] Though this legislation had the sponsorship, active support and backing of the Home Secretary, Roy Jenkins, on the insistence of the Prime Minister and many of the populist/labourist members of Cabinet these reforms were required to go through Parliament as private members' bills. While their origins undeniably lay in the revisionists' overall vision of society and its transformation, it was an indication of the political weakness of the revisionists in government that the reforms had to be passed without the full support of the Labour government, which was ostensibly committed to the modernisation of the archaic aspects of British society.

In many ways, these reforms were a story-book success of the revisionist approach to politics and social change – their top-down, expert approach. But ironically it was a success which was only possible in a field of policy which, while opposed to the deepest instincts of a certain significant right-wing tendency within many sectors within labourism, was nevertheless too unimportant to be obstructed. Nevertheless, as Home Secretary, Roy Jenkins had to fight for parliamentary time for this legislation and against pro-establishment pressures, even to the point of threatening resignation in the face of Wilson's interference in the case of theatre censorship. Clive Ponting contrasted the government's pragmatic, often less than liberal commitment to these reforms with the role of Jenkins:

> [W]ithout his help and advocacy the bills would have foundered amidst the doubts of his colleagues and in the morass of parliamentary procedure. Just how limited the government's commitment to modernisation could be was demonstrated in the case of theatre censorship. Virtually nobody could be found to defend the archaic and inconsistent censorship exercised by the Lord Chamberlain, but the Palace, Wilson and other members of the Cabinet felt personally threatened by its removal, and so made a major effort to replace it by another form of censorship to protect their own position and that of other members of the establishment. ... [The legacy of the reforms] has proved to be one of the lasting monuments, if not to the work of the government, at least to its period in office.[48]

Notes

1. Stephen Haseler, *The Gaitskellites*, Macmillan, London, 1969, p 246.

2. The principal parliamentary members of the Bevanite group, apart from Bevan himself, were Wilson and Freeman, who had resigned with him in 1951 over the issue of health charges and defence expenditure, the authors of *Keep Left* Richard Crossman, Ian Mikardo and Michael Foot, Jennie Lee and the former trade unionists Barbara Castle and Tom Driberg.

3. Mark Jenkins, *Bevanism*, Spokesman, Nottingham, 1979, p 1.

4. David Howell, *British Social Democracy*, Croom Helm, London, 1976, p 185.

5. *Ibid*, p 184. They were Bevan, Castle, Crossman, Driberg, Mikardo and Wilson.

6. *Parliamentary Socialism: A Study in the Politics of Labour*, Monthly Review Press, New York, 1972.

7. Gareth Stedman Jones, 'Editorial', *History Workshop Journal*, Number 12, Autumn 1981, p 5.

8. 'The Nature of the Labour Party' I and II, *New Left Review*, Numbers 27 and 28, September–December, 1964.

9. Lewis Minkin, *The Labour Party Conference*, Allen Lane, London, 1978, p 24.

10. Apart from the towering figure of Bevin, 'union representation in the Cabinet was unimpressive. By 1951, a cabinet of 17 included only 4 trade unionists, and in the remainder of the administration the proportion was 18 out of 66. It appears that leading Ministers were aware of the need to offer posts to younger trade union MPs, but were inhibited by generally unfavourable assessments of their potential.' Howell, *op. cit.*, p 163.

11. James Hinton, *Labour and Socialism*, Wheatsheaf, Brighton, 1983, p 182.

12. Anthony Crosland, *The Future of Socialism*, Jonathan Cape, London, 1956, pp 190–217.

13. Tom Nairn, *op. cit.*, p 58.

14. See Leslie Hunter, *The Road to Brighton Pier*, Arthur Barker Ltd, London, 1959, pp 129–131.

15. See *ibid*, pp 41–51, and Clive Ponting, *Breach of Promise: Labour in Power 1964–70*, Hamish Hamilton, London, p 4–5.

16. Fabian Tract Number 300, Fabian Society, London, 1956.

17. The Labour Party, *Industry and Society*, London, 1957.

18. Michael Foot, *Aneurin Bevan: A Biography, Vol. II 1945–60*, Davis-Poynter Ltd, London, 1973, p 575.

19. *Ibid*, p 579.

20. Hugh Dalton quoted in Philip Williams, *Hugh Gaitskell*, Oxford University Press, Oxford, 1982, p 314.

21. 16 October 1959.

22. Minkin, *op. cit.*, p 33.

23. Mark Abrams, *Must Labour Lose?*, Penguin Books, Harmondsworth, 1960, p 109.

24. See C.A.R. Crosland, 'Radical Reform and the Left', *Encounter*, October 1960, reprinted in *The Conservative Enemy*, Jonathan Cape, London, 1962.

25. *Ibid*, p 133.

26. Labour Party Conference Report, 1959, p 109.

27. 'The Future of the Left', *Encounter*, March 1960, p 7.

28. *Labour Party Conference Report*, 1960, p 201.

29. Williams, *op. cit.*, p 355.

30. Haseler, *op. cit*, p 198.

31. Lord Windlesham, *Communication and Political Power*, Johnathan Cape, London, 1966, p 148.

32. Williams, *op. cit.*, p 288.

33. Quoted in *ibid*, p 394.

34. *Labour Party Conference Report*, 1962, p 159

35. Chairman's remark, *ibid*, p 162.

36. See, The Labour Party, *Signposts for the Sixties*, London, 1961, p 8 and, C.A.R. Crosland, 'Production in the Age of Affluence' in *The Listener*, 25 September 1958, reprinted in *The Conservative Enemy*, Jonathan Cape, London, 1962.

37. Howell, *op.cit*, p 231. This concern, as noted earlier, first emerged in the late 1950s among Marxists and spread later, and in a less theoretically rigorous form, among mainstream intellectuals as well.

38. *Signposts*, p 9.

39. *Ibid*, p 10.

40. Ponting, *op. cit.*, p 18–19.

41. On the economic performance of the government see Wilfred Beckerman (ed), *The Labour Government's Economic Record: 1964–1970*, Duckworth, London, 1972. Clive Ponting's more recent work, *op. cit.*, Hamish Hamilton, London, 1989, provides a full and interesting record of the political as well as policy aspects of the life of that government.

42. C.A.R. Crosland, *The Future of Socialism*, p 515.

43. C.A.R. Crosland, 'The Role of Public Ownership', *Encounter*, May 1961.

44. Ponting, *op. cit.*, p 112.

45. From a 1963 TUC motion carried by a large vote quoted in Howell, *op. cit.*, p 236.

46. Peter Jenkins, *The Battle of Downing Street*, Charles Knight, London, 1970, p 165.

47. Ponting, *op. cit.*, p 260.

48. Ponting, *op. cit.*, p 268–69.

6

Origins of the 1981 Split: Common Market and Industrial Strategy

In the aftermath of the unravelling of revisionism in the 1964–70 Labour government, the revisionists failed to restate a credible set of policy alternatives. The period of opposition from 1970 onwards, according to the revisionists' own prognostications should have been an 'opportunity for reorientation',[1] with a fundamental reworking of the Croslandite revisionism of the 1950s. This, however, was not to be. Crosland himself, once Labour's foremost intellectual, although disappointed with the performance of the 1964–70 Labour governments, insisted that there was

> no analogy with the 1950s, when society had been changed out of recognition since the 1930s by full employment and the Welfare State and where a fundamental rethinking was required. This is not the position today. ... What we need is not some great shift of direction, but a clear reaffirmation of ... agreed ideals.[2]

As the principal author of 1950s revisionism, Crosland was perhaps now more reluctant than most to question its continuing relevance. In any case, for reasons explored below, Crosland's political path diverged from that of most other revisionists from the mid-1960s onwards. Some of the younger backbench revisionists (of whom there were many in the intakes of 1964 and 1966) had in the late 1960s sensed some of the difficulties of the revisionist strategy, and Roy Jenkins, their new leader, had made half-hearted gestures towards resolving them in the early years of opposition. However, the restatement of Labour's strategy came this time from the left of the party in the form of the Alternative Economic Strategy (AES). The truth was, as David Marquand admitted, that 'the [revisionist] right didn't have any doctrinal changes ... or really anything to say of a doctrinal nature in the 1970s ... [they] lost the battle of ideas with the Left by default really. Actually, they really didn't fight the battle for ideas.'[3]

There would be a neatness to the story if the roots of the political marginalization which the revisionists began to suffer in the 1970s, and which eventually led them out of the party in 1981, lay in this final intellectual failure. There is an intuitive justice in the fall of those who fail at their self-defined tasks. It would seem, however, that the causes of their marginalisation lay at least as much in the politics of the Labour Party in the 1970s as in any intellectual abdication. Fundamentally, it seemed to Bill Rodgers, with his sensitive ear to the ground, their marginalisation had to do with an unprecedented shift in the power relationships within the party:

> [Within the Labour Party] the 1970s were a watershed not in terms of ideas but politics, because the revisionist right and the centre were split. ... The dominant feature was the failure of the radical revisionist right and the centrist conservative right to make common cause on a common programme for the first time ever.[4]

The alliance between major trade union leaders and the intellectuals in the party, which had underwritten moderate and then revisionist ascendancy since the late 1940s, had begun to show cracks, as we have seen, even in the 1950s. The new trade union militancy which emerged in the late 1960s and which began to question the legitimacy and power of the parliamentary party and leadership positively destroyed this alliance. The exclusively parliamentarian revisionists were peculiarly ill-equipped to deal with, and uniquely capable of mishandling, this new configuration of power.

The Common Market issue dominated Labour's politics in the period of opposition from 1970–74, overshadowing other important questions such as the unions' extra-parliamentary opposition to the Tories' Industrial Relations Bill (which ultimately brought down the Heath government), or Labour's search for a new economic strategy. The new divisions which emerged in the party over this issue were a *résumé* of the new power configuration: they revealed the full extent of the revisionists' isolation. In the Great Debate on the Common Market the pro-European 'social democrats' (as the revisionists began to call themselves, in sympathy with Continental social democracy) were ranged against the rest of the party. This division became a matter for public record when, on 28 October 1971, 69 Labour MPs, led by the social democrats under the leadership of Roy Jenkins, voted with the Tory government for British entry into the European Community.

The new political configuration in the Labour Party of the 1970s is usually seen as the product of a significant shift to the left under the political momentum of trade union militancy and the ideological auspices of the AES. However, as this chapter demonstrates, despite the left's rhetorically greater radicalism, the AES remained largely within revisionist parameters. In fact, as its alliance with the centre in an essentially nationalist campaign against entry into the European Common Market demonstrates, the new Labour left actually rested on a resurgence of populist labourism. An inevitable consequence was that it further shrank the political space for traditional intellectuals in the party. Thus, the very moment of the revisionists' redefinition as the Europeanist social democrats was that of their isolation as intellectuals. This chapter explores the major dimensions of the complex political and ideological conjuncture of the early 1970s which precipitated Labour's principal intellectuals in their final form – the social democrats. It was also clear by this time that neither the former revisionists, nor the emergent new Labour left had a radically new programme with which to replace the exhausted revisionism. Their marginalization only deepened in the course of the 1970s and it was in this form that those who had hitherto been Labour's only intellectuals left the party to form the Social Democratic Party (SDP) in 1981: the division in the PLP over the Common Market closely prefigured the party split a decade later.

Labour in the 1970 General Election

The party leadership approached the 1970 general election expecting to win on the basis of the success of its post-devaluation economic performance which was, perhaps fetishistically, measured by the now comfortable balance of payments surplus. The postponed social expenditures could be undertaken in the expected climate of stability and growth – a situation in which the acquiescence of the unions in a planned, non-inflationary growth of incomes – i.e. an incomes policy – might also be more easily forthcoming. With the perceived failure of Wilson's economic modernisation policies of the 1960s, the Government had begun to focus on entry into the Common Market as the new key to modernisation and development; and now that de Gaulle had left the scene, it intended to re-apply for entry if re-elected. All of which is to say that the electoral appeal of the Labour Party was tacitly built within revisionist parameters, the left having failed, as usual, to present any alternative strategy. Indeed, with the decline of Bevanism and the absorption of many of the leading Bevanites into the Government there was no clearly defined left or right in the party, and certainly no left-wing policy platform.

But if the intellectual parameters of the party's election campaign were revisionist, the style was unmistakably Wilsonian in its combination of bluff and evasion. The campaign attempted to build an image of a government overcoming acute economic difficulties and finally creating a stable economic climate. There was no indication in party pronouncements of the disastrous vacillation on economic policy in the mid-1960s, or that any major problems of economic management remained to be solved. In essence the Labour government sought credit for having belatedly repaired the economic damage it had inherited and had then proceeded to exacerbate. Underlying this strategy was the (vain) hope that Labour was now becoming the 'natural party of government'. Even Tony Benn, soon to emerge as the leader of a new Labour left intent on binding the leadership to detailed manifesto pledges, warned at his 1970 adoption meeting at Bristol that 'there cannot be categorical promises to be carried out without regard to circumstances, many of which we cannot foresee.'[5] The *Financial Times* caustically commented on the vagueness of the manifesto: 'Either the government has run out of ideas, or with rather less excuse than the opposition, it is asking for a blank cheque. Its claim, in other words, is that it should be judged on its performance during its six years of office. This is a bold claim.'[6] While some revisionists did sense the policy problems and direction-lessness of the Government before the 1967 devaluation, the post-devaluation appointment of Roy Jenkins as Chancellor of the Exchequer, and his seemingly able direction of the economy, gave sufficient hope to the 'government-minded'. Peter Jenkins, a journalist noted for his consistent revisionist sympathies, expressed this attitude: 'A party which has been in power for six years with some successes, many failures and a large amount of its business unfinished has no need to set out on paper its detailed intentions for a further term.'[7]

But this united front presented by the leadership hardly implied a united party. The deep divisions in the parliamentary party of the 1950s might have become a thing of the past, but new divisions between the PLP and the rank and file prefigured Labour's troubles of the 1970s and 1980s. In the late 1960s the Labour Party had suffered an acceler-ated decline in membership, due principally to growing disillusionment and apathy amongst its activists and supporters. The labour movement at large had registered significant leftward shifts which were expressed at Conference in a series of defeats for government-backed resolutions. Wilson chose to deliberately ignore these verdicts on his Government's performance, saying 'the government must govern'; there was, however, a widespread feeling that the government had moved too far away from the party's grassroots, and this was exacerbated by the Government's mismanaged and highly unpopular proposal to regulate industrial relations in the 1969 White Paper, *In Place of Strife*. A disastrous Labour performance in the 1968 local elections, which had returned many Conservative councils in traditionally safe Labour strongholds, was another indication of popular discontent. The authority of government was used to override these forces and sentiments at Conference, however, and most former working-class Labour voters returned to the Labour fold in 1970 in a combination of traditional loyalty and fear of the Conservatives' even more draconian plans for union regulation.

Nevertheless, the Conservatives were able to win, largely, it seemed, by exploiting the industrial relations issue among the electorate at large.

The Left-ward Shift in the Trade Unions after 1970

Once in opposition, Labour's discontents resurfaced powerfully. Disillusionment with the Wilson governments, especially the unpopularity of the incomes policy and union regulation that had been attempted, was, of course, a central cause of rank and file militancy. But there were also important novel elements in it. Already in the late 1960s the slowdown in economic growth had resulted in a new kind of union militancy which pitted itself against the downward pressure on working-class living standards and increasingly by-passed the national union leadership to arrive at higher wage settlements. It also changed the basis of the relationship between the working class and the Labour Party. In a new working-class consciousness which Goldthorpe and Lockwood termed 'instrumental collectivism',[8] the attachment of the working class to the Labour Party was no longer characterised by effective links based on traditional working-class culture, but was conditional on a rational calculation of their collective interests. This meant that in order to retain the workers' loyalty, Labour would now have to work at articulating and perceptibly satisfying these interests. Perry Anderson hailed this new research as path-breaking as well as hopeful:

> The incursion of rationalism into the hermetic world of the English working class is a necessary stage in its emancipation – however limited or confusing its initial manifestations. It is the precondition of a genuinely ideological collectivism – founded on *ideas* not merely on instinct.[9]

However, in the period under consideration, the manifestations of this new consciousness remained 'limited and confusing', not to say labourist. The party leadership failed, inevitably perhaps, to respond to these potentially progressive aspects of the new consciousness, choosing instead to sow the seeds of a materialistic populism whose harvest Mrs Thatcher was to reap most successfully. Whatever the fate of 'instrumental collectivism', it was clear that from the mid-1960s onwards Britain's economic problems were being exacerbated by the increasing rate of unofficial strikes by workers who were 'not prepared to accept unemployment and downward pressure on wages without a struggle, [and who] thanks to the "affluent" fifties, when sometimes more job vacancies were recorded than job-seekers ... had become well placed to resist.'[10]

The more specific controversy over union regulation must also be placed in this context. As we have seen, competitive wage settlements in a slowly growing economy had inflationary consequences. The Government's preferred method of overcoming the problem was its attempt to regulate industrial relations. Indeed, the government's tacit revisionism, with its lack of any strategy for growth, left it with no other option. However, the Donovan Commission, which had been appointed in 1965 to look into the prospects of reforming industrial relations, delivered a disappointingly complacent and conservative report recommending few changes. In a dissenting 'Note of Reservation', however, the well-known economist Andrew Shonfield took the view that the industrial climate in Britain was in need of drastic reform if Britain wanted to be a modern competitive and dynamic society. The traditional immunities of trade unions were increasingly archaic and it was important to look positively at the role of the state and to rethink powerful social institutions like trade unions in terms of their obligations to society and not just their rights and immunities against it. While the state had made significant inroads in various aspects of industrial life it curiously stopped short at the door of the trade unions.

> [T]he myth that the act of regulation is a falling from grace and that each case is to be treated as a regrettable exception, which must not in any circumstances be generalised, continues to influence powerfully the judgement of many of those concerned with industrial relations. ... I start from the proposition that the deliberate abstention of the law from the activities of mighty subjects tends to diminish the liberty of the ordinary citizen and to place his welfare at risk.[11]

The revisionists in the Labour Party naturally favoured a reform of industrial relations along the regulatory lines favoured by Shonfield and there was widespread pressure on the Labour government to reform industrial relations – a pressure which the Conservatives were only too willing to exploit. Certainly Wilson viewed the need to appear to be doing something on the issue as very urgent, and eventually the Minister for Employment, Barbara Castle produced the 1969 White Paper, *In Place of Strife*. It included financial penalties on unions for unofficial strikes or for not agreeing to the proposed arbitration processes; among the rank and file this reinforced the impression that the Labour government had moved far away from its trade union base. Barbara Castle, however, herself a former Bevanite, firmly believed that *In Place of Strife* was 'first and foremost a charter of trade union rights'; it contained measures which would 'make it unlawful for an employer to prevent an individual joining a trade union; enable the Commission on Industrial Relations (CIR) to recommend the recognition of a trade union; create a development fund, with government support, to assist union mergers; provide compensation or reinstatement for unfair dismissal.'[12] The union leadership, however, jealous of its traditional immunities won through a long history of industrial and political struggle, and increasingly distrustful of the Labour leadership, refused to countenance any state regulation, and so the Government's attempt to limit unofficial strikes and generally create a more stable and predictable industrial climate in Britain foundered on forceful union resistance.

Strikes and 'direct occupations' increased under the new Conservative government from 1970 onwards, especially in light of its own industrial relations legislation and its neo-liberal policies towards the closure of lame duck industries. The unprecedented union militancy directed, in the early 1970s at least, against the openly neo-liberal policies of Edward Heath, seemed to offer new possibilities for a class-based socialist politics. And, of course, this union militancy was flavoured with much left-wing rhetoric and hope. However, while indicative of one of Britain's most serious economic problems, this militancy and mobilization occurred within well-defined labourist intellectual limits. As in the 1930s, the sense of betrayal did not lead to a challenge to the political leadership by the industrial wing. The union leaders at no time

> [saw] themselves as rivals for the political leadership of the labour movement even when they had sharp strategic as well as policy disagreements with the leaders of the Parliamentary Labour Party ... even left-wing leaders respected the autonomy of the party leadership and saw the way forward in terms of a more effective 'elite accommodation' between the industrial and political leadership.[13]

But the feeling that the parliamentary leadership could not be trusted to listen to the union rank and file did lead to a demand for greater union say in the policies of any future Labour government. The demand for extra-parliamentary influence on the parliamentary leadership had always been a slogan of the left, and now the new trade union demand for policy influence became articulated with that of the emerging new Labour left. The unions' position substantially amounted to a 'soft' corporatism in which a *voluntary* incomes policy would give trade union leaders privileged access to any future Labour government, in order to be able to prevent further fiascos like *In Place of Strife* and to co-operate with the Government on economic management. Further, any voluntary incomes policy was conditional on a positive programme for salvaging Britain's industrial position through increased state intervention. But how this might be done was not specified, and the ability of the national unions to control their rank and file in the traditionally loose structures of the trade union movement was, as always, in doubt. Nonetheless, this was the substance of the trade union position over which the new Labour left sought to hoist the banner of socialism, and which formed the political basis of the Alternative Economic Strategy and the Social Contract of the 1974–79 Labour government. While the bulk of the parliamentary party remained sceptical, not to say opposed, to the AES, the opportunists in the leadership were able to deal with this turn of events by the time-honoured use of ambiguity. The revisionists however, with their more clearly stated ideological positions, could not so easily sidestep the new political challenges this represented.

Labour Party Policy-Making in Opposition

The Alternative Economic Strategy, as it was embodied in party documents of the early 1970s, emerged out of the party's established policy-making apparatus. The prominence of the party's formal policy-making apparatus in the policy reorientation of the 1970s was partly the product of a reaction against the domination of the parliamentary leadership. During the years of the Wilson government the Labour Party's official policy process had became a near irrelevance. While a number of channels of 'dialogue and liaison' existed between the party, the PLP and the Government, party institutions lacked effective influence. A left-wing sympathiser, Terry Pitt, had become secretary of the Labour Party Research Department (LPRD), and although in the late 1960s the party's conference decisions had moved considerably to the left of the government, these had no visible impact on party policy and the manifesto of 1970 papered over any differences with ambiguous wording.

Those who occupied the leading positions in the apparatus of the party used the 1970 defeat to assert the importance of party structures. In analysing the defeat, the party headquarters staff pointed to the declining constituency parties, many of which were now very small and in some cases almost non-existent. By one account membership had declined from 1,150,000 in 1956 to 634,000 in 1970.[14] While the absolute numbers were, as usual, dubious, the trend towards decline of membership in the party did indicate widespread disaffection among the rank and file. According to Paul Whiteley, a number of different factors may have been responsible for this syndrome: the decreasing importance of public meetings, the increasing use of television in election campaigns, and the decline in the influence of Conference during the Wilson years, all of which reduced the importance of constituency activists. However, confirming Goldthorpe and Lockwood's analysis of the new working-class consciousness, the most important cause, according to Whiteley, was the new instrumental relationship of the working class to the Labour Party: 'Individuals who join the party for instrumental reasons are inherently more likely to defect than those who join for affective reasons'.[15]

An early party initiative sought to deal with both policy problems and rank and file disaffection. From 1969 onwards the LPRD under Terry Pitt had initiated a programme which attempted to revitalise the Constituency Labour Parties (CLPs) under the title 'Participation'. Its strategy consisted of sending questionnaires to CLPs on various policy issues to determine the direction of party feeling, and culminated in a grand *Participation 1972* exercise which polled CLPs on a comprehensive list of policy areas. Nothing much came of it, however, not least because of the fundamental ambiguity about the purposes – mobilizational or policy-making – it was supposed to serve. At best the results of such an exercise could only be a broad guide to policy-making. The amount of popular input that could be achieved through simple devices such as questionnaires on complex policy matters was, in any case, strictly limited. Polling assumed that the members of CLPs already knew what the right policies were and that all that needed to be done was to communicate these to the party leadership. If the function of Labour's leadership was to creatively articulate the genuine concerns of the people into a progressive political platform, one has to agree with the comment that the whole Participation exercise was an 'extraordinary confession of political bankruptcy.'[16]

This is not to say that there was no need for grassroots mobilisation. Paralleling the depleting membership rolls of local Labour parties in the late 1960s and early 1970s there had been a rise of activist groups like the Child Poverty Action Group and Shelter which mobilised the energies of the younger generation and reflected the failures of the welfare state in providing for the extremely disadvantaged and in keeping up the quality and quantity of social services. There was also the general trend towards participation and popular power which had emerged in the 1960s, of which the Institute for Workers' Control was a good example. Most of the political activity around these groups (not to mention the many ultra-Left groups which also thrived in this period) was unconnected to the Labour Party, which correspondingly suffered a loss of recruitment among the young. Very little of this new activist thinking was reflected in the policy processes of the party. The *Participation* policy exercise having (inevitably) failed, it is true to say, there was no 'bottom-up' policy-making process: the real process of policy-making remained fairly top-heavy. While grassroots disaffection remained a genuine problem, the opportunities afforded by the 1970 election defeat resulted in little more than the assertion of party structures as a counterweight to the power of the parliamentary leadership. The extra-parliamentary party – Conference and the machinery of the Labour Party – was also the principal terrain on which the left advanced, thanks largely to the new militancy in the unions. By contrast, the pre-eminent position of former ministers in the PLP continued into the 1970 Conference; Roy Jenkins's election as Deputy Leader in 1970 was a symptom of the respect the parliamentary revisionists continued to enjoy in the PLP at that date.

It was after the 1970 Conference that the task of party policy-making was resumed in earnest in the Home Policy Committee of the NEC and its sub-committees. In 1970 the status of these committees had been upgraded from 'advisory' (to which they had been demoted in 1964, so as to avoid 'embarrassment if they produced proposals which ran counter to Labour Government policy')[17] to 'consultative' status. This change 'offered an opportunity to set up high-level committees to attract outside experts who were national figures'.[18] Six sub-committees were set up: Finance and Economic Affairs, Industrial Policy, Regional and Local Government, Science and Education, Social Policy and Agriculture. There were four major sets of actors on these policy committees. The trade union representatives sought mainly to ensure that some effective strategy of government intervention emerged whose goal would be to improve British economic performance. Only on the basis of their satisfaction on this score could their compliance in any incomes policy be secured by a future Labour government. Secondly, the old Labour left from the NEC, where the left had come to have a majority in the late 1960s, was represented by people like Ian Mikardo and Judith Hart (both ex-Bevanites) whose status and credibility in the policy sub-committees was enhanced in the new left-wing climate, distrustful of the parliamentary leadership. Third, from the Labour front bench came MPs who included among their number many revisionists as well as MPs associated with the left like Barbara Castle, Michael Foot and the new Labour left's most celebrated leader, Tony Benn. The fourth group consisted of outside intellectuals, many of national stature, who were sympathetic to Labour but who were not MPs or office-holders in the party. The principal intellectuals to sit on the various committees included the economists Professor Richard Pryke, Lords Balogh and Kaldor and the social researchers Professors Brian Abel-Smith, Richard Titmuss and Peter Townsend. Stuart Holland, though much younger and less well-known, was the most significant figure in view of the importance of economic issues and the left-wing industrial programme that emerged from the Industrial Policy Committee, based on his analysis and recommendations. The dominant impulse in these committees was leftward, both in terms of moving party policy to the left, and in terms of demonstrating to the party that by the time of the next election the parliamentary leadership would be bound to policies reflecting the concerns of the rank and file.[19] Despite the fact that the revisionists were well represented in these committees they were to have little impact on the evolution of Labour's new policies.

From Croslandite Revisionists to Jenkinsite Social Democrats

The fact was that policy renewal was not anywhere near the top of the revisionist agenda in the early 1970s. They had emerged from government at least partially relieved to be freed from the constraints of office. Even though no love was lost between them and Harold Wilson, several revisionists had served in fairly senior positions in his governments and could now claim to be regarded as credible and well-known Labour figures. With the election defeat they fully anticipated a resurgence of left-wing ideas on the model of 1951, but they were, by the same analogy, also confident of winning the party back to a 'sane' and realistic path. What they had not anticipated was the strength of left-wing pressure, and of the opposition on the all important European question, coming this time not from a group of parliamentarians (which the Bevanites had been) over whom they could prevail through their intellectual ascendancy in the PLP and trade union loyalism outside it. Not only did trade union loyalism and labourism no longer work in their favour, this left-wing pressure built up in the extra-parliamentary party – an arena where they had little presence or organisation. As the revisionists regrouped, there were internal political matters amongst them which were settled in interesting ways. Hugh Gaitskell had died in 1963, and the Campaign for Democratic Socialism had been largely wound down with the election of the Labour government in 1964. Thereafter the revisionists had little organised presence in the Labour Party. There had been an informal discussion group called the 1963 Club, started by Bill Rodgers, but apart from holding rather free-ranging discussions it engaged in no organised political activity. Meanwhile the question of the succession to Gaitskell as leader of the revisionists brought about some realignments even in this informal grouping.

On the face of it, there were two possible contenders for Gaitskell's mantle, Tony Crosland and Roy Jenkins. Crosland's intellectual synthesis, *The Future of Socialism*, had earned the revisionists many of their younger recruits in the late 1950s and 1960s. Crosland was naturally the first figure they looked to for leadership. He appeared to have the breadth of vision and a grasp of the technicalities of various national problems to make a potential leader. However, beginning in the late 1960s he increasingly distanced himself from his fellow revisionists, a fateful development full of unexplained paradoxes. Perhaps his long-standing rivalry with Jenkins, dating back to the days of Dalton's patronage and craftily exploited by Wilson in his disbursement of ministerial portfolios in order to neutralise the revisionists, played some role. Many younger revisionists also felt that Crosland had not lived up to their expectations as a leadership figure, and that he was increasingly betraying them intellectually and politically. He demonstrated a lack of the one ability which, it soon seemed to the revisionists, every leader must have – the ability to cultivate and retain loyalty. He had always been very much an individualist, eccentric, even arrogant, and disdainful of coteries. Many of the young recruits of the 1960s found him unresponsive.[20] Bill Rodgers summed up the view of Tony Crosland which many revisionists came to hold in the late 1960s and early 1970s.

> [Tony Crosland] had a difficult and ambivalent relationship with younger men, whereas Roy Jenkins felt he had a duty to help younger men. Take a very obvious example. A Cabinet Minister can really choose his own junior ministers. Roy Jenkins's attitude was that he was loyal to those who had been loyal to him. Tony Crosland very characteristically would say, 'Well *they* are friends already, I can count on their loyalty. I will give *him* or *her* a chance'. And in fact, what he was doing was leaving those who were loyal to him out in the cold. You can't do that in politics. I think you cannot separate the failure of Tony Crosland to emerge as leader from his personal short-comings.[21]

Apart from this political dilettantism, which Crosland had indulged in fairly consistently throughout his political life, there seemed, by the 1970s, to be two other factors which rendered him unpalatable as a leader to most of the emerging social democrats. Firstly, his intellectual superiority seemed to have evaporated, leaving behind only what the revisionists saw as a politically counterproductive sophistry. An index of this change was his unwillingness, or inability, to produce a work of the scale and scope of *The Future of Socialism* in the manifestly changed circumstances of the 1970s. As we have seen, he refused to admit the necessity of a revision of his revisionism, insisting, perhaps pro-prietorially, on its continued relevance. There was also a distinct lack of grace in his attitude towards those who begged to differ. In the post-1970 policy process, for example, having already taken the view that the failures of the Wilson governments lay in technical mistakes and that there was no need for any great revision of party strategy, Crosland refused to accept the arguments of Stuart Holland. Holland argued for a new kind of industrial intervention which Crosland could, if he wished, take credit for, and which could be said to carry forward the analysis and implications of Crosland's own proposals for competitive public enterprise.

Secondly, Crosland now began to affect a romantic populism which he used against arguments of principle on many social and political issues. Peter Jenkins, a close friend, assessed Crosland's later years:

> Towards the end of his life he increasingly affected a sort of cloth cap popul-ism. He'd dress up in this black cap, was a tremendous football fan and went to official banquets where he'd leave the table rather rudely and go to watch football with the policemen and messengers outside. Though a middle-class intellectual with some private money himself, he took considerable delight in ribbing the metropolitan intelligentsia and saying to them, 'I'm afraid you'd find that pretty low on my constituents' list of priorities'. More and more questions, particularly libertarian ones and those relating to foreign policy, he brushed aside in this way, concentrating on the 'gut' issues.[22]

For example, on the question of Europe, which most revisionists considered the most important issue of the 1970s, he now claimed to favour British entry marginally on a finely balanced economic case, but he refused to vote with the other revisionists, arguing, much to their chagrin, that it was not the most important issue to working-class voters. This, according to many revisionists, was a dramatic turnaround. In another striking example of this attachment to what he took to be authentic working-class attitudes, Crosland was indifferent if not opposed to many of the progressive social reforms that Roy Jenkins initiated during his tenure at the Home Office. Anthony Lester QC, who was involved with Roy Jenkins on race relations issues in this period, remarked:

> The Croslanders and the Jenkinsites took fundamentally different positions on the race question as they did on many libertarian questions. Jenkins was regarded as a namby-pamby soft liberal who was out of touch with the real world, who wanted pornography, homosexuality and race equality. And the Croslanders felt that they had a much closer link with working-class values. ... Because Crosland was one of the ones lobbying Labour Peers in the House of Lords to vote for the East African Asians Bill, I remember being in the lobby with Nicholas Deakin watching Crosland deal with this ... and we then had a great row with Crosland, who said something along the lines of 'You people in NW1 make me sick with your libertarian values'.[23]

Perhaps because of this seemingly rather contrived loyalism, Crosland was perceived to be a weak minister by his revisionist followers, unable to stand up for a principle against Harold Wilson, as Roy Jenkins had to do on numerous occasions at the Home Office.

David Marquand has suggested an underlying psychological consistency in what seemed to most of Crosland's former supporters to be a gross political inconsistency. He traces it to his upbringing in a family committed to a most extreme form of religious dissent, the Plymouth Brethren. For Marquand a hint of the connection is provided, wittingly or otherwise, in Susan Crosland's dedication of her biography of her late husband to the 'people of Grimsby [Crosland's constituency] and the Labour Party'.

> He did identify himself with the 'people of Grimsby', or at least with what he imagined the people of Grimsby to be. It was not a pose: it was part of him. By the same token, and probably for the same reasons, he identified himself with the Labour Party. It was for him what the exclusive Brethren had been for his parents: the unquestioned structure giving meaning to his life; the embodiment of a commitment which was now beyond argument.[24]

Whatever the reasons, Crosland's distance from his revisionist colleagues, and his increasing closeness to the one man who was to prove himself a populist *par excellence*, Jim Callaghan, the 'keeper of the cloth cap',[25] led him along a solitary and not always consistent path in the course of the 1970s. By the late 1970s, Crosland was even distinguishing himself from his former revisionist colleagues by calling himself a 'democratic socialist', although many of his closest friends did not understand the doctrinal significance of this distinction. He even went so far as to describe a 'social democrat' as 'somebody about to join the Tory Party'.[26] This political course was not entirely unrewarded, as in 1976 Callaghan offered him the Foreign Office over the more ministerially senior (and by then politically larger) figure of Jenkins, two years before Crosland's untimely death in 1978. Thus the revisionists lost the one potential leader who might, it had seemed at one time, have had the stature to reassert their position at the centre of party policy-making.

It may be argued that Denis Healey, who had held the Defence portfolio all through the Wilson governments, was also a prominent revisionist intellectual and as such also a leadership contender. However, he had always followed a path of his own and was seen by the revisionists/social democrats as an opportunist. From their lofty position in the PLP, the revisionists viewed Healey, with his more intimate links with the structures of the party, as something of a 'superior apparatchik' in the Labour Party machine.[27]

The leadership of the revisionists thus fell on Roy Jenkins, a turn of events full of ironies. His claim was based above all on his ability to inspire loyalty. Under his often distant or diffident-seeming manner, his supporters affirmed time and again, was warmth and genuine concern and an ability to take principled and consistent stands, as on the social reforms of the mid-1960s and on Europe in 1971. However, a forward-looking, modernising group of proto-Fabian social-science-oriented intellectuals could hardly have found a leader who was more identified with past eras, one more self-consciously cast in the established literary historical mode of British intellectual life – an intellectual more at home writing elegant and erudite biographies of Asquith or Sir Charles Dilke than undertaking a social-scientific synthesis like Crosland's. Though a skilled politician and statesman, Jenkins was temperamentally incapable of an effort such as *The Future of Socialism*. Having tutored his sensibilities to what he saw as the best in British culture, in his urbane eclectic humanism he also fell under the spell of much of its 'anti-Benthamism', if not of its basic unintellectualism. With Jenkins as their leader, the intellectual tradition the revisionists/social democrats represented in British political life had indeed entered its terminal phase.

The group was also weakened by the absence from it of Crosland and Healey. Out of the running for the leadership of the revisionists, they could also no longer be counted among them. While Gaitskell had been able to unite the young revisionists, even the most ambitious among them, under him, Crosland and Healey, arguably figures of

equal substance to Jenkins, could hardly allow themselves to be numbered as mere members of a group led by him.

Moreover, as the leader of what now became known as the Social
Democrats Jenkins was more closely identified with liberalism than
social democracy, and had even excised the word 'socialism' from his
personal vocabulary since the late 1950s. On Europe, however, the one
issue which in the early 1970s seemed most important to the social
democrats, Jenkins appeared the natural leader, and they increasingly
adopted the label Social Democrats in order to demonstrate their
political affinity to Continental social democracy and their continuing
attachment to the cause of British entry into the Common Market.

The European Imagination

The revisionist stand on Europe was both a central element of their
outlook and one of its most characteristic fruits. The distinctive strength
of their intellectual stance lay in perceiving underlying historical trends
and setting new horizons for politics. The revisionists had been the first
to acknowledge that the Attlee governments had run out of intellectual
steam after 1948 and that full employment, the removal of absolute
poverty and the increase in social security for the ordinary citizen had
fundamentally altered the parameters of socialist politics: and so, they
reasoned, the socialist programme had to change. The contrast could
not be greater with the stand taken by the left, whose vague but strongly
accusative stance of 'not enough socialism' (highlighted by Bevan's
resignation from Cabinet in 1950), while being substantially true, also
prevented it from appreciating how much the terrain of politics had
been changed by the measures of the Attlee period, however limited
they had been. A similar acknowledgement of post-imperial realities
underlay the revisionists' ability to tear themselves away from the
illusions of Empire and train their sights on the emerging European
Common Market.

The initial pro-European impetus was provided by the émigré 'idealism' of *Socialist Commentary*. Already in 1952, when the dominant view
was still that Britain's superior position ought to be maintained by
staying out of any projected European organisation, *Socialist Commentary*
staked its position clearly in opposition to the prevailing mood of smug
parochialism. Rather than the prevalent lofty disdain towards the
project, the journal argued that a positive attitude was the *sine qua non*
of a constructive and beneficial British participation in the evolving
community. With a view to the 'many flexible forms which can be
devised for positive association', the journal urged that 'the debate
should now move away from recriminations and into the realm of
institutional innovation and compromise in which the British pride

themselves on their competence'.[28] By September 1957, when the Community of six nations (excluding Britain) had just been formed, *Socialist Commentary* made a clear and prescient argument. Britain might still appear to have much to lose by joining the Community, including a higher standard of living and a stable political system. However,

> The trouble about all these arguments is that they refer to Europe as it was, perhaps as it still is, but not as it is becoming. They are bound to the past and blind to the future. ... If they go forward while we stand aside, our superior living standards will not remain superior for long. If by joining in, we are compelled into readjustments, how much more will we be compelled by standing out. Of course there are risks in closer association, but there is no safety outside it. This is what we have yet to understand.[29]

And, further, it addressed the concerns of socialists in Britain:

> It is true that many European countries are weak in socialist forces and dominated by governments of a very different political complexion. But, surely this is no reason for keeping apart. Europe is the home of democratic socialism; socialist success or failure there will be decisive for the movement everywhere in the world. If it fails British socialists would stand isolated. ... Have we no interest, then, in helping to strengthen the socialist parties in Western Europe? Or have we ceased to believe that socialism is a universal creed?[30]

This vision of a continental social democracy infected the native revisionists. In 1958 Shirley Williams, for example, recommended that the European Free Trade Area (proposed by Britain as an alternative to membership of the Common Market and seen by revisionists as a prelude to closer British integration within the EEC) agree on measures of 'social harmonisation' already accepted within the EC: a forty hour basic working week, equal pay, and three weeks holiday with pay. A European vision and perspective were important because 'In ten or twenty years we will be trying to win the control of Europe as a whole for socialism, not just of national states'.[31]

By the early 1960s European reconstruction had already clearly made the Common Market a more attractive prospect. Nevertheless, the Labour Party still cherished Britain's 'splendid isolation', the left because of Britain's links with the Commonwealth, the right because of the 'special relationship' with the United States. In contrast, the revisionists in Parliament were combining a socialist Europeanism with an analysis of Britain's objective position in the world. Behind the rhetoric which accompanied the emergence of the New Commonwealth, not a little tinged with a post-imperial contrition, they saw the reality of disintegrating economic links. Moreover, while most social democrats were Atlanticists, their 'grand tours' of the United States also forced upon them a candid recognition of the insubstantial basis of any putative 'special relationship' with the US, or the idea of an 'Atlantic community'.

Roy Jenkins had already made the point when Britain first applied for entry to the Common Market under Macmillan in 1961:

> So far as our 'special relationship' with the United States is concerned there is surely something faintly ludicrous about our believing we must preserve this by staying out while the United States government is strenuously engaged in urging us to go in. A 'special relationship' is not likely to have much value if it is only cherished by the weaker partner.[32]

The signs of Britain's declining political and economic stature in the world, increasingly apparent since the late 1950s, were also read by the Social Democrats. Britain was clearly a small and increasingly uncompetitive, if still relatively prosperous, post-imperial nation which needed a more stimulating and appropriate set of trading links and markets to put it on the path to economic growth, modernisation and dynamism. Despite signs of economic sluggishness, Britons remained complacent and a factor in favour of entry was that the salutary shock it would surely administer might break this complacency. 'Without doubt the more conservative choice would be to stay out and the more adventurous choice, and the one more likely to lead to social change would be to go in; we believe that this factor too should weigh with the party.'[33] Early entry would also put Britain in an advantageous position to play a constructive and positive role in the still evolving Common Market. Arguments, both from left and right in the Labour Party, against the loss of sovereignty it would entail, seemed 'blimpish and nationalistic ... neither a natural or desirable position for a left-wing party.'[34]

The attraction of Europe for the social democrats was ultimately the prospect of modernising Britain, not just economically but also institutionally, culturally and socially. Retrospectively David Marquand summed it up as follows:

> What one felt ... and I don't think this is hindsight, was that Britain was a deeply conservative country ... It wasn't so much that Europe was a magic panacea which would automatically stop Britain being conservative but it was that the emotions and attitudes which were hostile to Britain being part of Europe were fortifying the conservatism and insularity. That if the argument was won by the opponents of entry that would simply set the seal, so to speak, for conservatism because that was the whole nature of the argument against entry. Basically it was that these benighted wogs across the channel who don't speak English and have these funny ways and we don't want anything to do with them, thank you, we're perfect. Or if not perfect, then very nearly perfect and we've nothing to learn from anybody else, we invented parliament and the Magna Carta and cricket and all these people ought to be jolly grateful that we're there and not start all this talk.[35]

Added to an intellectual appreciation of Britain's situation in the world was the development of an emotional affinity to European, especially German, post-Bad Godesberg Social Democracy. To an important extent this affinity was cultivated at annual gatherings of the Anglo-German Koenigswinter social democratic conferences of the 1960s, and the meetings of the Council for Europe. This contact with European Social Democracy also immunised the British social democrats against the fear, widespread on the Labour left, that the Rome Treaty was a recipe for a *laissez-faire* Europe. By the early 1970s European instances of planning and welfare were already outstripping the once-shining example of Britain. Moreover, contrary to the arguments of the left that the 'loss of sovereignty' entailed in joining the Common Market would render economic planning impossible, many kinds of economic regulation that were being increasingly experienced as problematic (and whose chief symptoms were the balance of payments crises) were now seen as having a better chance of being performed at a European rather than national level. Certainly, the extent to which the European Commission (as opposed to international financial forces) would inhibit national economic planning was greatly exaggerated by the left.

The economic case for Europe had always seemed finely balanced between the short term disadvantages and long term advantages, and economists accordingly tended to divide nearly evenly on the issue. However, the strictly economic arguments that raged on the merits of entry obscured more than they illuminated. As Tom Nairn acidly commented: 'Politicians who in office had been consistently unable to estimate the balance of payments correctly to within 100 million pounds now knew what the price of butter would be in five years time'.[36] But the social democratic case for entry was essentially political not economic, a fact overlooked by the left as it polemicized on the economic consequences of entry, making predictions about the prices of beer or sausages. While acknowledging that the immediate economic impact would be drastic, and that Britain should negotiate terms to cushion this impact, the social democrats argued that Britain's longer term interests nonetheless lay with Europe.

The actual pace of advance towards integration was, however, dictated by interests and motives quite different from the hopes and vision of the social democrats. Britain's two previous applications for entry had been vetoed by de Gaulle. His departure from the scene in 1969 left too little time for Labour to renew its application, and it was the Conservative government which successfully negotiated entry in 1971. The City of London, the dominant fraction of British capital, rallied behind the European cause only after the dollar crisis in the spring of 1971. Now the only solution was seen as entry into the Common Market.

And once the City was converted, all varieties of objections, including the legitimate ones of domestic industry, were suddenly swept away. The result was 'a rapid acceleration of the hitherto dignified and portly "imperial" approach to the matter. The gentlemanly perambulation turned into a run' for British membership.[37]

The Split on Europe

Political divisions on the issue of Europe have, as is well known, always cut across party lines. However when, on 28 October 1971, sixty-nine Labour MPs voted with the Tory government for entry into the Common Market, its implications went far beyond the issue of British entry and created a deep schism in the PLP. And it was rooted more in the realignments which had taken place in the party than in the substance of the issue itself. In the first place, the sixty-nine Labour MPs were not simply an agglomeration of MPs who severally felt strongly about the issue. They were organised and led by the revisionists or 'social democrats' under Jenkins's leadership. Moreover, unlike thirty Conservatives who also crossed the division lobbies to vote against Common Market entry (they had a free vote), the sixty-nine Labour MPs were voting against a three-line whip, against the decision of a special party conference on the issue, against the majority in the party as well as in the PLP, and *with* a particularly unpopular Tory government. In the loyalist culture of the Labour Party there could be few graver misdemeanours. The social democrats knew this and in crossing the division lobbies they were making a public statement about their relationship with the new Labour Party they clearly saw emerging. This action was also a reflex which betrayed, for the first time since the revisionist ascendancy of the post-war period, the original ambivalence and conditionality of the intellectuals' relationship to the Labour Party.

If the revisionists had lacked an organised presence in the Labour Party after 1964, the European issue precipitated them once again as an identifiable intellectual tendency, the social democrats. The press had no difficulty identifying the core group of a couple of dozen intellectuals who led the split, the most serious to wrack the party since the days of Bevanism. Moreover, then the revisionist intellectuals, with the backing of the moderate leadership and right-wing trade union leaders, had seemed to merge indistinctly into the new party leadership: that is, their status as intellectuals in the party was less and not more apparent in the days of their ascendancy. By contrast, the split of 1971, which signalled the beginning of their marginalization, also precipitated their identity as intellectuals more clearly than before. Tom Nairn saw this in countering the left's claim that it was a split between 'left' and 'right' in the party on the Common Market issue:

Far too many right-wing and centrist leaders joined the anti-Market movement for this to be an adequate explanation. It corresponds more closely to
a split between old 'party men' (with a strong phalanx of opportunists and
right-wing populists around them) and 'new men' of bourgeois origin, less
dependent on the party machine and the old Labourist spirit ... The 'old
faithfuls' (both right and left) of Labour national socialism and those who
thought they still needed the old cow for career motives were on one side –
except for a few pensioners like Lord George Brown – while the *nouvelle vague*
of middle class professionals (much closer both in appearance and spirit to
continental social democracy) stood on the other.[38]

Not surprisingly then, allowing for some deaths, and many retirements
from politics, the division of 1971 prefigured almost exactly the later
split.[39] Admittedly, there were a few notable exceptions. David
Marquand's later speculations about Tony Crosland were meant to
explain not only his distance from the rest of the revisionist intellectuals
(and, as a consequence, his equivocation on Europe), but also
Marquand's conviction that Crosland's attachment to the Labour Party
would also have prevented him, had he lived, from leaving it in 1981.
And the party retained the loyalties of several others whom the social
democrats were able to win over on the issue of Europe, but the nature
of whose association with the Labour Party was fundamentally different;
few of these figured in the SDP split. A leading case in point was Roy
Hattersley who, while voting with the Jenkinsites on Europe in 1971,
remained in the Labour Party in the 1980s and weathered the storm of
left-ward lurches to become deputy leader in 1985. He had something
of an intellectual reputation and had been a committed Europeanist
and a revisionist. However, younger than most revisionists, by his
background and his path of entry into the Labour Party, Hattersley was
very much a party machine man. Other exceptions surely also included
some, like Harold Lever, who felt they were too old to bother with the
trauma of splitting after a lifetime in the Labour Party.[40] On the other
hand, if only political tendencies are considered, no other identifiable
tendency apart from the Jenkinsites broke the Labour whip in 1971;
moreover, many of these social democrats who voted for Europe in 1971,
but were no longer in Parliament by 1981 (having left the Labour Party
in the 1970s at different junctures, as the rise of the new Labour left
increasingly frustrated them – e.g. Dick Taverne, Roy Jenkins and David
Marquand), rallied to the SDP in 1981.[41]

The Labour Party context of the 1971 vote on Europe also needs to
be kept in mind. Already at the 1970 conference the new mood among
trade union leaders was apparent. The old labourist loyalism seemed to
give way to an 'instrumental collectivist' assertiveness. Jack Jones, speaking against industrial regulation, called for an unequivocal understanding of the unions' 'complete and total opposition to restrictions on

collective bargaining, whether it be incomes policy or by ministerial intervention', while Hugh Scanlon declared that the only way to overcome the problem of low productivity in British industry was through a policy of high wages, which would in turn compel high investment and high productivity. This new trade union aggressiveness went well with long-standing impulses of the Labour left, both doctrinally in that it could be steered towards more socialist (interventionist) policies and politically in giving the extra-parliamentary party more say in the party's policies and direction. This clearly did not bode well for the social democrats in view of their conception of the role of the parliamentary party in representing the electorate as a whole, rather than the party or union rank and file alone, and of the functions of the leadership as having the political space to 'objectively' devise the party's strategy.

The forces arrayed against the social democrats were distinctly novel in many respects. The small but long-standing forces of opposition to the Common Market, which included both left and right elements, and which continued to oppose entry, were not the main problem for the social democrats. The latter had always respected the consistency of the position of these opponents. The real problem lay with the bulk of the centre and right of the party who now saw it as politically prudent to execute a timely about-face on Europe.

Sensing the anti-Market mood of the already clamorous rank and file of the party, the bulk of the party's centrist leadership, including Harold Wilson, adopted a 'wait and see' stance on the terms of entry the Conservatives could negotiate, but with a very audible negative undertone. The motive which underlay this shuffling away from what had been agreed policy only months ago went to the heart of the new politics which was emerging in the Labour Party. With the increase in union militancy from the late 1960s onwards, class-based issues were acquiring a salience which the party leadership could not control or direct. The labourist impulses of the leadership ruled out any unequivocally *socialist* articulation of those new forces and concerns: any such move would also alienate much of Labour's middle-class support. Instead the leadership opted for a populist-nationalist appeal. If the Tory government had to be opposed, and the labour movement rallied, it was safer to do this on issues of nationalism, however parochial, than on the explicitly class based ones that the labour movement also confronted in the shape of the Industrial Relations Bill. Thus, as Nairn rightly noted, 'the noisy debate about the Common Market *took the place* of the political and ideological disputes which had failed to emerge after 1970. It occupied the vacuum. There was not a single new notion about socialism in the air'.[42] The party of the working class became, ironically enough, the spearhead of the nationalist challenge to the 'internationalism' of the ruling class.

The social democrats, alienated by the display of trade union muscle at the 1970 Conference and disgusted by the craven line of the centrist leadership, were limited to making statements of high principle. Trying nevertheless to fall into the mood of the Conference in a largely anti-Tory speech, Roy Jenkins did manage to reiterate the need for a 'new deal for the relationship of incomes to our economic problems'.[43] On the question of Europe, he warned, however:

> I hope there will be no question of our taking a different attitude in opposition from the one we would have taken in government. Let us think the matter through afresh by all means. The ability to do this is always an advantage for an Opposition, and a reasonable one. But, we must think it through on its merits, and not on the basis of tactical considerations.[44]

Public opinion might seem to be against Europe, but that, as far as the social democrats were concerned, could no longer be a conclusive argument. As Jenkins wrote in *The Times*, 'I do not believe it is the duty of those who seek to lead to follow public opinion.'[45] In their view, it was only through a twist of electoral fate that it was a Tory government which was to negotiate entry. While 'good transitional terms are necessary', Jenkins nevertheless went on to argue, 'the terms themselves are not in any circumstances going to sound overwhelmingly attractive. An admission fee never does...But, anything will appear extortionate unless we have a lively idea that we want to join.'[46] The rationalistic political style of the social democrats, however, now revealed its complete ineffectiveness in the face of the forces of resurgent labourism which confronted them. At a political level, the issue was the test of wills: would the extra-parliamentary party, which seemed by then overwhelmingly anti-Common Market, be able to bend the parliamentary leadership, which had itself recently applied for entry, to its will? The answer, as far as the bulk party leadership went, was 'yes'.

When the terms of entry became known the left, more legitimately perhaps than the centrist leadership, claimed that they fell far short of Labour's standards and rejected them, even though Labour's own former negotiator, George Thomson, had just affirmed that even a Labour government would not have been able to obtain significantly better terms. Although the opposition to the Common Market within the Labour Party, both left and right, singularly lacked realistic alternatives to it, the special party conference on the issue opposed 'entry on the terms negotiated by the Conservative government' and called for a general election on the issue. It then invited the PLP to 'unite wholeheartedly in voting against the government's policy.'[47]

The social democrats had expected this and had determined to vote with the Conservative government. This was the crucial decision. Added to the unpopularity of the European cause in the Labour Party there was the Tory government's unpopularity. There was some hope that provided enough of the Conservatives broke ranks to vote against their Government, it would lose a major vote in Parliament and thus precipitate another election. Furthermore, Roy Jenkins had only weeks before been elected Deputy Leader of the Party, and it was a fairly serious matter that in this capacity he set an example for others, not merely to abstain but to defy the whip outright. Bill Rodgers organised and persuaded many potential back-sliders into voting with the Conservatives to arrive at the final tally of sixty-nine.

In the highly charged atmosphere of the time, the left insisted that the social democrats had enabled the passage of the European Communities Bill, although the social democrats pointed out that if they had not voted for entry, fewer Conservatives would have voted against their Government. In an understandable way the more general disillusionment which stemmed from the 1964–70 government, and which ought more appropriately to have been focused on the labourist centre, now became focused on the social democrats, represented as elitist parliamentarians with little concern for the concerns of the extra-parliamentary party and movement. As the smell of betrayal now hung about them, the social democrats had a grave handicap.

> There was no split in Labour's history, I think, to equal that. There was a certain sort of convention that you could, at a pinch, abstain in a vote like that, but to actually vote with the enemy, to actually go through the division lobbies and in doing so keep the government in office. ... Pretty strong stuff! Pretty wicked stuff![48]

Here lies the crux of the explanation of the prefigurative nature of the split over Europe. It ranged the social democrats against the rest of the party in a way that highlighted their rational but politically disastrous stand on the issue. While it also revealed, by contrast, the non-ideological, unintellectual and pragmatic, if not actually pusillanimous, nature of the bulk of the Labour Party leadership, faced with a resurgent labourism, this was obviously not high on Labour's list of misdemeanours. The revisionists had wanted to transform the historical accretion of institutions, and the defensive barricades of an oppressed class, which the Labour Party was, into a doctrinally unambiguous, progressive, forward-looking, modernising and successfully reformist, party. While revisionism may legitimately be criticised for lack of socialist radicalism, and it had other more practical shortcomings, its successful hegemony over the Labour Party would at least have transformed Labour into a clearly doctrinal party within which (and against which) genuinely theoretical and ideological struggles were finally possible. Now that moment seemed truly past, as the bulk of the party's leadership chose to respond to the most myopic element in Labour discontents –

nationalism. Even the left, in its new-found workerism, was all too eager to find solace in traditional arguments for a 'true internationalism', or, in a thoroughgoing contradiction, in the autarkic urgings of the economists of the Cambridge Economic Policy Group. The social democrats, neither numerically preponderant nor politically hegemonic, were isolated and marginalised.

The unpopularity into which the social democrats fell as a result of their stand on Europe further undermined their ability to put up a fight. Peter Jenkins later commented:

> I think it is a very important point historically that the fight over Europe so preempted the energies of the [social democrats] that it incapacitated them from fighting on the main ideological and organisational issues which by then were central to the character of the Labour Party. I remember talking to Roy Jenkins on the train coming back from the Conference at Blackpool in 1970. This was after the loss of the election. It was the conference where Jack Jones and Hughie Scanlon were at their most overweening, bullying the Labour Party, telling it what it should do and so on. Roy and the right hated all this and saw the dangers of it. I said to Roy, 'You know that you have got to stand up to Jones and Scanlon'. He said, 'Well we can't fight on two fronts'. So over the next two years, in fact right through to the referendum in 1975, they were so preoccupied with European issues that everything else that happened, like the great left-wing policy document of 1973, and so on, passed them by. Then they discovered that a Labour Party was emerging which was very uncongenial to them, which they found it difficult to support; and it was too late then and Roy Jenkins went off to Europe and eventually, as matters got worse, some of them did try to fight, but could not.[49]

An interesting part of the fall-out of the social democrats' decision to vote with the Tory government was the 1972 dismissal of Dick Taverne, MP for Lincoln, as candidate for the next general election by his constituency party, which had a sizeable and active group of left-wing anti-marketeers. The dismissal was upheld by the Organisation Committee of the then left-wing NEC, against the findings of a special committee appointed to inquire into the matter. Taverne decided to resign and fight the by-election held in 1973 as an Independent Labour candidate, and won with a respectable majority of 8,000 votes. This incident gained a lot of publicity at the time and was regarded later as a portent for things to come for the social democrats – a warning, in effect. In truth it was a single isolated case of de-selection, as 'the combination of a left-wing party and a right-wing MP was unique.'[50] Or almost so. With the exception of Neville Sandelson, the intellectual social democrats generally had good relations with their CLPs and none faced deselection.

After the Common Market vote in the Commons the 'mainstream' press, now unambiguously backing entry, lionised Jenkins as a man of courage and principle, a man fit to lead the Labour Party out of what it saw as its mire of struggles with the left. But within the Labour Party the social democrats' position had in reality reached a crisis point. Many of Jenkins' followers, including Bill Rodgers, David Owen, David Marquand and Bob Maclennan, wanted him to seize this opportunity and widen the issue to the future of social democracy against what they saw as the growing tide of unthought-out 'leftism' and perhaps even challenge Wilson for the leadership. Dick Taverne, already in trouble with his constituency party, even urged Jenkins to lead a breakaway party. He felt he could clearly see the way things would develop as left-wing militants captured one local party after another and the party as a whole drifted farther to the left. But at the time they still hoped to make a political comeback.

> Roy Jenkins' tack was to say 'let's keep our heads down, Labour is going to lose the next election anyway. It deserves to lose and it will lose it'. And then, I suppose his view was, I don't think he said it publicly, but he expressed it to me in private [that the Labour Party] would come around to sanity again … he stayed because he thought he could still be the leader of the Labour Party … it was better to win from within than to go out and start something very new and very uncertain.[51]

In the hope of an ideological and political turnaround in a prolonged period of opposition, Jenkins fought shy of such decisive actions; he felt rather the need to reiterate his fundamental commitment to the party. He did this by voting with the Labour Party against the Second Reading of the European Communities Bill and the subsequent stages of enabling legislation. At the very least, this was inconsistent.

Confusion was piled on top of inconsistency when in 1972 Roy Jenkins resigned from the Deputy Leadership on the issue of a referendum on the Common Market. From his point of view this served at least two purposes. More immediately it was supposed to take a stand against the willingness of the Shadow Cabinet to take opportunistic positions on an issue which he regarded as so much a matter of principle. More generally, he and the social democrats needed to distance themselves from a leadership which they considered opportunist and cowardly in face of left-wing and trade union pressures. But although the revisionists were willing to defend their opposition to the referendum, and although it was clearly a case of opportunism on the part of the party leadership, it was widely seen as a bad issue on which to resign. Jenkins was followed reluctantly by George Thompson and Harold Lever, who both resigned shadow cabinet positions, and by Dick Taverne, David Owen and Dickson Mabon who resigned their seats on the front bench. Quite apart from projecting an anti-democratic image, this action was ill-judged, as Jenkins' biographer pointed out, for another, more serious reason: 'For the principle of not committing the party to a referendum, the social democrats who were most disturbed at Labour's leftward drift handed the future direction of policy over to those whose resistance to the left was weakest'.[52]

Just how fatal this development was is underlined in the following reflection by David Marquand:

> It is difficult to exaggerate the impact of the split over Europe. I was a Labour back-bencher in this period. In fact, for a very short time I was front bench spokesman when Roy Jenkins was shadow Chancellor of the Exchequer. He was in a very central position inside the Labour Party in 1970 and might have been well placed to succeed Wilson as leader. To him and people like myself who were closely associated with him, the Europe split actually did two things. It absorbed almost the whole of our political energies so that there was no time left for anything else and secondly, it totally destroyed, for a time anyway, our influence within the party. We were a kind of sect within the party, which was tolerated, just, by the rest of the party, but regarded with a great deal of suspicion. ... We were engaged in a life and death political struggle for survival within the party, at the time most of us wanted to stay within the party and thought it would eventually come around to being in favour of Europe and then we might be able to exert some influence in it, but for the moment it was a question of hanging on. But, I promise you, the sense of isolation we all had was enormous.[53]

Nonetheless, believing the Labour Party to still be redeemable, the strategy of the social democrats was now to try to build up the image of Roy Jenkins as a serious contender for the leadership of the Labour Party, in spite of his post-1972 marginalization. The main problem here was that he was becoming exclusively connected in the public mind with the European issue. The social democrats therefore now sought to give him the image of a man of many issues, and with a broad grasp of the new problems facing Britain. This they attempted through a series of speeches Jenkins gave across the country on various issues, starting with a general philosophical one which attempted to restate the social democratic philosophy. Some of the leading younger social democrats, including David Marquand and his wife Judith, an economist at the Treasury, and other like-minded intellectuals like Matthew Oakshott, Nicholas Bosanquet and, initially at least, Stuart Holland, all contributed to the speech-writing effort.

Social Democracy and the Alternative Economic Strategy

However, this effect hardly amounted to a genuine intellectual advance. In fact, the social democrats were ill-equipped to provide, in doctrinal terms, what the new Labour Party needed most urgently – a strategy for economic growth. The revisionists had never had one and, in the 1970s, the social democrats also failed to deliver. On the contrary, under the auspices of the left, the policy process set up in the party in 1970 resulted in *Labour's Programme for Britain: 1972*, the 'longest, most comprehensive programme in Labour history', and widely regarded as the most left-wing. It also 'signalled the erosion of the reformist social democrats' hegemony over the formulation of party policy'.[54] The social democrats remained primarily preoccupied with the European issue. Moreover, unlike the policy-making processes set off by the 1951 and 1955 defeats, described in Chapter Four, the social democrats were stylistically and temperamentally unsuited for the one that began in 1970, in which the trade unions and the extra-parliamentary party had such a large influence. In the 1950s revisionism had emerged out of select discussion groups of the young and talented with the sponsorship and blessing of an indulgent Labour Party leadership secure in its prestige and power. The inclusion of revisionist views into party documents came later and relatively smoothly. By contrast, the policy-making process of the 1970s was much more politicised. The formalised committees set up by the LPRD and the Home Policy committee were arenas of political negotiation and they reflected the shifting balance of power in the labour movement and the revisionists were bound to face vocal opposition. In these very different circumstances, as Bill Rodgers pointed out, the social democrats 'were not so very keen on sitting in committees'.[55]

The new configuration of power within the Labour Party also seemed to undermine any basis of the kind of intellectual role the social democrats had played in the past as the locus of power moved from the parliamentary party and leadership to the extra-parliamentary Conference and the unions. The unions now wanted the party completely behind them in the struggle against the Tories' industrial relations legislation and attempts at controlling the rise of workers' incomes. Predictably, this escalation of class war left the Labour Party doctrinally stumped. A socialist party might have attempted to articulate this militancy to a socialist transformation of society. The only political response that the Labour Party's centrist leadership (as well as much of the Labour left) was capable of was a nationalistic populism, a central element of which was opposition to Common Market entry.

The left of the Labour Party also had its own version of workerist populism (although it was hailed as socialist). It amounted, in effect, to picking up all the new leftist trade union slogans – trade union rights, free collective bargaining and workers' control – rather than making any strategic commitment to a socialist strategy. John Mackintosh pinpointed the underlying political attitude:

Many on the traditional Left, from Michael Foot to Stan Orme, support populist class-oriented demands not because they derive from socialist philosophy but because they come from 'their people'. This means that they can support car workers or dockers demanding wage increases far above the national increases in productivity simply because they were made by a group of organised workers acting in a class conscious way and united by a common feeling of alienation, boredom and resentment at the standards enjoyed by the university trained, white collar managerial staff.[56]

While this was hardly an objective view, Mackintosh was not wrong in pointing to the essentially tribal rather than doctrinal impulses which underlay it – impulses which necessarily left out the intellectual social democrats. An important right-wing strand of working-class populism was represented in the writings of Stephen Haseler and John Gyford. Their basic thesis was that the Labour Party had ignored real working-class concerns, which had to do with better living standards. Only by addressing these now could it recoup the electoral losses it had suffered and survive. Thus Haseler and Gyford:

[S]ocial democracy should re-assert the primacy of its concern for the social and economic rights of its labour constituency and avoid being led down such enticing byways as fashionable libertarianism, the 'new politics' of technological revolution, or 'students' and workers' power'.[57]

For his part Crosland, who seemed so anxious to respond to working-class concerns, was also led to espouse a right-wing populism which was not entirely unlike the appeals which Enoch Powell had made in the late 1960s and which had prominently figured in the 1970 election campaign. Crosland's growing closeness to the one Labour figure who would carry this to its limits in the late 1970s, James Callaghan, was hardly fortuitous, and it seemed almost to sap his intellectual vitality. While re-iterating the importance of growth for any redistributive strategy, and even admitting that he had been 'too complacent about growth',[58] he continued to adhere to a rather dogmatic Keynesian conception of macro-economic management. Crosland sat on the Industrial Policy sub-committee of the NEC, where Stuart Holland had put forward his arguments about the increasing 'meso-economic' power of multi-national corporations and their ability to thwart national economic strategies through techniques of transfer pricing and the export of capital, and where he recommended a new approach to state intervention in industry. In face of these arguments, which were being supported by the left, Crosland attributed the economic slowdown to technical errors on the part of the Labour government. The central economic problem was still growth and here, in his view, the new policies being advanced were of little use.

The reason why the economy did not grow up to the level of this higher productive potential [in the late 1960s] was that the final *demand* was not there. This had nothing to do with too much or too little socialism; it was due to the deflationary policies which stemmed inexorably from the Labour Government's obsession with a particular parity for sterling. Thus the Labour Government's overall economic failure sheds no light on the rights and wrongs of alternative socialist policies.[59]

This remained the crux of Crosland's position in the 1970s.

Without a strategy for growth, Crosland became, willy-nilly, peripheral to the concerns and direction of Labour's policy in the 1970s. The social democrats were also without one. But they differed in deliberately distancing themselves from the clamour for growth and adjusting revisionist egalitarianism to the new assumption of low growth. Already in the economic slow-down faced by the Labour government in the late 1960s, some of the younger revisionists, mostly back-benchers from the intake of 1966, had attempted to point the revisionist way forward. The problem, according to David Marquand, John Mackintosh and David Owen, the co-authors of *Change Gear*, was not that there was a low rate of economic growth: 'It is that the Government has not yet spelled out how it intends to put the principles of equality, classlessness and democracy into practice within the context of the economic situation which now exists and the rate of growth it now expects to achieve.'[60] While they were in favour of devaluation as a means to stabilise the economy, even if at a lower rate of growth, they pointed to what they saw as the principal problem – that in the affluent societies of the West 'there is no inherent tendency towards a greater equality. On the contrary, there appears to be a built-in drive towards greater inequality and injustice'.[61] If this marked a clear (Galbraithian) break with the Croslandite faith in the egalitarian effects of capitalism, it also staked out a position at variance with the Labourism which had co-existed in a symbiosis with Croslandite revisionism in the prosperous 1950s: these younger revisionists were attempting to detach the ideal of equality from its (now paralysing) dependence on growth.

> Too often in the past few years we have been tempted to believe that economic growth would provide an automatic solution to the moral dilemma of a socialist party in an affluent society; that growth would give us equality without a fight, justice without tears. We now know that this was self-deception. No matter what the rate of growth may be, the enemies of socialism are the same: poverty on the one side and privilege on the other. And no matter how wealthy a society, privilege will always resist a determined effort to eradicate poverty.[62]

While this seemed to relieve them of any felt need to look for that strategy of growth which revisionism never had, this social democratic dissociation of equality from growth also allowed them to stay true to the stated ideals of revisionist socialism. Nevertheless, combined with their advocacy of parliamentary reform in the interests of individual and minority rights, regional government and so on, the younger social democrats still remained in an intellectual revisionist mode – seeking to elaborate explicit, progressive, modernising party principles. But this now put them, as intellectuals, even more clearly against the articulated concerns of the party's working-class base than Croslandite revisionism had been.

Croslandite revisionism had asserted the infinite reformability of capitalism in the service of an ethical commitment to socialism and equality. In the late 1950s and early 1960s much was made of this ethical commitment. But it had never placed socialism on a *purely* ethical basis. Rather, revisionist socialism had harnessed the benign, expansionary logic which capitalism seemed to have acquired to the party's already existing labourism. It yoked the political weight of the labour movement to progressive causes, rather than seek to alter it fundamentally. In the 1960s, as it became apparent that this original revisionist optimism about economic growth had been misplaced and that redistribution without growth could hardly be expected to make a substantial contribution to the cost of social reforms. Reform had been explicitly subordinated to growth both by the centrist leadership and by leading revisionists. The 1964 Manifesto had read, 'The key fact in determining the speed at which new and better levels of benefit can be introduced will be the rate at which the British economy can expand.'. The revisionists had done nothing to oppose this subordination of what was supposed to be an overriding goal. In a speech to the London Labour Party on May 13 1967, Roy Jenkins subscribed to this logic: 'The plain fact is that the only way in which we can marry our demand for protection of the lower paid and higher social expenditure with a buoyant standard of living for our most productive citizens is by a rapid rate of growth for the remainder of this Parliament.'[63]

But in the 1970s, if the revisionists wished to state a position distinct from Crosland's ostrich-like refusal to acknowledge the problems of a growth-led redistribution policy, without at the same time evolving a new strategy for growth, the only road open to them was an appeal to ethics. As they saw it, the challenge ahead was that of the defence of socialist principles for the welfare of the whole of society, especially the extremely disadvantaged, against all unreasonable demands. These included those of better-off workers. This challenge could only be met if the managers of the economy (including a Labour government) maintained detachment from sectional interests (including the most powerful elements of its own constituency), and applied impartial egalitarian principles for the benefit of the whole of society. By implication, the organised working class could no longer be relied upon to be progressive in its demands. As John Mackintosh put it,

Now it is no longer possible to blur the distinction between altruism and working-class demands. If poverty is to be alleviated, if there are to be proper pensions and hospitals, if there is to be adequate aid for the underdeveloped countries, it must be paid for in part by the better off workers. That they are not all socialists, that they are as open as any other section of the community to the 'I'm all right Jack' type of appeal, should always have been apparent. Indeed, it is becoming clear that considerable prosperity for the majority in Britain could be combined with a most unpleasant social atmosphere including racial prejudice, intolerance of the weaker sections of the community, increasing xenophobia and anti-youth, anti-student outbursts.[64]

Such a position clearly implied that a statutory incomes policy, which the labour movement opposed, had become necessary. The rhetoric of ethics would serve to justify it. This struck at the heart of the old revisionist/social democratic subsumption of labourist economism, a move already made in *Change Gear* and underlined in the 1970 election campaign.

The ethical position resurfaced more strongly as a central theme in the series of speeches Roy Jenkins gave in 1972 which sounded a distinctively social democratic note in the turbulent politics of the time.

[If] our attack on injustice is to be effective, it is not enough to devise an appropriate strategy. ... We have to persuade men and women who are themselves reasonably well off that they have a duty to forgo some of the advantages that they would otherwise enjoy for the sake of others who are much poorer than they are. We have to persuade motor car workers in my constituency that they have an obligation to lower paid workers in the public sector. We have to persuade the British people as a whole that they have an obligation to Africans and Asians whom they have never seen. It is a formidable task. We cannot hope to carry it out if we base our appeal on immediate self-interest.[65]

While this might possibly have had some appeal for middle-class non-conformity and working-class idealism, the revisionists' lack of organised presence in the labour movement ruled out a serious possibility of any such reorientation. The expectation of higher material standards to be financed through higher growth, fostered over the previous two decades, could hardly be turned off by a few speeches appealing to a vague altruism.

The left-wing Alternative Economic Strategy, evolved in the Labour Party's policy committees, and more attuned to the demands of the organised working class naturally stressed the goal of economic growth and the need for a strategy to foster it. It centred around a set of proposals for industrial intervention advocated by Stuart Holland in the Industrial Policy Sub-committee and its Public Sector Group, with his most active support coming from Judith Hart and Ian Mikardo. Holland elaborated the analysis on which his proposals were based in the book he was writing at the time, *The Socialist Challenge*. It analyzed the rise of the 'meso-economic' power of multi-national corporations which evaded macro-economic Keynesian management through practices such as transfer pricing, and through their relative flexibility in choosing investment sites globally. This was especially relevant, Holland felt, in the case of Britain, as it was peculiarly burdened with such companies which were in addition monopolistic. More than 80 per cent of overseas investment by British firms was controlled by 165 companies.

His solutions involved two basic proposals. The first entailed the creation of a State Holding Company which, in addition to co-ordinating the state's existing holdings in industry, would nationalise a significant number of the top manufacturing firms and turn them into competitive leaders of their respective industries, setting new standards in productivity, exports and industrial relations. The second proposal was to oblige large companies (with a turnover of over £50 million) to enter into planning agreements with the government with respect to long-term investment planning and exports. In contrast to the stodgy Morrisonian approach to public ownership, Holland advanced a more purposive and inventive industrial interventionism. Both of Holland's proposals were incorporated into *Labour's Programme for Britain*. Holland's analysis and proposals aimed primarily to enhance the government's ability to control the increasingly elusive and complex activities of international firms without, however, touching upon the deeper causes of Britain's industrial malaise. Nor was *Labour's Programme* despite the rhetoric which surrounded it and its promoters in the Labour Party, a socialist programme:

> It was by no means as Left-wing as the Conference resolutions of this period: indeed, ideologically it took as much from revisionist as from traditional Socialist conceptions. And there was a classic ambiguity to the central stated purpose of a 'fundamental and irreversible shift in the balance of power and wealth in favour of working people and their families'. The ambiguities were carried to the heart of the document in that it reflected the complex process of consultation, the varying balance of power in the study groups, not to mention different levels of completeness of the studies.[66]

Most of the instruments of state ownership and control stipulated by the Programme lay within the revisionist social democratic alternatives to outright nationalisation. What was more, they had consciously been borrowed from continental experiments in planning which Europeanist social democrats surely favoured. It was also not impossible to see them as extensions of revisionism so that it could transcend the external constraints on economic growth. The measures of nationalisation it promised were, in impeccable revisionist tradition, limited. They included the shipbuilding, aircraft industries and docks, with additional flexible state ownership to be effected through a National Enterprise Board (NEB) modelled on the Italian *Instituto per la Recostruzione Industriale* (IRI). The NEB was also to aid state planning of the economy along with the Planning Agreements (modelled after French and Belgian planning practice) envisaged with leading companies in key industrial sectors.

Unlike Crosland, the other social democrats did seem, initially at least, to have been intellectually open to these ideas. They looked favourably on Holland's arguments for more direct interventionist economic management. The strategy embodied in the AES was also a further extension of the more interventionist impulse of the 1960s, both in the previous Labour government's National Plan and Industrial Reorganisation Corporation, and further back still in the Macmillan Government's National Economic Development Council. The need for a more direct state intervention had already been accepted as part of the consensual economic management of the 1960s, as balance of payments difficulties made apparent time and again Britain's weak industrial position.

However, the social democrats evinced an ambiguity towards this new strategy, even while advocating elements of it. The Labour left sought new policy instruments to foster growth. By contrast, in a speech recognising the merits of a State Holding Company, Jenkins cited regional equality rather than economic growth as the principal objective.

> Britain needs an investment stimulus and especially a stimulus in the regions, that a State Holding Company is ideally fitted to provide. Such a company would be a flexible vehicle for direct government involvement to help achieve a broad-based mix of activities which is essential if the regions are to receive their fair share of national prosperity. The Holding Company could be supported by a Regional Development Bank equipped with substantial initial resources, which would make loans on specially advantageous terms. It would deploy its funds flexibly over the development areas to help a host of the smaller scale manufacturing and service industries such as tourism which are managed by private enterprise.[67]

Having initially endorsed elements of Holland's industrial strategy, however, the social democrats soon turned against it. As it became identified with the left, the social democrats alleged that it was based on old-fashioned Clause 4 nationalisation. Holland saw the matter thus:

> The arguments *per se* did not come from a left perspective, it had nothing to do with deciding it's time to regenerate Clause Four in order to strengthen the left within the party. Rather they came out of the actual experience of government at a fairly senior level, a critical evaluation of that in relation to European experience. This meant that there was a dimension of planning in it. We could have regenerated the National Plan. The right [social democrats]

felt that they had cornered the market in these arguments and polarised against them.[68]

But it was also true that policy debates were inevitably also bound up with political divisions and the AES – based on European models of economic and industrial planning – became, along with the autarkic proposals of the Cambridge Economic Policy Group, part of the anti-Common Market platform. In any case, it was unclear if the AES would have been effective in fostering growth. While Holland's analysis was based on the recognition of certain genuine problems faced by the government in controlling the economy in the context of the globalization of capital and production, it hardly went to the root of Britain's deep-seated industrial problems. Nor was it clear that the public resources or the administrative capabilities required for extensive industrial intervention and restructuring would be forthcoming. In fact, with the crisis of Croslandite revisionism, there was no viable socialist way forward. For their part the revisionists, without the growth which had been the basis for achieving a classless society, and without a strategy for fostering it, seemed to move towards a sort of default position – a more modest egalitarianism, where inequalities within the working class seemed to loom larger than those between classes. The chosen solution for this was an incomes policy. But this alternative remained to be fully elaborated and certainly its prospects under the resurgent labourism seemed few.

In any case, intellectual renewal was, for the social democrats as for the rest of the party, hardly at the top of the agenda. The shifts in Labour's power structure, whose politics would continue to dominate the 1970s, had already manifest themselves over the European issue. They eventually led the social democrats out of the party. But in the early 1970s, the social democrats still believed the situation not entirely lost. They hoped for a long period of opposition during which the need for electoral viability, and the need to be acceptable to a sufficiently broad range of progressive opinion in the country (to which the social democrats had always held themselves responsible, rather than to the party rank and file) would bring the party back from the extreme left deviations in which it was rhetorically indulging. By distancing themselves from the opportunist party leadership, the social democrats also hoped to be ready to take the party leadership for Roy Jenkins when the time came. They therefore committed themselves to a conservative, and at times, inconsistent strategy to demonstrate their allegiance to the party while they waited for this moment. This strategy was foiled when the Labour Party won office again, albeit barely, in 1974.[69]

Notes

1. Roy Jenkins, *Pursuit of Progress: A critical analysis of the achievement and prospect of the Labour Party*, William Heinemann, London, 1953, p 161.

2. C.A.R. Crosland, 'A Social-Democratic Britain', Fabian Lecture delivered in November 1970, reprinted in *Socialism Now and Other Essays*, Jonathan Cape, 1975, pp 72–73.

3. Interview with David Marquand, 13 October 1989.

4. Interview with Bill Rodgers, 27 June 1989.

5. *Times*, 30 May 1970.

6. *Financial Times*, 28 May 1970.

7. *Guardian*, 19 May 1970.

8. John H. Goldthorpe and David Lockwood, 'Affluence and the British Class Structure', *Sociological Review*, n.s., Volume II, Number 2, July 1963, pp 133–163.

9. Perry Anderson, 'Problems of Socialist Strategy', in Robin Blackburn (ed) *Towards Socialism*, Cornell University Press, Ithaca, 1966, p 265.

10. Colin Leys, *Politics in Britain: From Labourism to Thatcherism*, Verso, London, 1989, p 73.

11. *Royal Commission on Trade Unions and Employers' Associations 1965–1968, Report*, Chairman: Rt. Hon. Lord Donovan, HMSO, London, 1968, p 290.

12. Clive Ponting, *Breach of Promise*, Hamish Hamilton, London, 1989, p 353.

13. Leo Panitch, unpublished manuscript, Chapter Two, p 21. I am very grateful to Leo Panitch for allowing me to read this unpublished manuscript on the Labour Party. It has helped enormously in understanding the character of the new trade union climate in the early and mid-1970s.

14. Minkin, *op. cit.*, p 84–85.

15. Paul Whiteley, *The Labour Party in Crisis*, Methuen, London, 1983, p 79.

16. Political Editor of *The Times*, quoted in Michael Hatfield, *The House the Left Built: Inside Labour Policy-Making 1970–75*, Victor Gollancz, London, 1978, p 75.

17. Hatfield, *op. cit.*, pp 41–42.

18. *Ibid.*

19. The mood of the extremely varied left in this period is very well reflected in the pages of the Labour Left journal, *Tribune*, throughout the period of opposition.

20. See, for example, David Marquand's reminiscence, 'Tony Crosland: The Progressive as Loyalist', *The Progressive Dilemma*, Heinemann, London, 1991, pp 166–67.

21. Interview with Bill Rodgers, 21 July 1989.

22. Interview with Peter Jenkins, 26 October 1989.

23. Interview with Anthony Lester QC, 10 October 1989.

24. David Marquand, 'Tony Crosland: The Progressive as Loyalist', p 177.

25. Peter Jenkins, *The Battle for Downing Street*, Charles Knight and Co. Ltd., London, 1970, p 75.

26. Peter Jenkins in *Guardian Weekly*, 27 February 1977.

27. David Marquand, *op. cit.*, p 167.

28. 'Europe Asks Why' Editorial, *Socialist Commentary*, January 1952, pp 3–4.

29. 'Crossing the Channel', *Socialist Commentary*, September 1957, pp 4–5.

30. *Ibid*, p 5.

31. Shirley Williams, 'Uneasy Courtship', *Socialist Commentary*, April 1958, p 18.

32. Roy Jenkins and Robert Neild, 'Dissenting Note' in 'Britain and Europe' Second Draft of Report submitted to the Home Policy Sub-committee, 12 June 1961, quoted in Michael Newmann, *Socialism and European Unity: The Dilemma of the Left in Britain and France*, Junction Books, London, 1983, p 166.

33. *Ibid*.

34. *Ibid*.

35. Interview with David Marquand, 13 October 1989.

36. Tom Nairn, 'The Left Against Europe?', *New Left Review* Number 75, September–October 1972, p 67.

37. Tom Nairn, p 24.

38. Tom Nairn, *op. cit.*, p 75.

39. Social democrats who died between 1971 and 1981 included Arthur Blenkinsop, John Cronin, Maurice Edelman, Patrick-Gordon Walker, Ray Gunter, George Lawson, John Mackie, John Mackintosh, William Price, John Rankin. Social democrats who retired between 1971 and 1981 included Richard Buchanan, Freda Corbet, Edmund Dell, Maurice Foley, Gerry Fowler, Geoffrey de Freitas, Douglas Houghton, Richard Ivor, Carol Johnson, Dick Leonard, Bert Owram, George Strauss, Frank Tomney, William Wells.

40. Interview with Lord Lever, 26 September 1989. The other exceptions were: Leo Abse, Peter Archer, Joel Barnett, Tam Dalyell, Ifor Davies, Dick Douglas, Jack Dunnett, William Edwards, Andrew Faulds, Denis Howell, Alexander Lyon, Roy Mason, Arthur Palmer, Charles Pannell, Robert Sheldon, S.C. Silkin, John Smith, Michael Stewart, Phillip Whitehead, Fred Willey. These, although they remained politically active in 1981, did not join the SDP.

41. Those who, among the 69 pro-Common Market MPs who did join the SDP were: Austen Albu, Michael Barnes, Tom Bradley, Richard Crawshaw, Tom Ellis, David Ginsburg, William Hannan, Roy Jenkins, Edward Lyons, Dickson Mabon, Robert Maclennan, David Marquand, David Owen, William Rodgers, John Roper, Paul Rose, Neville Sandelson, Dick Taverne, George Thompson, and Shirley Williams. Christopher Mayhew joined the Liberal Party in 1973.

42. Tom Nairn, *op. cit.*, p 66.

43. *Labour Party Conference Report*, 1970, p 226.

44. *Times*, 29 September 1970.

45. *Times*, 10 May 1971.

46. *Ibid*.

47. *Labour Party Conference Report*, 1971, p 114.

48. Interview with David Marquand, 14 June 1989.

49. Interview with Peter Jenkins, 26 October 1989.

50. Interview with Dick Taverne, 8 September 1989.

51. Interview with Dick Taverne, 4 August 1989.

52. *Op. cit.*, p 145.

53. Interview with David Marquand, 14 June 1989.

54. Hatfield, *op. cit.*, p 17.

55. Interview with Bill Rodgers, 8 September 1989.

56. John P Mackintosh, 'Socialism or Social Democracy', *Political Quarterly*, Volume 43, 1972, pp 472–3.

57. John Gyford and Stephen Haseler, *Social Democracy: Beyond Revisionism*, Fabian Society, London, 1971, p 1.

58. Anthony Crosland, *A Social-Democratic Britain*, Fabian Tract 404, Fabian Society, London 1971, reprinted in *Socialism Now*, Jonathan Cape, London, 1974, p 72–73.

59. Anthony Crosland, 'Socialism Now' in *op. cit*, p 37.

60. David Marquand, John Mackintosh and David Owen, *Change Gear! Towards a Socialist Strategy*, Supplement to *Socialist Commentary*, October 1967, p iv.

61. *Ibid*, p vi.

62. *Ibid*, p xv.

63. Quoted in John Cole, 'Labour's Lost Souls', *Guardian*, 16 January 1970.

64. John P Mackintosh, 'Forty Years On?', *Political Quarterly*, Volume 41, 1970, pp 53–54.

65. Roy Jenkins, *What Matters Now*, Fontana, London, 1972, pp 21–22.

66. Minkin, *op. cit.*, p 338.

67. Roy Jenkins, *What Matters Now*, p 34.

68. Interview with Stuart Holland, 24 July 1989.

69. Dick Taverne recalls that 'Roy Jenkins was absolutely devastated by Labour's victory and he went through a period of 12 months of black depression because he felt that he'd helped the party win when it deserved to lose'. Interview with Dick Taverne, 4 August 1989.

7

The Dénouement

Labour's assumption of office in 1974 did mean, however, that power in the Labour Party shifted back to the parliamentary wing where the social democrats were based. But neither this nor the favourable verdict of the June 1975 referendum on British entry into the European Community could reverse the decline in the social democrats' position in the Labour Party which the split in the PLP over the Common Market had begun. It continued throughout the 1970s. Efforts such as the establishment of the Manifesto Group in the PLP to organise wider support for the social democrats on the right of the party, or Roy Jenkins' decision to enter the party leadership contest after Wilson's retirement in 1976 only succeeded in demonstrating the extent of their decline.

The middle and later 1970s thus mark the final stages of the unmaking of the relationship between the social democrats and the Labour Party. By the late 1970s, Roy Jenkins had departed for Brussels, Tony Crosland and John Mackintosh had died. By then too, the Labour government had negotiated a large loan from the International Monetary Fund. The accompanying deflation and restrictions on public expenditure underlined more widely the impossibility of advance towards equality by the methods prescribed by at least Croslandite revisionism. Social democracy began to be recognised as intellectually threadbare even by sympathetic observers and commentators.

Meanwhile, the further advance of the new Labour left in this period, principally through the party's extra-parliamentary wing, represented a mounting opposition to the philosophy and political approach of the social democrats. The victories scored by the new Labour left after Labour's General Election defeat in 1979 undermined the autonomy of the PLP. The social democrats, having no extra-parliamentary base in the party, were the most directly affected. However, they could do little to limit all this damage and, by that time had few intellectual or political resources with which to try. The eventual decision of the social democrats, in the face of the marginalisation they suffered in the party, was to leave it. In doing so they were congratulated for their political initiative by an overwhelmingly sympathetic press. In a political system which they saw as gravely polarised and possibly immobilised by Thatcherism on the right and the new Labour left imminently in control of the Labour Party on the left, the new Social Democratic Party were seen as representing a bold, well-judged initiative to break the deadlock of extremism. The analysis of this chapter indicates, however, that in their decision to leave the Labour Party the impotence before the political forces they faced in the Party was at least as significant as any foresight or boldness: by 1981 the political condition of the social democrats remaining in the party could only be described as a powerless inertia.

The Social Democrats and the Third Wilson Government

Contrary to the expectations of Roy Jenkins and the social democrats, Labour was in government by early 1974, and their fate in it confirmed their apprehension of this prospect. While power moved back toward the parliamentary party and the leadership (and had been doing so even in opposition with Wilson's attempts to curb the left-ward policy shifts, most notably by reserving a veto over the proposal to nationalise twenty-five profitable companies), Labour was nevertheless now precariously in government with a set of policies which the social democrats had openly opposed as potentially disastrous. What was more, the social democrats were politically even weaker than they had been in the previous Wilson governments. As a result of the advance of the new Labour left in the party in opposition it had to be more strongly and seriously represented in cabinet. Similarly, the trade union militancy of the late 1960s and 1970s and its eventual success in bringing Edward Heath's Conservative government down, secured the TUC a prominence in party and later government policy-making which was unprecedented in the history of the post-war Labour Party. The 'social contract' was the device by which the unions, in promising co-operation in a voluntary incomes policy, demanded legislation on price and rent controls, housing, transport, taxation and the interventionist industrial policies already outlined in the AES. The rapport which some leaders of the left, notably Michael Foot, enjoyed with the unions now became the axis around which the Government's policy turned. Such extra-parliamentarism was neither palatable nor possible for the social democrats and it was hardly likely that they would be given any important role in such a Government.

The social democrats had also yet to recover from the setback they had inflicted on themselves by resigning their shadow cabinet and front bench positions in 1972 (when Roy Jenkins, as deputy leader of the Labour Party and shadow Chancellor of the Exchequer, had been the second most important leader in the party). While they had returned to the front bench in 1973, they would have needed more time in opposition to consolidate their position in the PLP where the Common Market split had so deeply divided the right. Eventually Roy Jenkins had hoped to challenge Harold Wilson for the leadership of the party. In any such challenge, the social democrats figured, a Wilson defeat, which seemed more likely than a Jenkins victory, would at least create a new power balance. The General Election of February 1974 forestalled this, however, and after 1979 the constitutional victories of the new Labour left made it impossible to achieve power through the only methods the social democrats could successfully use.

In the delicately balanced new government, the social democrats did badly in the distribution of cabinet places and ministerial portfolios. Initially Jenkins' followers urged him to refuse to accept any office other than that of Chancellor of Exchequer, believing that with a small majority Wilson would not be able to deny it to him. Jenkins refused to insist on this, however, not least because, having once been Chancellor as well as Home Secretary, he now eyed the third important office of state, the job of Foreign Secretary.[1] Moreover, having made a show of reconciliation with the party in order that he might yet win it from within, he could hardly now choose not to serve. In the end he had to go back to the Home Office. For an ex-Chancellor of the Exchequer and ex-deputy leader of the party, this amounted to a demotion.[2] For the conduct of the crucial economic policies of the Government as well as the steering of its overall direction, the Home Office was irrelevant: as Jenkins had written in 1971, 'A man could, I believe, be a tolerable and even a good Home Secretary while not on speaking terms with most of his principal colleagues.'[3]

The Common Market Referendum: An Illusory Victory

The Labour Government had pledged in its manifesto to renegotiate the terms of British entry into the EEC, especially on aspects of the Common Agricultural Policy and the British contribution to the Community budget and declared further that '[i]f the renegotiations are successful ... the people should have the right to decide the issue through a General Election or a Consultative Referendum'.[4] The referendum on the renegotiated terms was held on 5 June 1975, resulting in a 2:1 majority in favour of remaining in the EEC, on a large turnout. The social democrats' campaign on the 'yes' side did enjoy some clear advantages including the far greater resources at the disposal of the pro-Market forces and their consequently much more professional campaign, and the general difficulty of getting anti-status-quo verdicts in referenda in general. But, the overwhelming 'yes' vote in the referendum on the Common Market did not reverse the social democrats decline. If anything, the campaign, which pitted the social democrats against members of their own party, and which forged (albeit temporary) links between the social democrats and pro-Common Market forces and figures of other parties, in providing a foretaste of possibilities, sowed the seeds of future rupture.

The social democrats had opposed the proposal for a referendum and in 1975 John Mackintosh mounted an able, if post-hoc, attack on its confused logic. Given that the leadership of the Labour party now favoured entry on suitable terms, the referendum was no longer on the broad question of the principle of membership. Rather, it invited voters to make an unequivocal judgement on complex and technical matters relating to the 'suitable terms' which should properly be the subject of negotiation. Moreover, Mackintosh contended, 'If Mr Callaghan gets every single concession he is asking for on Britain's contribution to the EEC budget (which he says is the key issue in the renegotiation), the sum involved will not exceed the cost of Mrs Judith Hart's overseas aid budget or our share of the research costs on Concorde or be equal to one fortnight's deficit on the balance of payments at the rate current in the last quarter of 1974.'[5]

Despite their (temperamental and) principled objections to the recourse to referendum, once it was announced, the social democrats campaigned enthusiastically. In contrast to their dismal lack of influence in the government, which in any case failed to arouse their enthusiasm for politics, the referendum was the one issue on which they could appeal directly to the quite apparent and widespread sympathy of the electorate at large and on which they could campaign with conviction and enthusiasm. Given their antipathy towards most of what stood for Labour policy, and given the importance of the European issue to them, the two social democrats in cabinet, Roy Jenkins and Shirley Williams, had also announced during the October 1974 General Election campaign that they would resign if the referendum registered a 'No' vote.

With Wilson's suspension of collective cabinet responsibility on the issue for the duration of the referendum, both the strong pro- and anti-Market factions in the Labour Party were free not only to put their views openly before the public, but also to campaign with members of other parties. While this led to cross-party alliances which might have appeared unnatural, they were less so for the social democrats on the 'yes' side than for the Labour left on the 'no' side. If Roy Jenkins sharing a platform with Edward Heath and Jeremy Thorpe might have seemed strange, the sight of Tony Benn and Michael Foot campaigning on the same side as Enoch Powell was even more so. The broad sympathy the social democrats encountered among prominent pro-Marketeers from other parties sowed hardy seeds of disaffection with the current division of the parties: it tore off 'the mental blinkers, making it that much easier to contemplate a departure hitherto almost unthinkable'.[6] Campaigning on the 'yes' side with members of other parties, pitted mostly against members of their own (for the anti-Market campaign was overwhelmingly Labour), once again drove home the realisation of the gulf which separated them from their own party on the one all-important issue.

The decisive vote in favour of remaining in the EEC seemed to many to imply the firm re-instatement of the social democrats in the Labour Party, now that the left had staked its claim and lost. It also devastated claims by the left and the trade unions to represent the true inclinations and concerns of working people. But, if the social democratic side regained any self-confidence at all, it was only temporary. To be sure, the new Labour left was in retreat with the indecently hasty transfer of Tony Benn from the important post of Minister for Industry responsible for implementing the industrial policy of the AES to that of Energy which Harold Wilson effected in the aftermath of the referendum.

But the decline of the new Labour left in government strengthened the centre of the party and their allies among the old left; it did not mean a revival of the fortunes of the social democrats. The core of the government's policies still depended crucially on the TUC's co-operation – a power nexus which left the social democrats stranded on the margins. This irrelevance was only further compounded because on the most pressing economic questions, they had nothing substantial to contribute. It was the left's Alternative Economic Strategy, which, albeit in a suitably watered down form, had formed the basis of the Manifestos of 1974. Initially at least, it seemed to have some prospect of success with Tony Benn installed at the Department of Industry and the creation of the National Enterprise Board. After his transfer to Energy and the progressive abandonment of various elements of the AES, it was clear that the centrepiece of the Government's strategy was the 'social contract' – an arrangement whereby the co-operation of the Trades Union Congress (TUC) with an incomes policy to bring inflation down was linked to the government's fulfilling certain public expenditure commitments which would go to increase the social wage.

The actual record of 1974–79 was even more dismal than that of the late 1960s. While the Government started out with a series of measures to increase services and benefits, the large balance of payments deficit and inflation it had inherited soon led to deflationary measures which by 1976 also included IMF-imposed public expenditure cuts. Despite the deflationary path the government decided to take, the TUC implemented wage restraint fairly faithfully until 1978. While the effectiveness of pay restraint under the social contract had been impressive, the social democrats had, from the beginning, not been very enthusiastic about it given their view that it gave too much power to the TUC in government policy and the ever-present uncertainty surrounding its ability to secure compliance. In cabinet, Roy Jenkins also intermittently urged a review of public expenditure stressing its value to the economy as part of a general attack on inflation. But it was not clear if any coherent conception of socialism, or for that matter, social democracy, underlay the social democrats' positions any longer. Thus without any clear philosophy, and without any real base of support in the party or the unions, the role of the social democrats in the Labour governments of 1974–1979 was not particularly memorable.

Harold Wilson resigned as Prime Minister in March 1976, at the beginning of a period of Sterling crises which were to last until the end of the year when Denis Healey negotiated the largest ever IMF loan. The leadership election that followed in March 1976 revealed the weak hold of the social democrats on the PLP, and actually worsened their political position in the Labour Party. Roy Jenkins contested the leadership election with the intention of at least making a respectable show of social democratic strength in the PLP and perhaps, with a bit of luck, even winning in a second or third ballot. He got only fifty-six votes, however, as against the eighty or ninety considered respectable on the first ballot.[7] Although he had come third, with three others balloting even lower than his own low vote, Jenkins decided to withdraw from the second ballot in what Barbara Castle called a 'further display of political daintiness'.[8] She, for one, saw that the leader of the social democrats did not have what it took be a leader of the Labour Party of the 1970s. It was important, one might not be mistaken in thinking, to stay and fight. And if both Crosland and Healey withdrew, Roy Jenkins might actually have picked up their votes with a good chance to win. But while Castle's surmise of Jenkins' political style was probably not wide of the mark, Peter Kellner and Christopher Hitchens' analysis of the vote in the PLP shows that objectively Jenkins' decision was as correct as the future was dismal for the social democrats.

> Jenkins's surprise decision was due to the simple fact that he had won 12 votes fewer than even his most pessimistic prediction. But this in turn reflected a more fundamental failure in Jenkins's campaign. Of all senior Labour politicians, he was the most fervently pro-Market; while this ensured majority support – though only just – among the 90 strongly pro-Market Labour MPs, it also denied him all but a handful of the neutral and anti-Market votes. Evidence collected by the Sunday Times and the London Weekend Television programme Weekend World from more than 250 MPs during the contest, suggests that Jenkins won only seven votes from the 227 MPs who were not passionate pro-Marketeers ... for Jenkins to have stayed in the race would

have been an act of insane hope rather than calculated judgement: his enemies on the centre and left massively outweighed his friends on the right.[9]

Jenkins now clearly faced the conclusion that as things were, he would never lead the Labour Party. Indeed he seems to have at least suspected it even earlier. He had already provisionally accepted a job in Brussels as President of the European Commission, a job with more prestige than power, but a suitable parking place for a politician with grave doubts.

The Demise of Social Democracy in the Labour Party

The Manifesto Group

More fundamental than the reduction in the social democrats' representation in Government and Cabinet was their diminished allure in the Labour Party as a whole. The advance of the left and its pre-eminence in policy-making had the effect of almost eliminating any new recruitment on the social democratic side.[10] In the landslide victory of 1966 revisionism had made such significant recruits as David Owen, John Mackintosh, David Marquand, Evan Luard and Robert Maclennan. This, however, was to be the last such major recruitment. By 1976, as John Horam put it, the intake of MPs had been 'selected when anti-European and pro-nationalisation feeling was at its height in the Party'. This meant that 'MPs of that vintage were bound to reflect this balance of opinion'.[11] Of the fifty new MPs elected in 1974, twenty-eight joined the left-wing Tribune Group. In fact the increasing strength of the Tribune Group was a source of some concern to backbench social democrats and they made an attempt to counter it in the PLP by setting up the Manifesto Group in December 1974. Some observers likened this to the Campaign for Democratic Socialism (CDS) of the early 1960s. But there were important differences. Then the revisionists had been in the ascendant and enjoyed official patronage in the Labour Party under the leadership of Hugh Gaitskell. The social democratic position in 1974 was a far cry from that. Further, unlike the CDS, the Manifesto Group was a purely parliamentary grouping attempting to unite the various anti-left tendencies in the PLP. It was temporarily successful at putting up slates of candidates for various back-bench policy committees and, in November 1975, winning the chairmanships of all but four of them. On the strength of this the political journalist, James Margach, deduced that 'the moderates are the masters now ... and it's the militants and extremists who are in retreat'.[12]

But the very description of the Manifesto Group as 'moderate' revealed its basic irrelevance to the cause of the social democrats in the Labour Party. It was at least partly a consequence of the existence of

many social democrats on the backbenches who in different circumstances would have expected to be in Government. On the backbenches,
they attempted to mobilise 'moderate' opinion divided and demoralised
since the European split, against the left. However, right-wing unity
could only be had by agreeing not to raise important issues such as the
Common Market and any gains for the Manifesto Group could only be
of dubious value to the social democratic cause.

The social democrats who were engaged in this attempt at recreating
this alliance of the revisionist right and the centrists in the Labour
Party knew well enough that in the prevailing political climate it was
of limited effectiveness. It was a half-hearted, only half-serious effort on
the part of those who probably knew that their tenure in the Labour
Party was now seriously in question – an exercise in premeditated
futility not unlike Roy Jenkins' bid for the party leadership. While there
was very little in the way of effective action they could take, they might
as well at least appear to be doing something as well as making things
slightly more difficult for the left. A despairing humour lay behind
establishing the group. On the face of it it aimed 'To work for the
implementation of the policies set out in the Labour Manifesto and to
support the Labour Government in overcoming the country's acute
economic difficulties'.[13] So what, one might well ask, were Labour's
revisionists doing, extending their support for the left-wing manifesto,
whose policies and entire thrust it had routinely condemned as impractical and dangerous? David Marquand wryly recalled the reasoning
of Jim Wellbeloved who initially suggested the name:

> [A] lot of us didn't like [the name] initially because we didn't agree with the
> manifesto all that much. Jim, I thought, was very clever and he said, 'Well,
> we are not saying we agree with the manifesto, but when we call ourselves
> the Manifesto Group, we don't mean that we like the manifesto, what we
> mean is that the manifesto is as far as we're prepared to bloody well go! This
> is our sticking point. Don't try to push us any further'. And it created some
> confusion. I remember somebody wrote to me ... I can't remember who it
> was, not someone who was in parliament, saying, 'I'm jolly glad to hear of
> this manifesto you've got, can I sign it?'[14]

The Tribune Group, now numbering some eighty–odd MPs was, however, much stronger, and the advance of the left inside the Labour
Party continued. The Manifesto Group could not effectively organise
to oppose it, especially after 1979: its membership was too diverse to
enable that. The active core of about twenty members mostly joined
the SDP after 1981. The rest of its paralysingly diverse members did
not have the same primarily intellectual relationship to the Labour
Party. The Group's ineffectiveness was also revealed in the meagre
support for Roy Jenkins in the party leadership election. Apart from

getting their slates elected to committees and having 'agonized discussions' about the government's series of public expenditure cuts, the Manifesto Group achieved little, least of all in the way of proposing policy alternatives.

Having chosen to support the Government in the interests of right-wing unity against the new Labour left, the Manifesto Group focused its criticism mostly on the minutiae of anti-inflationary policy – demanding more firmness and consistency. In the face of new and unanticipated problems, the group's policy statement is more interesting as (another) measure of the social democrats' intellectual and political decline than for the merits of the arguments. *What We Must Do: A Democratic Socialist Approach to Britain*,[15] backed a permanent but flexible incomes policy, as well as a careful review of public expenditure and anti-inflation measures. The latter plank represented another default adjustment to the facts of slow economic growth: while fast growth may have sustained increasing public expenditure, in conditions of low growth increases in public expenditure meant that the share of public expenditure in GNP might reach levels which would imperil 'freedom' in society. The Manifesto Group's overall analysis also focused on the need for change in the national mindset. 'Our main failing is a profound resistance to change' and a 'backward-looking national psychology and backward-looking institutions'. But this laudable modernising sentiment was unsupported by any clearly researched and documented strategy or perspective. The statement also had to avoid any mention of the EEC, a problematic omission made necessary by the fact that the committee which wrote it contained not only the social democrats but other right-wingers in the Labour Party who were opposed to the Common Market.

The Social Democrats and the Callaghan Government

With the election of James Callaghan as the leader of the party and Prime Minister, Roy Jenkins left for Brussels and the social democrats' fortunes slipped even lower. While Wilson had been no friend of the revisionists, he had become leader when the revisionist ascendancy under Gaitskell could hardly be wiped out overnight. Now, however, as the leadership elections most recently demonstrated, the social democrats were effectively a marginalised section of the party, not a focus of power. Callaghan's strongest rival for the leadership was the Labour left's Michael Foot, not the social democrats' Roy Jenkins. John Horam, Secretary of the Manifesto Group, writing in *Socialist Commentary*, surveyed the scene after the reshuffle:

> For the moment ... left-wing voting strength ... and the power it gave Michael Foot, was bound to have an influence on the composition of the government. In one respect it has been a savage influence. The Jenkinsites have got

nothing. Roy Jenkins himself has been denied the Foreign Office. Bill Rodgers has not got into Cabinet. Dick Mabon is not Secretary of State for Scotland. None of the four new Cabinet members voted for Roy Jenkins. An important section of the party which is third most important in terms of voting strength has received no recognition. It is true that Shirley Williams has been given an additional job as Paymaster General, and this will be welcome if it increases the power of her voice in economic policy making ... There is undoubtedly deep feeling about all this.[16]

Tony Crosland, however, perhaps as a reward for his loyalty to Callaghan, went to the Foreign Office, holding for the first time one of the three most important offices of state.

With many of their most prominent members absent from Parliament by the late 1970s, serious questions were being asked about the future of the social democrats in the Labour Party. David Marquand had accompanied Jenkins to Brussels. In 1977 and 1978 respectively, Tony Crosland and John Mackintosh met with untimely deaths. With the growing strength of the left in the Labour Party and, even, of the left outside it, the dwindling band of social democrats were isolated from the mainstream of Labour's political life. This situation was hardly mitigated by the fact that by 1979, in addition to Shirley Williams, both Bill Rodgers and David Owen were in the Cabinet.[17] It was now a largely labourist and centrist cabinet with little consistency or principle and only one overriding objective – to hold the fort against inflation and the trade unions until an election could safely be called. The social democratic cabinet members, committed to stemming the left-wing advance, became defenders of the Government (Shirley Williams, with her seat on the left-wing dominated NEC, the staunchest). And lacking a set of alternatives of their own, they ended up being identified with the increasingly unpopular government.

The End of Socialist Commentary

While the European issue had pre-empted the social democrats' energies in the early 1970s, no restatement of the goals and methods of socialism issued from the dwindling demoralised social democrats even after the referendum settled the issue once and for all in 1975.

And in the absence of a conscious attempt to rethink it, there was nothing to salvage Croslandite revisionism from the practical termination it reached in 1976. In the aftermath of the Sterling crises, negotiations for the IMF loan in November 1976 had brought with it conditions which effectively shattered any remaining illusions there might be about the viability of a Croslandite redistributive strategy. Peter Jenkins dramatised the event: 'When the IMF foreclosed on Britain it foreclosed on Croslandism'. In 1970, the primacy Crosland attached to growth – 'We may take it as a certainty that rapid growth is a precondition of any significant reallocation of resources' – 'was a pessimistic observation; after 1973, when the world was plunged into recession, it became tantamount to an admission that further redistribution had become impossible, or at least without the dire consequences which flowed from Crosland's own theory.'[18]

Throughout the middle and late 1970s, especially after Crosland's death in 1977, sympathetic observers, both scholars and journalists, commented on the need for intellectual regeneration of social democracy (or in the terms used by many, a moderate centre left policy for Labour) as a counter to the extremisms of left and right. As an institutional manifestation of this intellectual decline of social democracy in the Labour Party, in December 1978, the independent revisionist journal, *Socialist Commentary*, published its last issue. It had always operated on a shoestring budget which had to be supplemented by the dedication and persuasive power of Rita Hinden, its editor for most of its life. The respect in which she was held, both by the revisionists/ social democrats as well as the rest of the Labour Party, was crucial to the magazine's ability to solicit some of Labour's best writing without pay. It was already uncertain whether *Socialist Commentary* would survive her death in 1976. By 1978 inflation caught up with the small capital grant (a modest bequest) on which it had so far survived and there was no more money. In his assessment of the magazine's role in the past, Peter Stephenson, its last editor, underlined the even greater need for such a role in the late 1970s.

> We share the view of those who are concerned that there is increasingly an ideological vacuum in the Labour Party, and in particular that those who share the Manifesto Group position – that is to say the great majority of members and Labour voters – find it much easier to define themselves in terms of their difference from the simplifications of the Left than putting forward their own inevitably complex positive policies of democratic socialism.[19]

Whatever the merits of Stephenson's claim that social democrats represented 'the great majority of members and Labour voters', the more immediate and urgent reality was that their kind of socialist position was now under attack from both the 'New Right' in the Conservative Party and the new Labour left. According to Stephenson these certainly made the task of restating the social democratic position more difficult: 'A growing awareness of the complexities of modern society, growing understanding of the difficult choices facing us in economic and social policy, have caused some loss of confidence amongst democratic socialists ... .'[20] In such a situation, the intellectual simplicities of the far left or far right were, it seemed, bound to appeal more than the demands of a more balanced and nuanced perspective.

1979–1981: Retrospective Certainties and Prospective Hopes

Labour emerged from the 1979 election defeat even more bitterly divided than in 1970. The unions' co-operation in the social contract had earned them the first cut in real wages since the depression of the 1930s. The resentment and sense of betrayal among the unions was hardly diminished when, with the reversal of some of the decline in wages of the industrial strife and wage settlements of 1978–79, Callaghan seemed to blame them for having lost Labour the election after the 'Winter of Discontent'. The new Labour left campaign for intra-party democracy mobilised this union sentiment, and by 1981 had won two of their three major proposals – compulsory reselection of MPs and the election of the party leader by an electoral college. (They lost on the proposal for the control of the election manifesto to be vested in the NEC.) The Wembley special conference of January 1981, where the election of the leader by an electoral college was carried, prompted the departure of the social democrats. Without a base in the assertive unions and extra-parliamentary party, any hopes that might have remained of playing an intellectual role in the Labour Party could no longer be reasonably sustained.

So much has been written about the run-up to the formation of the SDP after 1979, replete with intimate anecdotes and detailed polling figures, that an analytical study such as this has neither the need for nor the cause to add anything factually new. There is certainly no call for another narrative of the meetings, understandably imbued with conspiratorial trepidations. While these undoubtedly dominated the perspective for those involved, in themselves they were only the con-junctural guise in which a more subterranean change in British political life manifested itself. This was the intellectual break which the defection of the social democrats represented and a more worthwhile task for the present study would be to demonstrate the basically intellectual nature of the split.

In 1979, the social democrats' assessment of their positions in the Labour Party were diverse: David Owen, Shirley Williams and Bill Rodgers, who had recently been in Cabinet or government, seemed to think the situation still recoverable; Harold (by then Lord) Lever was of the opinion that, as in the late 1950s, the social democrats ought to have fought for their political position in the Labour Party; Roy Jenkins, David Marquand and Dick Taverne seemed to think the split merely a matter of timing and tactics. The story of the split from 1979, as told and retold in various accounts, was a matter of the gradual convergence of these views toward the last. A few years away from party politics had, it seemed, given Roy Jenkins time to reflect and he put forward his vision in the well-known Dimbleby Lecture, which clearly established his claim to the paternity of the SDP.

For those still within the party, who now served in shadow positions, the break could not come without much dithering. In the aftermath of the 1979 election defeat, as the social democrats fully expected, the advance of the left resumed and the 1979 Conference voted for both the mandatory reselection of MPs and resting control over the manifesto in the NEC. (They were, however, constitutional amendments and would also have to be ratified the following year.) The immediate reaction of the 'Gang of Three' was to resolve to stay and fight. They still harboured the hope that other centre-right leaders, like Healey, Hattersley and others, would be allies. Thus when Jenkins' Dimbleby Lecture posed the question of a 'Centre Party' it was met with public hostility from the leading social democrats in the Labour Party. Most famously, Shirley Williams dismissed such a party as having 'no roots, no principles, no philosophy and no values'. It took some time, and further advance of the left in the following conferences for this resentment to be converted into a readiness to contemplate withdrawal. Much further equivocation about the intentions of the Gang of Three was to follow. The resulting confusion and flux was further exacerbated by the differences between Jenkins on the one hand and the Gang of Three on the other about the purpose and philosophy of the new party – the former having for some time displayed rather openly Liberal proclivities while the latter clung to an exhausted 'social democracy'. The political question of the relationship of any new party with the Liberals corresponded to the philosophical one. And there was also the inevitably contentious question of party leadership. All these were to wrack the fledgling SDP, but the tempo of the break with the Labour Party was set in very different quarters.

The 1980 Party Conference which agreed to Mandatory Reselection of MPs and to change the method of electing the leader seemed to have been decisive. 'What had formerly been a matter of principle now became primarily a matter of timing'.[21] Finally, the 'Gang of Three' became the 'Gang of Four', and jointly, if not entirely with a single mind, embarked on the 'Road to [and beyond] Limehouse'.[22] The new formula for the election of the party leader adopted at the Wembley Conference on 24 January 1991 which gave the extra-parliamentary party a much larger say in the election of the party leader (trade unions got 40 per cent of the vote, Constituency Parties 30 per cent and the PLP 30 per cent), seemed to have been the last straw. The 'Gang of Four' formed the 'Council for Social Democracy' the next day as a prelude for the launching of the SDP on 26 March 1981.

The decision to split, in each individual case, was a question of judgement and it may have been wrong or right. It was certainly not without consequences for each social democrat and, when considered collectively, for the Labour Party both politically and electorally. And it involved a complex assessment of prospects, especially of any small break-away party in the British electoral system, and one about the social democrats' future in the Labour Party as well. Here the balance was surely tipped in favour of a break with Labour by the verdict of various opinion polls following Roy Jenkins' Dimbleby Lecture (in which he first proposed the idea of a new 'Centre Party'), which put the popular support for a Centre Party at dizzyingly high levels and by the advice of sympathetic political scientists like Anthony King and Ivor Crewe that 'a new Social Democratic party would have significant electoral support'.[23]

Roy Jenkins' Dimbleby Lecture is rightly seen as the genesis of the SDP. It made the case for the SDP most elegantly by combining the prospects for a fourth party and an historical view of the party system – in a single bold prospectus. Delivered on 22 November 1979, after the election of Mrs Thatcher's government, and the further surge of the left in the Labour Party, it identified the polarisation of British politics into extremes of left and right as the single most important cause of the lack of effective choice for the British electorate. The voters' political apathy, and their alienation from the two major parties in particular, had become increasingly evident over the past decade. Jenkins criticised what he saw as the wild fluctuations of policy (such as on nationalisation) which were a politically lethal result of the electoral system when injected with the right dose of extremism, and concluded: 'The paradox is that we need more change accompanied by a greater stability of direction'.[24] There was a clear implication that he considered the Labour Party as good as taken over by the left. This was no longer, as far as Jenkins was concerned, a doctrinal dispute of the sort which is both inevitable and creative in political parties. It seemed more like an unending and highly destructive feud. 'The response to such a situation, in my view, should not be to slog through an unending war of attrition, stubbornly and conventionally defending as much of the old citadel as you can hold, but to break out and mount a battle of movement on new and higher ground'.[25]

With an eye to future developments he dismissed the traditional antipathy towards coalitions, pointing out that the old Labour Party of Attlee and Gaitskell was a coalition of liberal social democrats and 'industrially responsible' trade unionists.[26] The clear implication of Jenkins' speech was that the first of these two elements, for whom the Labour Party had ceased to be a political home, must now find another home or build a new one. Not unreasonably, it was interpreted as a call to his fellow social democrats in the Labour Party to take his lead, even if it was not perceived as either helpful or convenient by those to whom it was primarily directed – the social democrats still bogged in the 'low ground' of the Labour Party.

However elegant or relevant Jenkins' analysis of the political situation, this speech had more to do with the future of the social democrats outside the Labour Party than with their (in retrospect much longer) past inside it. (And it focused on the political situation in Britain as a whole rather than in the Labour Party in particular.) In some ways Jenkins was the natural person to undertake this task. He had always been interested in the party system and its history. In his book, *The Pursuit of Progress*, he had made this his principal theme. While his detached political style had disappointed some of his followers in the Labour Party (although it can hardly be said to have been an important factor in the marginalisation of the social democrats), Jenkins was now the man of the hour. His leadership of the social democrats was suited to a radical resolution of their predicament. While he may not, like Crosland, have had an intellectual temperament suited to the task of producing a vision of social democracy articulated to the practical problems it would be called upon to resolve, what he did have was a historical vision capable of appreciating political changes, and an ability to set forth creative responses.

He was also an appropriate leader for the social democrats on their way out of the Labour Party in another more specific sense. Since any fourth party would have had to have some electoral understanding with the Liberals, Roy Jenkins, with his natural attraction to Liberalism, was well-suited to engineer it. The rhetoric of 'moderation' and 'stability', which was partly a reflection of the social democrats' theoretical exhaustion and partly an effort not to prejudice the future direction of any new party, also came naturally to Jenkins.

However, the founding text of the SDP, with its eye to the future and its society-wide perspective, cannot be considered a text of the social democrats' break with the Labour Party. That distinction must go to David Marquand's essay in *Encounter*, written immediately after the 1979 election. In contrast to Jenkins' lecture, delivered a few months later, it looked backward to the social democrats' history in the Labour Party and to the reasons why it was next to impossible for them to remain in it any longer. For one thing, the right and left wings of the party were now divided, not by a manageable political difference but an unbridged chasm.

> To pretend, in this situation, that socialists and social democrats are all part of the same great Movement – that Shirley Williams and Bill Rodgers and Roy Hattersley really have more in common with Tony Benn and Eric Heffer and Stanley Orme than they do with Peter Walker or Ian Gilmour or Edward Heath – is to live a lie. But it is a lie which the Labour Party has to live if it is to live at all.[27]

Marquand also recognised the underlying character and causes of the polarization in the party. Marquand traced the lineage of the social democrats as the heirs to the liberal social democratic, or what he called the Radical, intelligentsia in the Labour Party, who had been attached to it since the 1920s and whose contribution was essentially intellectual. They 'could and did lay down the intellectual framework within which the battle for votes took place. They asked the questions which the politicians had to answer: and in asking the questions, they helped to determine what the answers would be'.[28] While recognising that the revisionist doctrine had been flawed, Marquand concentrated on another deeper failure – that of the Labour Party – which accounted for the social democrats' impasse. The Labour Party had been unable and unwilling to effect an unambiguous doctrinal revolution in the party of the sort that Hugh Gaitskell had attempted in the 1950s. This failure was vastly compounded in the 1970s by the growth of what he called 'proletarianism' or, more picturesquely, 'the cult of the tea room' in the Labour Party. A central element of this was a pronounced anti-intellectualism:

> The central tenets of the 'cult of the tea room' are that the Labour Party is, or at any rate ought to be, not merely a predominantly but an exclusively working-class party: that the working class can be properly represented only by people of working-class origin who alone understand its aspirations and have its interests at heart: that middle-class recruits to the party, so far from being assets, are liabilities, who have no rightful business in it and who, if they do manage to join it, ought at least to keep their origins dark; and that the elaborate intellectual constructs of the middle-class Radical are therefore, at best, unnecessary, since the party can be guided much more satisfactorily by the gut reactions of its working-class members, and at worst positively dangerous, since they may lead the party away from its working-class roots.[29]

While allowing for a measure of polemical exaggeration (Marquand did, however, caution that no particular Labour MP would actually put it quite that way), as an account of the attack on the position of the traditional intellectuals in the Labour Party, for Marquand, it explained a lot – from the virulence of the Common Market split in the party, and the treatment of Dick Taverne, to the 'metamorphosis of the second Lord Stansgate into Mr. Tony Benn'.[30] This 'cult of the tea room' got an extra fillip when in 1974 the unions took on a Conservative government and won, 'not only on the industrial ground where they knew they were strong, but on the Government's chosen electoral ground as well'. This '1926 in reverse' also ensured the Labour Party's 'total identification' with the TUC.[31] The inevitable left-wing conclusion was:

> The proletarianists, it seemed, had been proved right: and right electorally as well as emotionally. The clever people, the intellectuals, the claret-drinkers,

the barristers, the academics, the frequenters of London Clubs, the article writers and the television-appearers, with their glib phrases and their disloyal attitudes, their outside interests and their European friends, had been shown up. The party did not need them, after all. They were surplus requirements: superfluous baggage on the Movement's back, which it could, if it wished, shrug off at no cost to itself. What you had to do to win an election was to keep in with Jack Jones. The Radical intelligentsia could jump in the river.[32]

The traditional doctrinal ambiguity Labour had retained had made the resurgence of labourism possible, and the political basis of the Labour government in 1974 had reinforced this. Indeed, in the revived anti-intellectualist atmosphere no sort of worthwhile intellectual effort seemed possible, especially by the middle-class social democratic intellectuals. For the most part this was a rather intangible mood, but one familiar enough from the past. In the atmosphere of the 1970s, it became transformed into a sort of hubris, Marquand claimed – a hubris which consisted in 'spurning new ideas at the very point when it most needed them'.[33]

Notes

1. John Campbell, *Roy Jenkins: A Biography*, Weidenfeld and Nicholson, London, 1983, p 157.
2. In 1974 the only other social democrat in Cabinet was Shirley Williams (Prices and Consumer Protection), Tony Crosland went to Environment. Junior ministerial offices went to Edmund Dell, Robert Sheldon, David Owen, Evan Luard, William Rodgers, James Wellbeloved and Dickson Mabon.
3. *Sunday Times*, 17 January 1971.
4. *Let Us Work Together – Labour's Way Out of the Crisis, Labour Party General Election Manifesto*, February 1974.
5. John Mackintosh, 'The Case Against a Referendum', *Political Quarterly*, Volume 46, 1975, p 75.
6. John Campbell, *op. cit.*, p 171.
7. The full result of the first ballot was as follows: Foot (90), Callaghan (84), Jenkins (56), Benn (37), Healey (30), Crosland (17).
8. It proved, she said further 'what I have always known: That Jenkins will never lead the Labour Party. I bet Denis [Healey] stays in ring, despite his derisory thirty votes. But then, he's a pugilist, not patrician. Wedgie's [Benn's] withdrawal in favour of Mike [Foot] was foregone conclusion ... I am not surprised by Crosland's dismissal with a seventeen votes. Despite the endless build-up he gets in the press, he isn't a serious contender at all.' Barbara Castle, *The Castle Diaries*, 1974–76, Weidenfeld and Nicholson, London, 1980, pp 704–5.
9. Peter Kellner and Christopher Hitchens, *Callaghan: The Road to Number Ten*, Cassell, London, 1976, p 171.
10. While they regarded the left's policy stance as no more than sloganeering, the social democrats nevertheless had to admit that 'the left at least had some good and attractive slogans. We didn't even have that'. Interview with David Marquand, 30 August 1989.

11. John Horam, 'After the Change', *Socialist Commentary*, May 1976.

12. James Margach in the *Sunday Times*, 30 November 1975.

13. Quoted in 'Let Umpteen Flowers Flourish', *Socialist Commentary*, February 1975, p 1.

14. Interview with David Marquand, 13 October 1989.

15. The Manifesto Group, March 1977.

16. John Horam, 'After the Change', *Socialist Commentary*, May 1976, p 3.

17. Bill Rodgers entered cabinet in the reshuffle which followed Roy Jenkins' departure for Brussels in September 1976 (Shirley Williams was moved to Education at the same time). David Owen replaced Tony Crosland as Foreign Secretary upon the latter's death in February 1977.

18. Peter Jenkins, *Mrs. Thatcher's Revolution: The Ending of the Socialist Era*, Pan Books, London, 1989, p 8. He is quoting Crosland from *Socialism Now*, Jonathan Cape, London, 1974, p 75.

19. Editorial, 'The Future of Socialist Commentary', *Socialist Commentary*, December 1978, p 3.

20. *Ibid.*

21. Ian Bradley, *Breaking the Mould: The Birth and Prospects of the Social Democratic Party*, Martin Robertson, London, 1981, p 82.

22. Hugh Stephenson, *Claret and Chips: The Rise of the SDP*, Michael Joseph, London, 1982, p 13.

23. Ian Bradley, *op. cit.*, p 84.

24. Roy Jenkins, 'Home Thoughts from Abroad', Dimbleby Lecture, reprinted in Wayland Kennett (ed), *The Re-Birth of Britain*, Weidenfeld and Nicholson, London, 1982, p 27.

25. *Ibid*, p 26.

26. *Ibid*, p 27.

27. David Marquand, 'Inquest on a Movement: Labour's Defeat and its Consequences', *Encounter*, July 1979, p 17.

28. *Ibid*, p 8.

29. *Ibid*, p 14.

30. Marquand, *op. cit.*, p 14.

31. *Ibid*, p 15.

32. *Ibid*, p 16.

33. *Ibid.*

8

Conclusion

Through their presence in the Labour Party, the revisionist social democrats had represented its link with Britain's principal intellectual tradition. Conversely Labour, like previous critical political tendencies in modern Britain, was the avenue through which this intellectual tradition had exerted its influence in British politics more widely. The media glitz, technologico-democratic fads, and opinion-poll euphoria amid which the SDP was born tended to draw attention away from the historic break the SDP split represented. This aspect of its significance went unremarked and unnamed, because most commentators focused on the future electoral prospects of the SDP in the British political system and not on the past of the social democrats in the Labour Party.

The SDP was the last political vehicle of Britain's principal intellectual tradition. In the inter-war period this tradition had given the Labour Party its most memorable and effective programme. Despite the wide prestige it enjoyed as a result, it proved unable to hegemonise a primarily labourist, unintellectual party and this lay at the root of the eventual break with Labour. The resurgent labourism of the 1970s, whose crest the new Labour left rode, challenged the authority of Labour's parliamentary leadership through its campaign for intra-party democracy. While it offered an important threat to the power of the centrist leadership, it undermined the political position of the exclusively parliamentarian social democrats even more. This bleak assessment formed the basis of their case for leaving the Labour Party.

The SDP: Intellectuals without a Philosophy

Once the new party had been launched, it became subject to the external and relentless logic of the highly disproportional British electoral system. Its electoral performance in 1983, and in subsequent general elections, hardly did justice to the high hopes amid which it had been launched. The support for the Alliance between the SDP and the Liberal Party announced soon after the formation of the SDP, which opinion polls reported at 50 per cent, failed to translate into as many votes and yielded, under the prevailing electoral system, even fewer seats.[1] To the vagaries of the British electoral system was added the destructiveness of personal rivalries such as that between Roy Jenkins and David Owen for the leadership of the party. The settlement of the issue in favour of David Owen had a paradoxical effect. While his charisma, relative youth and general 'potential-Prime-Minister' air were undeniably assets, the slightly megalomaniac tendency which went with them eventually split the party over the equally vexed question of its relationship with the Liberal Party. After its even worse electoral performance in 1987, Owen opposed the merger between the SDP and the Liberal Party to the point of splitting the SDP on the issue. By the late 1980s, the SDP's breakthrough to power, or even the balance of power seemed even more distant than before and it was abundantly clear that the SDP had failed in its declared objective to 'break the mould' of two party electoral competition by posing a more acceptable left-of-centre alternative to the Labour Party. By the same token it also failed in its real objective which was to *preserve* a mould of politics in which its intellectual progenitors could play a central role.

The true root of this failure was, however, deeper than these personal and electoral impediments. If, despite their intellectual shortcomings, the social democrats' fate in the Labour Party had been governed primarily by Labour's unintellectualism, once outside the Labour Party the intrinsic limitations of their outlook caught up with them. Their original (Croslandite) revisionism had not been crowned with the kind of success that had ensured the Attlee governments an almost sacred place in Labour folklore. Indeed, theirs had been largely a record of failure. They failed to revise Crosland's ideas in the 1970s and by the time of the SDP's creation, as we have seen, the social democrats had reached a point of intellectual exhaustion. And if the social democrats had failed to reformulate revisionism in the 1970s while they were still in the Labour Party, they were no more successful outside it in the 1980s.[2] Ironically for a party launched by intellectuals, it failed to present a viable positive programme, philosophy and strategy. According to the late Peter Jenkins, a long time sympathiser of the social democrats and later the SDP, the failure of the social democratic project lay in 'something much more basic'. It was

> their own lack of real purpose and conviction. What were they offering? What exactly was their alternative? What was the nature of their project? Why were they there? It had been a noble enterprise at the beginning. A stand had been taken for something open and democratic which would tackle the problems of the country in a decent and moderate spirit. Yet in some way the enterprise had brought out the worst in them all, turned them against each other, and destroyed four good careers.[3]

The dominant certainty in 1981 had been that the Labour Party could no longer accommodate them, as intellectuals. While this constituted a sufficient reason to leave the Labour Party, the social democrats were much less clear about the philosophical contours and political identity of the new party and never really overcame such ambiguities over the years. Surprising as it may seem, David Owen seemed more aware of the philosophical vacuum than the rest of the SDP's top leadership. His opposition to the merger of the two parties is usually attributed to the near certainty that the merged party (which would include the Liberals' battalions of community activists who, on most issues, stood considerably to the left of Owen and towards whose 'anarchism' and 'moralism' Owen had publicly expressed contempt) was highly unlikely to elect him leader. Owen also feared, however, (and he was not wrong) that the SDP element would lose its identity in the merged party. Roy Jenkins had long since come to comfortable terms with the SDP's lack of philosophy or radicalism and resorted to a distinctly 'immoderate moderation'.[4] Owen's miscalculation lay in his assumption that his increasingly 'sub-Thatcherite' themes would prove attractive to a broad enough segment of the SDP's membership. Not surprisingly Owen's own rump of the SDP failed to survive the 1988 merger by many years.

Without a distinct philosophy or strategy, the platoons of political novices the SDP had successfully mobilised in the early 1980s dissolved indistinctly in the merged party while their remaining shallow differences took on a destructive salience.[5] By the late 1980s, when the hopes of the SDP's early years had definitely evaporated, some, like Bill Rodgers, took heart at Labour's 'new revisionism', believing that it would never have happened without the electoral pressure represented by the SDP, while others, such as David Marquand, acknowledged that it might have been a mistake of judgement to leave the Labour Party.[6] While the merged Social and Liberal Democrats (SLD) debated such world-shaking issues as the name of the party, the founders of the original SDP had all but retired from politics.[7] The serious story of the Social Democrats was finished.

Labour: a Party Without Intellectuals

The fate of the Labour Party after the SDP split further underlines the historic importance of the intellectual amputation it suffered. While the SDP breakaway certainly damaged Labour's electoral fortunes, it increasingly became clear that it could not fully explain Labour's political impasse. Not only did Labour not replace its defunct tacit revisionism with a new philosophy, it remained oblivious of the need to do so. Labour's astonishing record of failure, its loss of four consecutive general elections, must be partly traced to the leadership's self-inflicted intellectual poverty.

In the 1970s, the new Labour left had never questioned, indeed, had chosen to abet, unintellectual labourism and it suffered the consequences in the following decade. Far from capturing the party, it was soon routed – and routed, ironically, by the first leader of the party elected under the new electoral system which it had fought so hard for. The 'soft' Tribunite left, whose numbers had swelled in the 1970s and which had ensured Kinnock's victory in 1983, also supported his campaign to make Labour 'electable'. It was ostensibly against the 'hard' left but the real target was the plural but active grassroots, extra-parliamentary left which challenged the increasingly irrelevant parliamentary orientation of Labour's leadership, old and new.[8] Kinnock's campaign was also supported by a new union leadership rendered even more defensive and anxiously moderate by Thatcherite attacks on them. In its anxiety to appear moderate, Labour suppressed the only spark of political vitality to grace the party since 1970, the grassroots activists of the new Labour left. And even then, it suffered a third consecutive election defeat in 1987. The verdict of the election only further underscored that of 1983: 'Labour strengthened its position in its traditional bases but failed to break out of them.'[9] Labour's appeal was restricted to the few remaining bastions within its former strongholds – the north of England and Scotland and Wales – the declining industrial heartland of Britain.

Kinnock's inference was that if the purge of the left had not, by itself, made the party electable, then many of the longstanding policies of the party, still discernably products of the period of left dominance in the early 1980s (albeit repackaged) would now have to go: the second stage of Neil Kinnock's purge, now of the party's policies, began. Policies deemed unpopular, like unilateralism, were renounced in often quite bitter confrontations with Conference. Opposition to British membership of the EEC was replaced with an uncritical Europeanism. Nationalisation was renounced in favour of a vague 'common ownership'. All this, it was hoped, would work to woo back Labour's lost middle-class and skilled working-class voters. Twenty-five years after Gaitskell's fight to renounce Clause 4, it seemed to many observers – and not least some social democrats feeling the first twinges of regret at their decision of 1981 – that Labour might have become a Gaitskellite Party. However, unlike Gaitskell, Kinnock still refused to challenge labourism by proposing a clear doctrinal basis for the party. Unlike the revisionism of the 1950s, Kinnock's Policy Review was not so much a restatement of socialism (however flawed), as a cynical image-building capitulation to a seemingly hegemonic Thatcherism (which ironically, however, came too late, at a time when Thatcherism's own appeal and radicalism were waning). Rather than any concern with policy and philosophy, new-fangled media techniques were harnessed to old-fashioned labourism in an obsession with Labour's image. Even the mild reformism of the soft left gave way to the 'market-research socialism' of the Policy Review. Policies were now to be weighed not in terms of their effectiveness or viability as part of any coherent strategy to deal with important issues facing Britain, but rather in terms of their popularity as gauged through opinion polling.[10] Labour's philosophical bankruptcy became glaringly apparent. In the event, a party almost entirely concerned with image and media strategies failed to convince the electorate and lost its fourth consecutive general election.

British Intellectuals in the Late Twentieth Century

With socialism everywhere at an impasse there are now few among its sympathizers so undiscerning as to make any unequivocal predictions about its future. In Britain, the 1981 split in the Labour Party repres-ented a major electoral and political reconfiguration of the left and of politics in general. However, with the left half of the political spectrum divided once again between the Liberals and Labour, and with the electoral dominance this permitted the Conservatives, the prospects of socialist or progressive advance at the close of the century were to say the least modest. While the exact shapes of any left renewal are difficult to predict, if the past experience analysed in this book is any guide, in addition to political reconstitution, an important component of any renewal will be an intellectual or philosophical refoundation. The argument of this book has been that the split also represented a historical discontinuity in the political affiliations of British intellectual life, and any theoretical refoundation of socialism will be a product of an altered intellectual terrain.

In fact, the 1981 split was an aspect of a wider reconfiguration of British intellectual life. As we saw in Chapter Three, the agenda-setting power of British intellectuals in the dominant tradition came to be exercised through the Labour Party and lasted until the 1970s. The exhaustion of revisionism therefore had implications beyond the fate of Labour Party. The crisis of revisionism was also the beginning of the unravelling of the hegemonic post-war consensus of which revisionism had been the intellectual-directive core. But, unlike Labour's revisionist programme which had filled the programmatic vacuum of the 1950s, the 1970s had brought no significant theoretical departures from the politically beleaguered revisionists. Nor did the left's Alternative Eco-nomic Strategy, which foundered in face of the party leadership's opposition, represent any notable advance. Instead, for the first time in modern British history, a new governing philosophy was introduced into British politics by the far right. It was this complex of events which brought in its train the deeper historical break which Perry Anderson noted: 'a marked disjuncture between high culture and politics in Britain'.[11]

Under Thatcherism the relationship between high culture and politics was broken in at least two ways. In the first place, 'high politics' fell under the intellectual influence of a sectarian grouping of neo-Liberal intellectuals who had managed to survive during the post-war consensus on the fringes of British intellectual life, lodged not in the major universities but largely in meagrely-financed think-tanks. Secondly, the long period of Conservative political dominance which Mrs Thatcher inaugurated put the mainstream of British academics for the first time in an at least semi-permanent oppositional stance. Indeed, a strong antipathy began to develop between the universities and the Thatcher governments. This was spectacularly revealed in the letter signed by 364 economists against Mrs Thatcher's economic policies, and later in the refusal of Oxford University to grant her an honorary degree. British intellectuals, including those in the major universities, (hitherto, in Noel Annan's words, so 'secure and established', conforming rather than rebelling) were now 'not so much, perhaps, disaffected as dis-established.'[12]

Longer term developments had also begun to jar the 'harmony if not unison with the established powers of the day' which British intellectuals had until recently enjoyed. One of the most important conditions for this – the relative 'underproduction' of intellectuals in Britain – ceased to hold just when these intellectuals' post-war influence was at its peak. The expansion of the universities had, by the 1970s, brought with it an unprecedented 'overproduction' of intellectuals, which for the first time led to a significant bifurcation of British intellectuals into left and right tendencies. Not only did it create a small intellectual base for the right in Britain for the first time, but the sheer expansion in the numbers of graduates, now increasingly employed in newer and less privileged positions in the new professions, provided an opening for the development of a far more radical left culture. The left activists of the 1970s, many of whom joined the new Labour left, were largely professionals of this kind: 'The main line of cleavage ... ran between those employed by the private or profit-oriented sector and the public sector, including the non-profit-making institutions such as universities, churches and charitable foundations.'[13] Moreover, the campus radicalism of the 1960s and 1970s played a significant in forming the outlook of important sections of these intellectuals and, in interaction with the work of past generations of socialist intellectuals, produced a lively left-wing intellectual ferment in journals, magazines and conferences. More generally, under new influences – from the left and social movements, especially feminism and from Europe and North America – British culture seemed to shed many of its native deficiencies: sociology, theory, historicity, sexual difference and internationalism figured more prominently on a fast-changing intellectual landscape. In the more variegated intellectual life Britain now enjoyed, what had once been the principal intellectual tradition now became merely the 'centre' persuasion. Moreover, in a hopeful development for the prospects for left renewal, the right, politically ascendant but not exactly hegemonic, was clearly recognised by many centre and left intellectuals by the late 1980s as their common target. And this intellectual stance was not without political consequences.

Even as the political centre-left remained divided between the Liberals, Labour, and a non-party left, many of its intellectuals seemed to converge on a common political issue – that of political reform. Can this be seen, on the analogy of the emergence of the New Liberalism in advance of the political move of intellectuals from Liberalism to Labour during the early years of the twentieth century, as foreshadowing the future of progressive politics in Britain?

Opening the Political Front

By the late 1980s a number of factors contributed to the gathering strength of the case for political reform, best represented by the non-party political movement, Charter 88. They included Scottish nationalism, European integration, the disproportionality of the electoral system and the archaic and undemocratic character of Britain's political institutions made more evident than ever by Mrs Thatcher's abuse of the elastic rules which governed them. This case was strengthened by the fact that any progressive advance on economic and social questions seemed stalled. Many centre-left intellectuals invested much hope in the prospect that the 1992 General Election would produce a hung parliament. The Liberal Democrats, whose platform already included proportional representation, would then make it the price of their co-operation with the Labour Party. This would also open up further possibilities for democratising and modernising reforms. By forcing co-operation between Labour and the Liberals it would break the logjam on the left which had enabled more than a decade of Conservative government, and, for the socialist left, it would finally open up political space for an authentically socialist party, unshackled by labourism.

While the outcome of the 1992 General Elections sorely disappointed these immediate hopes, the case for political reform retained its cogency: indeed it could be argued that in the 1990s it had become the precondition of any advance in social and economic spheres. This reversal of the traditional socialist order of priorities emerged on the centre-left in the first systematic attempt to grapple with the limitations of the long-defunct Croslandite socialism. David Marquand, the leading intellectual among the younger social democrats, and more committed than most to such a revision of what he called Keynesian social democracy, made a persuasive case that contrary to the dominant lesson drawn from this experience – that social democracy had to be abandoned – the true lesson was that, 'Keynesian social-democratic policies were frustrated by Keynesian social democratic politics'.[14] A new style of politics was necessary to underpin what was still a very attractive combination of egalitarian, progressive, and modernising policies.

Marquand argued that the record of government attempts to control the economy in the 1970s clearly revealed that Britain's inherited political framework was inadequate for the more interventionist policy which had become a precondition of full employment. Westminster politics could provide neither the institutional basis for the kind of relationship between the state and producer groups such intervention presupposed, nor could it afford the sort of legitimacy which any government needed to engage in such intervention. Only a further democratization and institutional modernization could provide these.

The weight of Marquand's revision of Keynesian social democracy was borne by its politics, not its policies and this has an important implication. In this guise social democracy no longer aims to transform capitalism. And it truly parts company with socialist currents. Kitted out with a new political framework it would be better able to promote egalitarianism within conditions of low capitalist growth without questioning the wider framework of economic power.

Even so, others farther to the left, like Perry Anderson, have granted that a 'social-democratic concertation' probably represents the best chance of a progressive politics within capitalism

> In all probability, a condition of relative industrial revival in Britain is now some political reorganization, as the decline of the economy appears inseparable from the arrest of the state. ... But so far there is only one kind [of strategy] that has linked economic success to democratic deepening. Social-democratic concertation only works where political representation is fully equitable, and governments can negotiate and ensure common lines of economic growth because they rest on genuinely broad social forces.[15]

Such an agreement across formerly significant political divides is an expression of a real intellectual convergence on the question of the archaism of the British state, as well as of the blurring of boundaries between socialism and social democracy in the West. Truly, any intellectual renewal of the left in this conjuncture of its crisis must be undogmatic and fresh. And the case for political reform is clearly indisputable. However, it is unclear if this more modest 'social-democracy-as-a-progressive-strategy' is any more firmly grounded in an analysis of the possibilities offered by capitalism than its predecessor, revisionism. For if revisionism's reliance on the pace of capitalist growth for its advance towards socialism eventually undermined it, this new social democracy, while realistically shelving sustained growth as a condition of its modest egalitarianism, relies just as much on capitalism's ability to *maintain* present levels of economic activity whose fruits, given the right political framework, it would then be possible to partially redistribute. This, from the perspective of the mid-1990s at least, seems dubious. While on the one hand the outer limits of global resource constraints seem rapidly being reached, on the other it is at least plausible that capitalism is genuinely unable to provide a decent standard of living to a substantial majority (as opposed to opulence to a small and diminishing minority and inadequate material access to a majority even within the OECD countries, let alone globally), at least for the foreseeable future. While political reform does seem to be a precondition for any new left project, a vision of the social and economic order which may be achieved through it, based on a thorough analysis of the problems posed and possibilities offered by contemporary capitalist civilisation, remains to be elaborated. And this is despite the many developments over the last couple of decades which, both in expanding the numbers of the educated and 'disestablished', and remarkably advancing progressive scholarship, could be expected to favour such endeavour.

Intellectuals and the Future of Socialism

Chapter Two ended with a survey of important observations on western intellectual life which pronounced it to be in deep crisis, noting its academicisation, lack of political engagement and social connection, general media and market domination and a fragmentation which seemed to destroy the very notion of social thought. And with the increasing internationalisation of intellectual life – the traffic in ideas and the conditions in which they are generated – these larger problems affect British intellectuals as much as any others. Moreover, it is very clear to these commentators that the very developments which otherwise seemed bound to enhance intellectual life play an important part in its crisis as, for example, the increase in the numbers of the educated has itself implied academicisation and specialisation. With such changes in what Regis Debray called the respective national 'bodies' of intellectual life, its 'spirit' necessarily undergoes a change.

H. Stuart Hughes noted that younger post 1968 generations of European intellectuals who replaced older ones have played roles significantly different from their predecessors – renouncing larger social theorisation and the more ambitious politics which went with it in favour of a variety of localised, particular, limited and pragmatic out-looks and political strategies. He called them 'sophisticated rebels'. Hughes attributed this to the realisation by this generation that the capacity of the system to defuse challenges was very considerable. But perhaps equally important, at least in Britain, was the fact that while the New Left had represented important radical impulses which shaped the outlook and politics of generations of radicals, it failed 'to offer any structural analysis of British society'[16] which might have been a base for a wider movement, and spawned instead a variety of social struggles which could not be accommodated within the already dwindling class basis of labourism. Rooted in these new struggles, and drawn from a wider social base, many of the younger generation of intellectuals who represented these important if localised critical perspectives eventually forced their way into the Labour Party, constituting the new Labour left. Despite their critiques of its leadership and outlook, the Labour Party dominated the space of the left and needed to be worked in and on: it could *not* be ignored. But their own experience in the Labour Party was itself instructive of the price of neglecting social theorisation.

In the Labour Party, these radical intellectuals and professionals concentrated 'on political advance through internal structural reforms [intra-party democracy] ... at the expense of developing a radical pro-gramme which combined intellectual credibility, practical application and popular support'.[17] The AES inherited from the early Labour left and never seriously re-examined by the activists was more significant for its potential for mobilising support for their cause within the party than as a strategy for socialism.

But for all that they were also representative of the shift in Labour's appeal towards the professional class, and constituted genuinely a new intellectual element in the party who were 'just as highly educated and articulate as the MPs and party leadership ... [and] unlikely to defer to the superior knowledge and ability of the latter.'[18] These activists differed from previous generations of Labour's intellectuals in being products of the expanded system of higher education. But this was in many ways an important difference. They were rooted in a very different political milieu. Their participation in movements of people bypassed or victimised by the welfare state – squatters groups, tenants' associ-ations, welfare and benefit claimant groups and, not least, women's groups – gave them fresh insights into the administrative and intellectual strategies which the welfare state embodied. Also, unlike the speedy upward trajectory of the revisionist generation, most of them entered Labour politics at the local level and local government remained the arena of their greatest successes. Nor was their upward advance in the party an easy one. This vastly more numerous intelligentsia could hardly be absorbed by the shrunken PLP of the 1970s as the revisionists had been in the 1950s. Indeed, as activists they were critical of the relationship between Labour's existing 'official' intellectuals and those for whom they claimed to speak. In this sense it was not surprising that they battened on and fanned the positive anti-intellectualism which pervaded the Labour Party in the 1970s.

Their critique of the traditional intellectual role as it had come to be practised, while genuine, remained untheorised. It could, however, be seen in their political practice rather than in their pronouncements. Their principal platform within the Labour Party, that of intra-party democracy, unified their diverse concerns. While their critique of representative democracy remained cloudy, Hilary Wainwright's sympathetic study of the new Labour left makes it clear that it involved giving those 'directly affected by ... policy'[19] a role in making it. In this respect their practice reflected a critique of the past role of traditional intellectuals, including that of the social democrats in the Labour Party.[20] And as a critique of the remoteness and insularity which came to characterise Labour's intellectual life from the 1950s onwards, this is undoubtedly valid. In fact, as Gramsci's concept of organic intellectuals (which was designed precisely to overcome this tendency of intellectuals) shows, the intellectuals' tendency towards an objectifying positivism, to become remote from the concerns they are supposed to represent, has been a long-standing concern. But Gramsci also held that the kind of local and partial rootedness that the new Labour left stood for had also to be overcome if intellectuals were to truly perform their role in hegemonic politics – to become directive in a wider social and political movement or party.

Many intellectuals among the new Labour left remained aware of the need to fulfil a policy-strategic role more usually associated with traditional intellectuals. The formation of the Labour Co-ordinating Committee (LCC) in 1978 was explicitly based on a recognition of the need to fill the policy lacuna of the Labour left, as was the Socialist Society founded in 1981. While these organisations failed to fulfil their role, they were based on a realisation that it was necessary.

The analysis of the intellectuals' role and decline in the Labour Party thus suggests that socialism, or for that matter any project which aims to transform society, cannot do without a cadre of intellectuals who are centrally concerned with the creation of overarching strategies, while retaining a capacity to adapt these to changing social, economic and political realities. The conceptual and technical rigour which is brought to bear on this task is a crucial determinant of its potential for success, while overall coherence is crucial in making it a hegemonic doctrine capable of both challenging other doctrines and organising social forces and the numerous functionaries needed to sustain it administratively and politically. The significance of the revisionists lies in their effort, however flawed, and however lacking in radicalism, to do this for the Labour Party. In present conditions of intellectual life this may seem a tall order, but it is one which must be filled by any viable left strategy.

Notes

1. The combined SDP-Liberal vote in 1983 was 25.2% (23 seats). In 1987 the vote fell to 22.6% (22 seats) while, despite many by-election successes, the merged Liberal Democrats did even worse in 1992 with 17.9% (20 seats).

2. David Marquand, *The Progressive Dilemma*, Heinemann, London, 1991, p 170.

3. Peter Jenkins, *Mrs. Thatcher's Revolution: The Ending of the Socialist Era*, Pan Books, London, 1989, p 367.

4. I borrow this delightful and prescient phrase from Alasdair MacIntyre, 'The end of ideology and the end of the end of ideology' in *Against the Self-Images of the Age*, Shocken Books, New York, 1971. See p 3.

5. For a survey of the main events and issues in the formation of the of the Alliance see Jeremy Josephs, *Inside the Alliance: An Inside Account of the Development and Prospects of the Liberal-SDP Alliance*, John Martin Publishing, London, 1983.

6. Interviews with David Marquand (30 August 1989) and Bill Rodgers (27 June 1989).

7. To account for the most prominent, after winding-up the three person army which his own SDP had become, Dr. David (now Lord) Owen became an international statesman. Roy Jenkins had become the Chancellor of Oxford University. Shirley Williams, married to Prof. Richard Neustadt of Harvard University, was now teaching at the Kennedy School of Government. Bill Rodgers had become the Executive Director of the Royal Institute of British Architects. Lord (Michael) Young of Dartington had rejoined the Labour Party. David Marquand was back in the academic profession and Dick Taverne was back practising law.

8. For a detailed and sympathetic analysis of this left see Hilary Wainwright, *Labour: A Tale of Two Parties*, Hogarth Press, London, 1987.

9. Doreen Massey, 'Heartlands of Defeat', *Marxism Today*, July 1987, p 18. For her analysis of the 1983 General Election results see 'Contours of Victory: Dimensions of Defeat', *Marxism Today*, July 1983.

10. Richard Heffernan and Mike Marqusee's *Defeat from the Jaws of Victory: Inside Kinnock's Labour Party*, Verso, London, 1992, is a scathing expose of the cynical manipulation and media-obsession in the conduct of the policy review.

11. Perry Anderson, 'A Culture in Contraflow', *English Questions*, Verso, London, 1992, p 300.

12. *Ibid*, p 199.

13. Harold Perkins, *The Rise of Professional Society*, Routledge, London, 1989, pp 437–8.

14. David Marquand, *The Unprincipled Society: New Demands and the Old Politics*, Jonathan Cape, London, 1986, p 58.

15. Perry Anderson, 'The Light of Europe', in *English Questions*, Verso, London, 1992, p 351.

16. Perry Anderson, 'The Left in the Fifties', *New Left Review*, Number 29, January-February, 1965, p 18.

17. Patrick Seyd, *The Rise and Fall of the Labour Left*, Macmillan, Houndmills, 1987, p 102.

18. Paul Whiteley, 'Who are the Labour Activists?', *Political Quarterly*, Volume 52, 1981, p 163.

19. Hilary Wainwright, *op. cit.*, p 100.

20. In *Arguments for a New Left: Answering the Free Market Right*, Basil Blackwell, London, 1994 Wainwright has since also attempted to elaborate and theorise the implicit politics of knowledge represented by these movements and intellectuals into a wider 'social' theory of knowledge.

Bibliography

Looking at the journals *Socialist Commentary* (1949–1978) and *Tribune*, (1970–1981) has been central in the research for this book. In addition, the newspaper cutting files at the Royal Institute of International Affairs at Chatham House, London have been an important resource.

Aaronovitch, Sam, *The Road From Thatcherism: The Alternative Economic Strategy*, Lawrence and Wishart, London, 1981.

Abercrombie, Nicholas, Turner, Bryan and Hill, Stephen, *The Dominant Ideology Thesis*, George Allen and Unwin, London, 1980.

Abrams, Mark, *Must Labour Lose?*, Penguin, Harmondsworth, 1960.

Addison, Paul, *The Road to 1945: British Politics and the Second World War*, Jonathan Cape, London, 1975.

Ali, Tariq and Hoare, Quintin, 'Socialists and the Crisis of the Labour Party', *New Left Review*, March–April 1982.

Althusser, Louis, 'Ideological State Apparatuses', in *Lenin and Philosophy*, New Left Books, London, 1971.

— *Reading Capital*, New Left Books, London, 1970.

Amis, Kingsley, *Socialism and the Intellectuals*, The Fabian Society, London, 1957.

Anderson, Perry, 'The Light of Europe', *English Questions*, Verso, London, 1992.

— 'The Ends of History' in *A Zone of Engagement*, Verso, London, 1992.

— 'Culture in Contraflow', Parts I and II, *New Left Review*, March–April and July–August 1990, reprinted in *English Questions*.

— 'Figures of Descent', *New Left Review*, January–February, 1987, reprinted in *English Questions*.

— 'The Antinomies of Antonio Gramsci', *New Left Review*, November 1976–January 1977.

— 'Components of the National Culture', *New Left Review*, July–August 1968, revised and reprinted in *English Questions*.

— 'Problems of Socialist Strategy', in Perry Anderson and Robin Blackburn (eds), *Towards Socialism*, Cornell University Press, Ithaca, NY, 1966.

— 'The Left in the Fifties', *New Left Review*, January–February 1965.

— 'Critique of Wilsonism', *New Left Review*, September–October 1964.

— 'Origins of the Present Crisis', *New Left Review*, January–February 1964, revised and reprinted in *English Questions*.

— 'Sweden II: Study in Social Democracy', *New Left Review*, May–June 1961.

— 'Sweden: Mr. Crosland's Dreamland', *New Left Review*, January–February 1961.

Annan, Noel, *Our Age: A Portrait of a Generation*, Weidenfeld and Nicholson, London, 1990.
— 'The Intellectual Aristocracy', in J.H. Plumb (ed), *Studies in Social History*, Longman, London, 1955.
Arnold, Matthew, *Culture and Anarchy*, Macmillan, New York, 1928.
Avineri, Shlomo, 'Marx and the Intellectuals', *Journal of History of Ideas*, Number 28, 1957.
Ashton, Joe, *Grass Roots*, Quartet Books, London, 1977.
Barker, Colin and Nicholls, David (eds), *The Development of British Capitalist Society*, Northern Marxist Historians Group, Manchester, 1988.
Barnett, Corelli, *The Audit of War*, Macmillan, London, 1986.
Barratt-Brown, Michael, 'Away with all the Great Arches: Anderson's History of British Capitalism', *New Left Review*, January–February 1988.
— Ken Coates and Tony Topham, 'Workers' Control versus Revolutionary' Theory', *Socialist Register*, 1975.
— and John Hughes, *Britain's Crisis and the Common Market*, New Left Review Pamphlet, London, 1971.
Bauman, Zygmunt, *Legislators and Interpreters*, Blackwell, London, 1987.
Bealey, Frank, *The Social and Political Thought of the British Labour Party*, Weidenfeld and Nicholson, London, 1970.
Beckerman, Wilfred (ed), *The Labour Government's Economic Record 1964–70*, Duckworth, London, 1972.
Beetham, David, 'Reformism and the "Bourgeoisification" of the Labour Movement', in Levy, Carl (ed), *Socialism and the Intelligentsia 1880–1914*, Routledge and Kegan Paul, London, 1987.
Bell, Daniel *et al*, 'Anthony Crosland and Socialism', *Encounter*, Volume XLIX, August 1977.
— *The End of Ideology and Other Essays*, The Free Press, New York, 1960.
Benda, Julian, *The Betrayal of the Intellectuals*, Beacon Press, Boston, 1955.
Benn, Anthony Wedgewood (Tony), *Conflicts of Interest: Diaries 1977–80*, Hutchinson, London, 1990.
— *Against the Tide: Diaries 1973–76*, Hutchinson, London, 1989
— *Office without Power: Diaries, 1968–72*, Hutchinson, London, 1988.
— *Out of the Wilderness: Diaries 1963–67*, Hutchinson, London, 1987.
— *Parliament, People and Power: Agenda for a Free Society: Interviews with New Left Review*, Verso, London 1982.
— *Arguments for Democracy*, Jonathan Cape, London, 1981.
— *Arguments for Socialism*, Jonathan Cape, London, 1979.
— *The New Politics: A Socialist Reconnaissance*, The Fabian Society, London, 1970.
Benton, Sarah, 'The Party is Over', *Marxism Today*, March 1989.
Berger, Peter, 'The Socialist Myth', *Public Interest*, Summer 1976.
— and Thomas Luckman, *The Social Construction of Reality*, Anchor Books, Garden City, New York, 1967.
Bevan, Aneurin, *In Place of Fear*, Heinemann, London, 1952.
Beveridge, William, *Full Employment in a Free Society*, Allen and Unwin, London, 1944.
Blackburn, Robin, 'The Ruins of Westminster', *New Left Review*, January–February 1992.

— 'Fin de Siècle: Socialism after the Crash', *New Left Review*, January–February 1991.

Blackwell, Trevor, and Jeremy Seabrook, *A World Still to Win: The Reconstruction of the Post-War Working Class*, Faber and Faber, London, 1985.

Bloom, Allan, *The Closing of the American Mind*, Simon and Schuster, New York, 1987.

Boddy, Martin and Fudge, Colin (eds), *Local Socialism? Labour Councils and New Left Alternatives*, Macmillan, London, 1984.

Boggs, Carl, *The Two Revolutions: Antonio Gramsci and the Dilemmas of Western Marxism*, South End Press, Boston, Massachusetts, 1984.

Boswell, Terry, 'Recent Developments in Marxist Theories of Ideology', *The Insurgent Sociologist*, Summer 1986.

Bradley, Ian, *Breaking the Mould*, Martin Robertson, London, 1981.

— 'Attempts to Form a Centre Party in Britain, 1880–1980', *History Today*, Volume 31, 1981.

Braunthal, Julius, *In Search of the Millennium*, Gollancz, London, 1945.

Briggs, Asa, and Saville, John (eds), *Essays in Labour History in Memory of G.D.H. Cole*, Macmillan, London, 1967.

Butler, David and Kitzinger, Uwe, *The 1975 Referendum*, Macmillan, London, 1976.

Callaghan, John, *The Far Left in British Politics*, Basil Blackwell, Oxford, 1987.

Callinicos, Alex, 'British Exceptionalism', *New Left Review*, May–June 1988.

Campbell, John, *Roy Jenkins: A Biography*, Weidenfeld and Nicholson, London, 1983.

Carvel, John, *Citizen Ken*, Chatto and Windus, London, 1984.

Cassirer, Ernst, *The Philosophy of the Enlightenment*, Tr. Fritz C. A. Koellen and James P. Pettegrove, Beacon Press, Boston, 1965.

Castle, Barbara, *The Castle Diaries, 1964–70*, Weidenfeld and Nicholson, London, 1984.

— *The Castle Diaries, 1974–76*, Weidenfeld and Nicholson, London, 1980.

Chomsky, Noam, 'The Responsibility of Intellectuals', in *American Power and the New Mandarins*, Random House, New York, 1967.

Clarke, Peter, *Liberals and Social Democrats*, Cambridge University Press, Cambridge, 1979.

Cline, Catherine Ann, *Recruits to Labour*, Syracuse University Press, Syracuse, N.Y., 1963.

Coates, David, *Labour in Power? A Study of the Labour Government 1974–1979*, Longman, London, 1980.

— *The Labour Party and the Struggle for Socialism*, Cambridge University Press, London, 1975.

Coates, Ken, *The Social Democrats: Those Who Went and Those Who Stayed*, Spokesman, Nottingham, 1983.

— *What Went Wrong? Explaining the Fall of the Labour Government*, Spokesman, Nottingham, 1979.

— 'Socialists and the Labour Party', *Socialist Register*, 1973.

Cole, G.D.H., 'An Open Letter to Members', *Fabian Journal*, May 1950.

— *A History of the Labour Party from 1914*, Routledge and Kegan Paul, London, 1948.

Cole, John, 'Labour's Lost Souls', *The Guardian*, 16 January, 1970.

— 'Wanted: A New Soul for Labour', *The Observer*, 9 October 1977.

Coleman, Peter, *The Liberal Conspiracy: The Congress for Cultural Freedom and the Struggle for the Mind of Post-war Europe*, The Free Press, New York, 1989.

Colletti, Lucio, 'Bernstein and the Marxism of the Second International', in *From Rousseau to Lenin*, Monthly Review Press, New York, 1972.

Collini, Stefan, 'Sociology and Idealism in Britain, 1880–1920', *European Journal of Sociology*, Volume XIX, Number 1, 1978.

Collins, H., 'The Marxism of the Social Democratic Federation', in Briggs, Asa and Saville, John (eds), *Essays in Labour History*, Macmillan, London, 1960.

Conference of Socialist Economists (London Working Group), *The Alternative Economic Strategy: A Labour Movement Response to the Economic Crisis*, Black Rose Press, London, 1980.

Cooke, Colin, *The Life of Richard Stafford Cripps*, Hodder and Stoughton, London, 1957.

Coser, Lewis, *Men of Ideas: A Sociologist's View*, The Free Press, New York, 1965.

Craig, F.W.S. (ed), *British General Election Manifestoes 1900–1974*, Macmillan, London, 1975.

Crick, Bernard, 'Intellectuals and the British Labour Party', *Revue Française de Civilisation Britannique*, Volume IV, Number 2. 1988.

— 'The Character of a Moderate (Socialist)', *Political Quarterly*, Volume 47, 1976.

— 'Some Socialist Books', *Political Quarterly*, Volume 48, 1977.

— 'Socialist Literature in the 1950s', *Political Quarterly*, Volume 31, 1960.

Crick, Michael, *The March of Militant*, Faber, London, 1986.

Cripps, Francis, *et al.*, *Manifesto: A Radical Strategy for Britain's Future*, Pan, London, 1981.

Cronin, James, 'Class and the Labour Party', *Studies in Political Economy*, Autumn 1986.

Crosland, Charles Anthony Raven (Tony), 'Equality in Hard Times', *Socialist Commentary*, October 1976.

— *A Social Democratic Britain*, Fabian Society, London, 1971.

— *Socialists in a Dangerous World*, Supplement to *Socialist Commentary*, 1968.

— *The British Economy in 1965*, Nottingham University, Nottingham, 1965, Hugh Gaitskell Memorial Lecture.

— *The Future of Socialism*, Second edition, Jonathan Cape, London, 1964.

— *The Conservative Enemy: A Programme of Radical Reform for the 1960s*, Jonathan Cape, London, 1962.

— 'The Mass Media', *Encounter*, November 1962.

— 'Some Thoughts on English Education', *Encounter*, July 1961.

— 'The Role of Public Ownership', *Encounter*, May 1961.

— *Can Labour Win?*, Fabian Tract Number 324, The Fabian Society, London, 1960.

— 'Radical Reform and the Left', *Encounter*, October 1960.

— 'The Future of the Left', *Encounter*, March 1960.

— 'What Does the Worker Want?', *Encounter*, February 1959.

— 'Production in An Age of Affluence', *The Listener*, 25 September 1958.

Crosland, Susan, *Tony Crosland*, Jonathan Cape, London, 1982.

Crossman, R.H.S., *The Backbench Diaries of Richard Crossman*, Holmes and Meier Publishers, New York, 1981.

— *The Diaries of a Cabinet Minister*, Hamilton, London, 1975–77.
— (ed) *New Fabian Essays*, J.M. Dent and Sons Ltd., London, 1970.
— 'The Lessons of 1945', in Anderson, Perry and Blackburn, Robin (eds), *Towards Socialism*, Fontana, London, 1965.
— Introduction to Walter Bagehot, *The English Constitution*, Fontana, London, 1963.
— 'The Spectre of Revisionism: A Reply to Crosland', *Encounter*, April 1960.
— *Labour and the Affluent Society*, Fabian Tract Number 325, The Fabian Society, London, 1959.
— *Socialist Values in a Changing Civilisation*, The Fabian Society, London, 1951.
Curran, James (ed), *The Future of the Left*, Polity Press and *New Socialist*, Cambridge, 1984.
Dalton, Hugh, *Practical Socialism for Britain*, Routledge, London, 1935.
Dangerfield, George, *The Strange Death of Liberal England*, Paladin, London, 1970.
Davenport, Nicholas, *Memoirs of a City Radical*, Weidenfeld and Nicholson, London, 1974.
— *The Split Society*, Gollancz, London, 1964.
Davidson, Alastair, *Gramsci: Towards an Intellectual Biography*, Merlin, London, 1977.
Debray, Regis, *Teachers, Writers, Celebrities: The Intellectuals of Modern France*, Tr. David Macey, Verso, London, 1981.
Dell, Edmund, 'To Plan or Not to Plan', *Socialist Commentary*, December 1965.
Desai, Radhika, 'Second-Hand Dealers in Ideas: Think-tanks and Thatcherite Hegemony', *New Left Review*, January–February 1994.
Dews, Peter, *Logics of Disintegration: Post-Structuralist Thought and the Claims of Critical Theory*, Verso, London, 1987.
Donoghue, Bernard and George W. Jones, *Herbert Morrison: Portrait of a Politician*, Weidenfeld and Nicholson, London, 1973.
Dowse, Robert E., *Left in the Centre: The Independent Labour Party 1893–1940*, Longmans, London, 1966.
Drucker, H.M., *Doctrine and Ethos in the Labour Party*, George Allen and Unwin, London, 1979.
Duff, Peggy, *Left, Left, Left*, Allison and Busby, London, 1971.
Durbin, Elizabeth, *New Jerusalems: The Labour Party and the Economics of Democratic Socialism*, Routledge and Kegan Paul, London, 1985.
Durbin, Evan, *The Politics of Democratic Socialism*, Routledge, London, 1957.
— *Problems of Economic Planning: Papers on Planning and Economics*, Routledge and Kegan Paul, London, 1949.
— *Socialism: The British Way*, Essential Books, London, 1948.
Eagleton, Terry, *Ideology: An Introduction*, Verso, London, 1991.
Eden, Douglas, 'Crosland: An Alternative View', *Encounter*, June 1979.
Ehrenreich, Barbara and John, 'The Professional Managerial Class', in Pat Walker (ed), *Between Labor and Capital*, South End Press, Boston, 1979.
— 'Rejoinder', in Pat Walker (ed), *Between Labor and Capital*, South End Press, Boston, 1979.
Everett Charles, *The Education of Jeremy Bentham*, Columbia University Press, New York, 1931.
Fiori, Giuseppe, *Antonio Gramsci: Life of a Revolutionary*, Tr. Tom Nairn, New Left Books, London, 1970.

Foot, Michael, *Loyalists and Loners*, Collins, London, 1986.

— *Aneurin Bevan: A Biography*, Volume II, 1945–1960, Davis-Poynter Ltd., London, 1973.

Forester, Tom, *The Labour Party and the Working Class*, Heinemann Educational, London, 1976.

Foster, John, 'The Declassing of Language', *New Left Review*, March–April 1985.

Foucault, Michel, *Power/Knowledge*, Colin Gordon (ed), Pantheon Books, New York, 1977.

Freeman, Alan, *The Benn Heresy*, Pluto Press, London, 1982.

Fyvel, T.R., *Intellectuals Today*, Schocken Books, New York, 1968.

Gaitskell, Hugh, 'At Oxford in the Twenties', in Briggs, Asa and Saville, John (eds), *Essays in Labour History in Memory of G. D. H. Cole*, 1960.

— *Socialism and Nationalism*, Fabian Tract Number 300, The Fabian Society, London, 1956.

— 'The Future of Prosperity', *Encounter*, November 1955.

Gamble, Andrew, *Britain in Decline*, Macmillan, London, 1985.

Gandall, Keith, 'Michel Foucault: Intellectual Work and Politics', *Telos*, Spring 1986.

Gay, Peter, *The Dilemma of Democratic Socialism: Eduard Bernstein's Challenge to Marx*, Columbia University Press, New York, 1952.

Gilmour, Ian, *Inside Right*, Quartet Books, London, 1977.

Glees, Anthony, 'The SPD in Emigration and Resistance, 1933–1945', in Roger Fletcher (ed) *Bernstein to Brandt: A Short History of German Social Democracy*, Edward Arnold, London, 1987.

Goldthorpe, John and David Lockwood, 'Affluence and the British Class Structure', *Sociological Review*, July 1963.

Gordon-Walker, Patrick, 'On Being a Cabinet Minister', *Encounter*, April 1956.

Gould, Julius, 'End of a Movement', *Encounter*, November 1979.

Gouldner, Alvin, *The Future of Intellectuals and the Rise of the New Class,* Oxford University Press, New York, 1979.

— 'Prologue to a Theory of Revolutionary Intellectuals', Winter 1975–76.

Gowan, Peter, 'The Origins of the Administrative Elite', *New Left Review*, March–April 1987.

Gramsci, Antonio, *Selections from Cultural Writings*, Forgacs, David and Nowell-Smith, Geoffrey (eds), tr. William Bollhower, Harvard University Press, Cambridge, Massachusetts, 1985.

— *Selections from the Prison Notebooks*, tr. Hoare, Quintin and Nowell-Smith, Geoffrey, International Publishers, New York, 1983.

— *Selections from Political Writings (1910–1920)*, Hoare, Quintin (ed), tr. John Mathews. International Publishers, New York, 1977.

— *The Modern Prince and Other Writings*, International Publishers, New York, 1967.

Guttsman, W. L., *The British Political Elite*, MacGibbon and Kee, London, 1968.

Gyford, John, *The Politics of Local Socialism*, George Allen and Unwin, London, 1985.

— and Stephen Haseler, *Social Democracy: Beyond Revisionism*, Fabian Society, London, 1971.

Hain, Peter (ed), *The Debate of the Decade: The Crisis and the Future of the Left*, Pluto Press, London, 1980.

Halévy, Elie, *The Growth of Philosophic Radicalism*, tr. Mary Morris, Faber, London, 1972.

Hall, Stuart, *The Hard Road to Renewal*, Verso, London, 1989.

— 'The Problem of Ideology – Marxism without Guarantees', in Betty Matthews (ed), *Marx: 100 Years On*, Lawrence and Wishart, London, 1979.

— *Policing the Crisis: Mugging, the State, Law and Order*, Macmillan, London, 1978.

Halsey, A. H., 'Provincials and Professionals: the British Post-War Sociologists', *European Journal of Sociology*, Volume XXIII, 1982.

— 'British Universities and Intellectual Life', in Halsey *et al* (eds), *Education, Economy and Society: A Reader in the Sociology of Education*, Free Press of Glencoe, New York, 1961.

Hamburger, Joseph, *Intellectuals in Politics: John Stuart Mill and the Philosophic Radicals*, Yale University Press, New Haven, 1965.

Harrington, Illtyd, 'Young Turks of the Town Hall', *New Statesman*, 16 July 1971.

Harrison, Royden, 'Sidney and Beatrice Webb', in Levy, Carl (ed), *Socialism and the Intelligentsia 1880–1914*, Routledge and Kegan Paul, London, 1987.

Harvey, James and Hood, Katherine, *The British State*, Lawrence & Wishart, London, 1958.

Haseler, Stephen, 'Towards a Centre Party?', *Encounter*, April 1980.

— *The Death of British Democracy: A Study of Britain's Political Present and Future*, P. Elek, London, 1976.

— 'Can British Socialism Survive?', *Encounter*, December 1976.

— 'Don't Soak the Rich: They're Doing their Best', *Tribune*, 17 March 1972.

— 'Labour and the Whigs', *Tribune*, 26 November 1971.

— 'The Establishment, the Socialists and the Labour Movement', *Tribune*, 29 October 1971.

— 'The Gaitskellites and the Common Market', *Tribune*, 18 June 1971.

— *The Gaitskellites: Revisionism in the British Labour Party 1951–64*, Macmillan, London, 1969.

Hatfield, Michael, *The House the Left Built: Inside Labour Policy-making 1970–1975*, Gollancz, London, 1978.

Hattersley, Roy, *Choose Freedom*, Michael Joseph, London, 1987.

— 'Why I Will Stay and Fight', *The Sunday Times*, 25 January 1981.

— 'The True Crosland Creed', *The Guardian*, 15 January 1981.

Hayek, Fredrich A., 'The Intellectuals and Socialism', *Studies in Politics, Philosophy and Economics*, Routledge and Kegan Paul, London, 1967.

— *The Road to Serfdom*, Chicago University Press, Chicago, 1944.

Heffer, Eric, *Never A Yes Man: Life and Politics of an Adopted Liverpudlian*, Verso, London, 1991.

— *Labour's Future*, Verso, London, 1986.

— 'Inquest on a Coroner', *Encounter*, November 1979.

— 'Two Labour Parties or One', *Political Quarterly*, Volume 46, 1975.

— *The Class Struggle in Parliament*, Gollancz, London, 1973.

— 'Labour's Future', *Political Quarterly*, Volume 43, 1972.

Heffernan, Richard and Marqusee, Mike, *Defeat from the Jaws of Victory: Inside Kinnock's Labour Party*, Verso, London, 1992.

Hewison, Robert, *Too Much: Art and Society in the Sixties*, Methuen, London, 1986.

— *In Anger: British Culture and the Cold War 1945–1960*, Weidenfeld and Nicholson, London, 1981.

Heyck, T. W., *The Transformation of Intellectual Life in Victorian England*, Croom Helm, London, 1982.

Hindell, Keith and Williams, Philip, 'Scarborough and Blackpool: An Analysis of Some Votes at the Labour Party Conferences of 1960 and 1961', *Political Quarterly*, July 1962.

Hindess, Barry, *Parliamentary Democracy and Socialist Politics*, Routledge and Kegan Paul, London, 1983.

— *The Decline of Working Class Politics*, MacGibbon and Kee, London, 1971.

Hinton, James, *Labour and Socialism*, Wheatsheaf, London, 1983.

Hobsbawm, Eric, 'The Crisis of Today's Ideologies', *New Left Review*, March–April 1992.

— (ed), *The Forward March of Labour Halted?*, Verso, London, 1981.

— 'Intellectuals and the Labour Movement', *Marxism Today*, July 1979.

— 'Labour's Lost Millions', *Marxism Today*, October 1973.

— 'The Fabians Reconsidered', in *Labouring Men*, Weidenfeld and Nicholson, London, 1964.

Hogdson, Geoff, *Labour at the Crossroads: The Political and Economic Challenge of Labour in the 1980s*, Martin Robertson, London, 1981.

Hoffman, John, *The Gramscian Challenge: Coercion and Consent in Marxist Political Theory*, Blackwell, Oxford, 1984.

Hofstadter, Richard, *Anti-Intellectualism in American Life*, Knopf, New York, 1963.

Hoggart, Richard, *The Uses of Literacy*, Chatto and Windus, London, 1957.

Holland, Stuart, *The Socialist Challenge*, Quartet, London, 1975.

Horam, John, 'After the Change', *Socialist Commentary*, May 1976.

Houghton, Walter E., *The Victorian Frame of Mind: 1830–1870*, Yale University Press, New Haven, 1957.

Howard, Anthony, *Crossman: The Pursuit of Power*, Jonathan Cape, London, 1990.

Howell, David, *British Social Democracy*, Croom Helm, London, 1976.

Hughes, H. Stuart, *Sophisticated Rebels: The Political Culture of European Dissent 1968–1987*, Harvard University Press, Cambridge, Massachusetts, 1988.

— *Consciousness and Society: The Reorientation of European Social Thought 1890–1930*, revised ed. Vintage Books, New York, 1977.

Hughes, Colin and Wintour, Patrick, *Labour Rebuilt*, Fourth Estate, London, 1990.

Hughes, John, 'The British Economy: Crisis and Structural Change', *New Left Review*, October 1963.

Hunter, Leslie, *The Road to Brighton Pier*, Arthur Baker Ltd, London, 1959.

de Huszar, George Bernard (ed), *The Intellectuals: A Controversial Portrait*, The Free Press, Glencoe, Illinois, 1960.

Hynes, Samuel, *The Edwardian Turn of Mind*, Princeton University Press, Princeton, 1968.

Inglis, Fred, *Radical Earnestness: English Social Theory 1880–1980*, Martin Robertson, Oxford, 1982.

Jacoby, Russell, *The Last Intellectuals: American Culture in the Age of Academe*, Basic Books, New York, 1987.

Jay, Douglas, *The Socialist Case*, Faber, London, 1971.

— *After the Common Market: A Better Alternative for Britain*, Penguin, Harmondsworth, 1968.

— and Jenkins, Roy, *The Common Market Debate*, The Fabian Society, London, 1962.

Jay, Martin, *Fin-de-Siècle Socialism and Other Essays*, Routledge, New York, 1988.

Jenkins, Mark, *Bevanism: Labour's High Tide*, Spokesman, Nottingham, 1979.

Jenkins, Peter, *Mrs Thatcher's Revolution: The Ending of the Socialist Era*, Pan Books, London, 1989.

— 'The Future of the Labour Party', *Political Quarterly*, 1975.

— 'Weak Link', *Guardian*, 26 November 1975.

— *The Battle of Downing Street*, Charles Knight and Co. Ltd., London, 1970.

— 'The Crumbling Old Order', in Kennett, Wayland (ed), *The Re-birth of Britain*, Weidenfeld and Nicholson, London, 1982.

— 'The Labour Party and the Politics of Transition', *Socialist Register*, 1977.

Jenkins, Robert, *Tony Benn: A Political Biography*, Writers and Readers, London, 1980.

Jenkins, Roy, *European Diary 1977–1980*, Collins, London, 1989.

— *Baldwin*, Collins, London, 1987.

— *Truman*, Collins, London, 1986.

— *Partnership of Principles*, Secker and Warburg, London, 1985.

— *Britain and the EEC: Proceedings of Section F (Economics) of the British Association for the Advancement of Science*, Macmillan, London, 1983.

— 'Home Thoughts from Abroad', in Wayland Kennett (ed), *The Re-birth of Britain*, Weidenfeld and Nicholson, London, 1982.

— *The Role of the European Community in World Affairs*, Samuel D. Berger Memorial Lecture, Georgetown University, Washington, 1981.

— 'What's Wrong and What Could Be Set Right: Reflections after 29 Years in Parliament', *Encounter*, February 1978.

— *Nine Men of Power*, Hamilton, London, 1974.

— *What Matters Now?*, Fontana, London, 1972.

— *Afternoon on the Potomac? A British View of America's Changing Position in the World*, Yale University Press, New Haven, 1972.

— *Sir Charles Dilke: A Victorian Tragedy*, Collins, London, 1965.

— *Asquith*, Collins, London, 1964.

— 'Hugh Gaitskell', *Encounter*, February 1966.

— 'From London to Rome', *Encounter*, September 1961.

— *The Labour Case*, Penguin, Harmondsworth, 1959.

— 'Obscenity, Censorship, and the Law: The Story of a Bill', *Encounter*, October 1959.

— *Essays and Speeches*, Collins, London, 1957.

— 'A Genius for Compromise? A Debate on the British Party System', *Encounter*, March 1956.

— *Mr. Balfour's Poodle: An Account of the Struggle between the House of Lords and the Government of Mr. Asquith*, Heinemann, London, 1954.

— *Pursuit of Progress: A Critical Analysis of The Achievement and Progress of the Labour Party*, William Heinemann, London, 1953.

— *Fair Shares for the Rich*, Tribune, London, 1951.

— *Post-war Italy: A Report on Economic Conditions by Four Observers*, Fabian Society, London, 1950.

Joseph, Jeremy, *Inside the Alliance: An Inside Account of the Development and Prospects of the Liberal-SDP Alliance*, John Martin Publishing Ltd., London, 1985.

Jessop, Bob, 'Accumulation Strategies, State Forms and Hegemonic Projects', *Kapitalstate*, Double Issue 10/11, 1983.

Joad, C. E. M., 'The End of An Epoch I and II', *New Statesman and Nation*, December 1 and 8, 1934.

Johnson, R.W., 'Third Party Insurance', *New Statesman and Society*, 19 January, 1990.

Johnstone, J. K., *The Bloomsbury Group: A Study of E. M. Foster, Lytton Strachey, Virginia Woolf, and their Circle*, The Noonday Press, New York, 1963.

Kaufman, Gerald, *The Left: A Symposium*, Blond, London, 1966.

Kautsky, Karl, *Selected Writings*, Macmillan, London, 1983.

Kellner, Peter and Christopher Hitchens, *Callaghan: The Road to Number 10*, Cassell, London, 1975.

Kennett, Wayland (ed), *The Re-birth of Britain*, Weidenfeld and Nicholson, London, 1982.

— 'The Policies of the Party', *Political Quarterly*, 1972.

Kiernan, V. G., 'Notes on the Intelligentsia', *Socialist Register*, 1969.

King, Anthony, 'Never Another Crosland', *Socialist Commentary*, April 1977.

Kitzinger, Uwe, *The Second Try: Labour and the EEC*, Pergamon Press, Oxford, 1968.

Knights, Ben, *The Idea of a Clerisy in the Nineteenth Century*, Cambridge University Press, Cambridge, 1978.

Kogan, D. and M. Kogan, *The Battle for the Labour Party*, Fontana, London, 1981.

Labour Party, *Signposts for the Sixties*, London, 1961.

— *Industry and Society*, London, 1957.

Laclau, Ernesto and Mouffe, Chantal, 'Post-Marxism without Apologies', *New Left Review*, November–December 1987.

— *Hegemony and Socialist Strategy*, Verso, London, 1985.

Laclau, Ernesto, *Politics and Ideology in Marxist Theory*, Verso, London, 1977.

Lasch, Christopher, 'The Cultural Cold War: A Short History of the Congress for Cultural Freedom', in *The Agony of the American Left*, Alfred Knopf, New York, 1969.

Laski, Harold, *Parliamentary Government in England*, Allen, London, 1938.

— *The Crisis and the Constitution*, Hogarth Press, London, 1932.

Lenin, V.I., *What is to be Done?*, in *V.I.Lenin: Collected Works*, Volume 5, Foreign Languages Publishing House, Moscow, 1960–1970.

Lipsey, David and Dick Leonard, *The Socialist Agenda: Crosland's Legacy*, Jonathan Cape, London, 1981.

Lele, Jayant, 'Orientalism and the Social Sciences', Mimeo.

Lester, Anthony, 'Fundamental Rights: The United Kingdom Isolated?', *Public Law*, Spring 1984.

— *Race and Law in Great Britain*, Penguin, Harmondsworth, 1972.

Levy, Carl (ed), *Socialism and the Intelligentsia 1880–1914*, Routledge and Kegan Paul, London, 1987.

Leys, Colin, *Politics in Britain: From Labourism to Thatcherism*, revised edition, Verso, London, 1989.

Luard, Evan, *Socialism at the Grass Roots*, Fabian Society, London, 1980.

— *Socialism without the State*, Macmillan, London, 1979.

Lukes, Steven, 'The Future of British Socialism', in Pimlott, Ben (ed), *Fabian Essays in Socialist Thought*, Heinemann, London, 1984.

— *Emile Durkheim: His Life and Work*, Penguin, Harmondsworth, 1973.

MacIntyre, Alasdair, *Against the Self-Images of the State*, Shocken Books, New York, 1971.

Macintyre, Stuart, *A Proletarian Science: Marxism in Britain 1917–1933*, Cambridge University Press, Cambridge, 1980.

Mackenzie, Norman (ed), *Conviction*, MacGibbon and Kee, London, 1958.

Mackintosh, John, *J. P. Mackintosh on Parliament and Social Democracy*, edited with an Introduction by David Marquand, Longman, London, 1982.

— *People and Parliament*, Saxon House, Farnborough, 1978.

— 'Has Social Democracy Failed in Britain?', *Political Quarterly*, Volume 49, 1978.

— *Britain's Malaise: Political or Economic?* University of Southampton, Southampton, 1977.

— 'Is Labour Facing Catastrophe?', *Encounter*, Volume XLVIII, Number 1, January 1977.

— 'The Case against a Referendum', *Political Enquiry*, Volume 46, 1975.

— 'The Report of the Royal Commission on the Constitution 1969–1973', *Political Quarterly*, Volume 45, 1974.

— 'How Much Time Left for Parliamentary Democracy?', *Encounter*, August 1974.

— 'The BBC and the General Election', *The Listener*, 25 July, 1974.

— 'Do We Want a Referendum?', *The Listener*, 22 August 1974.

— 'Socialism or Social Democracy', *Political Quarterly*, Volume 43, 1972.

— 'The Problems of the Labour Party', *Political Quarterly*, Volume 43, 1972.

— 'Anybody Still for Democracy? Troubled Reflections of a Westminster M.P', *Encounter*, November 1972.

— 'Forty Years On', *Political Quarterly*, Volume 41, 1970.

— 'Britain and Europe: New Opportunities', *Socialist Commentary*, February 1970.

— 'The Boredom and the Excitement: On Reforming Local Government', *Encounter*, September 1969,

— *The Devolution of Power: Local Democracy, Regionalism and Nationalism*, Chatto and Windus, London, 1968.

— 'Defence and the Backbencher', *Socialist Commentary*, April 1967.

— 'The Reform of Parliament', in Ben Whitaker (ed), *A Radical Future*, Jonathan Cape, London, 1967.

— 'Wanted: A Sense of Direction', *Socialist Commentary*, December 1966.

— 'Cabinet Alternatives', *Aspect*, January 1964.

Mackintosh, Maureen and Hilary Wainwright (eds), *A Taste for Power: The Politics of Local Economics*, Verso, London, 1987.

Maclean, Ian, Alan Montefiore and Peter Winch (eds), *The Political Responsibilities of Intellectuals*, Cambridge University Press, Cambridge, 1990.

Macmillan, Harold, *The Middle Way*, Macmillan, London, 1938.

Manifesto Group, *What We Must Do*, March 1977.

Mannheim, Karl, *Ideology and Utopia*, Harcourt, Brace and Jovanovich, New York, 1936.

Marquand, David, *The Progressive Dilemma*, Heinemann, London, 1991.

— 'Keep Right On', *New Statesman and Society*, 2 June 1989.

— *The Unprincipled Society: New Demands and Old Politics*, Jonathan Cape, London, 1988.

— 'Is There New Hope for the Social Democrats?', *Encounter*, April 1983.

— 'Social Democracy and the Collapse of the Westminster Model', in *The Re-birth of Britain*, Kennett, Wayland (ed), Weidenfeld and Nicholson, London, 1982.

— *European Elections and British Politics*, Longman, London, 1981.

— 'The Politics of Economic Recovery', *Political Quarterly*, Volume 51, 1980.

— 'Why Labour Cannot be Saved', *The Spectator*, 27 September 1980.

— *Parliament for Europe*, Jonathan Cape, London, 1979.

— 'Inquest on a Movement', *Encounter*, July 1979.

— 'Towards a Europe of the Parties', *Political Quarterly*, Volume 49, 1978.

— *Ramsay MacDonald*, Jonathan Cape, London, 1977.

— 'The Challenge to the Labour Party', *Political Quarterly*, Volume 46, 1975.

— 'Tory Idealists', *New Society*, 9 April 1970.

— 'The Politics of Deprivation', *Encounter*, April 1969.

— 'May Day Illusions', *Encounter*, August 1968.

— 'Treat Us Like Adults', *Socialist Commentary*, October 1968.

— John Mackintosh and David Owen, *Change Gear! Towards a Socialist Strategy*, Supplement to Socialist Commentary, October 1967.

— 'Europe', in *A Radical Future*, Ben Whitaker (ed), Jonathan Cape, London, 1967.

— 'Myths about Ideology', *Encounter*, February 1966.

— 'Labour and the Honours' List', *Socialist Commentary*, July 1964.

— 'Passion and Politics', *Encounter*, December 1961.

— 'Labour and the European Cause', Number 4, October 1961.

Martin, Kingsley, *Harold Laski 1893–1950: A Bibliographical Memoir*, Gollancz, London, 1953.

Marwick, Arthur, 'Middle Opinion in the Thirties: Planning Progress and Polit-ical "Agreement"', *English Historical Review*, Volume LXXIX – 79, 1964.

— 'The Independent Labour Party in the Nineteen-Twenties', *Bulletin of the Institute of Historical Research*, Volume XXXV, 1962.

Marxism Today, 'Manifesto for New Times', *Marxism Today*, October 1988.

Massey, Doreen, 'Heartlands of Defeat', *Marxism Today*, July 1987.

— 'The Contours of Victory...Dimensions of Defeat', *Marxism Today*, July 1983.

McBriar, A. M., *Fabian Socialism and English Politics 1884–1918*, Cambridge University Press, Cambridge, 1963.

Meade, J. E., *The Intelligent Radical's Guide to Economic Policy: The Mixed Economy*, George Allen & Unwin, London, 1971.

— 'The Restoration of Full Employment', in *The Re-birth of Britain*, Kennett, Wayland (ed), Weidenfeld and Nicholson, London, 1982.

Meiksens-Wood, Ellen, *The Retreat from Class*, Verso, London, 1986.

Merrington, John, 'Theory and Practice in Gramsci's Marxism', in *Western Marxism: A Critical Reader*, Gareth Stedman Jones (ed), New Left Books, London, 1977.

Michels, Robert, *Political Parties: A Sociological Study of the Oligarchical Tendencies of Modern Democracy*, The Free Press, New York, 1966.

— 'The Intellectuals', *Encyclopaedia of the Social Sciences*, Volume III, Macmillan, London, 1932.

Miliband, Ralph, 'The New Revisionism in Britain', *New Left Review*, March–April 1985.

— *Parliamentary Socialism: A Study in the Politics of Labour*, Second edition, Monthly Review Press New York, 1972.

Mill, John Stuart, *Mill on Bentham and Coleridge*, Leavis, F. R. (ed), Chatto and Windus, London, 1950.

Minkin, Lewis, *The Labour Party Conference: A Study in the Politics of Intra-Party Democracy*, Allen Lane, London, 1978.

— 'The Labour Party has not been hi-jacked', *New Society*, 6 October 1977.

Mirsky, Dimitri, *The Intelligentsia of Great Britain*, Victor Gollancz, London, 1935.

Mitchell, Austin, *Four Years in the Death of the Labour Party*, Methuen, London, 1983.

— 'Inquest on a Coroner', *Encounter*, December 1979.

Mitford, Nancy, 'The English Aristocracy', *Encounter*, September 1955.

Momsen, Wolfgang J., 'Max Weber and German Social Democracy', in *Socialism and the Intelligentsia 1880–1914*, Carl Levy (ed), Routledge and Kegan Paul, London, 1987.

Morgan, Kenneth O., *Labour People: Leaders and Lieutenants: Hardie to Kinnock*, Oxford University Press, Oxford, 1987.

— 'Edwardian Socialism', in Read, Donald (ed), *Edwardian England*, Rutgers University Press, New Brunswick, New Jersey, 1982.

— *Labour in Power 1945–51*, Oxford University Press, Oxford, 1985.

Mouffe, Chantal, 'Working-Class Hegemony and the Struggle for Socialism', *Studies in Political Economy*, Number 12, Fall 1983.

— 'Hegemony and Ideology in Gramsci', in Chantal Mouffe (ed), *Gramsci and Marxist Theory*, Routledge and Kegan Paul, London, 1979.

Mulhern, Francis, *The Moment of Scrutiny*, Verso, London, 1979.

— Introduction to Regis Debray, *Teachers, Writers, Celebrities: The Intellectuals of Modern France*, Verso, London, 1981.

Murdoch, Iris, 'A House of Theory', in Mackenzie, Norman (ed), *Conviction*, Macgibbon and Kee, London, 1958.

Nairn, Tom, *The Break-up of Britain*, Verso, London, 1981.

— 'The Crisis of the British State', *New Left Review*, November–December 1981.

— 'The Future of Britain's Crisis', *New Left Review*, January–April 1979.

— 'The English Literary Intelligentsia', in Tennant, Emma (ed), *Bananas*, Quartet, London, 1977.

— 'Twilight of the British State', *New Left Review*, February–April 1976.

— 'The Left Against Europe', *New Left Review*, September–October 1972.

— 'British Nationalism and the EEC', *New Left Review*, September–October 1971.

— 'The British Meridian', *New Left Review*, March–April 1970.

— 'The Nature of the Labour Party I & II', *New Left Review*, September–October, 1964.

— 'Hugh Gaitskell', *New Left Review*, May–June 1964.

— 'The English Working Class', *New Left Review*, March–April 1964.

— 'The British Political Elite', *New Left Review*, January–February 1964.

Nettl, J. P., 'Ideas, Intellectuals and Structures of Dissent', in Phillip Rieff (ed), *On Intellectuals*, Anchor Books, New York, 1970.

Neumann, Michael, *What's Left? Radical Politics and the Radical Psyche*, Broadview Press, Peterborough, Canada 1988.

Newman, Michael, *Socialism and European Unity: The Dilemma of the Left*, Junction Books, London, 1983.

Next Five Years Group, *The Next Five Years: An Essay in Political Agreement*, Macmillan and Company, London, 1935.

Nicholson, Max, *The System: The Misgovernment of Modern Britain*, Hodder and Stoughton, London, 1967.

Norman, William, 'Signposts for the Sixties', *New Left Review*, September–October 1961.

Norris, Christopher, 'Old Themes for New Times: Basildon Revisited', *Socialist Register*, 1993.

Oakshott, Matthew, *The Road from Limehouse to Westminster: Prospects for a Radical Realignment at the General Election*, Radical Central for Democratic Studies in Industry and Society, London, 1989.

O'Brien, Conor Cruise, 'Some Encounters with the Culturally Free', *New Left Review*, July–August 1967.

Orwell, George, *The Lion and the Unicorn: Socialism and the English Genius*, Secker and Warburg, London, 1962.

Osborne, John, *Look Back in Anger*, S.G. Phillips, New York, 1957.

Outwin, Denis, *The SDP Story*, Hartswood Publications, Maidenhead, 1987.

Owen, David, *Time Has Come: Partnership for Progress*, Weidenfeld and Nicholson, London, 1987.

— *David Owen: Personally Speaking to Kenneth Harris*, Weidenfeld and Nicholson, London, 1987.

— *A Future That Will Work: Competitiveness and Compassion*, Praeger, New York, 1984.

— 'The Enabling Society', in Kennett, Wayland (ed), *The Re-birth of Britain*, Weidenfeld and Nicholson, London, 1982.

— *Face the Future*, Jonathan Cape, London, 1981.

— William Rodgers and Shirley Williams, 'Open Letter to the Labour Party', *The Guardian*, 1 August 1980.

— 'Britain and Europe: At 6's and 7's Between Nine and Twelve', *Encounter*, January 1979.

— *Human Rights*, Jonathan Cape, London, 1978.

— *In Sickness and in Health*, Quartet Books, London, 1976.

— *The Politics of Defence*, Jonathan Cape, London, 1972.

— Peter Townsend and Brian Abel-Smith, *Social Services for All*, Fabian Tract 385, Fabian Society, London, 1968.

Panitch, Leo, Unpublished Manuscript on the Labour Party in the 1970s.

— *Working Class Politics in Crisis*, Verso, London, 1986.

— 'Socialist Renewal and the Labour Party', *Socialist Register*, 1988.

— *Social Democracy and Industrial Militancy: The Labour Party, The Trade Unions and Incomes Policy*, Cambridge University Press, Cambridge, 1976.

Parkin, Frank, *Middle Class Radicalism*, Manchester University Press, Manchester, 1968.

Paterson, Peter, *The Selectorate: The Case for Primary Elections in Britain*, MacGibbon and Kee, London, 1967.

Parsons, Talcott, ''The Intellectual': A Social Role Category', In *On Intellectuals*, Phillip Rieff (ed), Anchor Books, New York, 1970.

Perkins, Harold, *The Rise of Professional Society*, Routledge, London, 1989.

Pierson, S., *Marxism and the Origins of British Socialism*, Cornell University Press, Ithaca, 1973.

Pimlott, Ben, *Hugh Dalton*, Jonathan Cape, London, 1988.
— (ed), *Fabian Essays in Socialist Thought*, Heinemann, London, 1984.
— *Labour and the Left in the 1930s*, Cambridge University Press, Cambridge, 1977.
— 'The Socialist League: Intellectuals and the Labour Left in the 1930s', *Journal of Contemporary History*, Volume 67, Number 3, 1971.
— Anthony Wright and Tony Flower, *The Alternative: Politics for a Change*, W.H. Allen, London, 1989.
Pitcairn, Lee, 'Crisis in British Communism: An Insider's View', *New Left Review*, September–October 1985.
Ponting, Clive, *Breach of Promise: Labour in Power 1969–70*, Hamish Hamilton, London, 1989.
Powell, J. Enoch, *The Common Market: The Case Against*, Kingswood Elliott, London, 1971.
Price, Richard, *An Imperial War and the British Working Class: Working Class Attitudes and the Reaction to the Boer War*, Routledge and Kegan Paul, London, 1972.
Przeworski, Adam, 'Social Democracy as a Historical Phenomenon', *New Left Review*, July–August 1980.
Pugh, Patricia, *Educate, Agitate, Organise: 100 Years of Fabian Socialism*, Methuen, London, 1984.
Radice, Giles, *Labour's Path to Power: The New Revisionism*, Macmillan, London, 1989.
— 'Why the Labour Party Must Not Split', *Guardian*, 12 January 1981.
Radice, Lisanne, *Beatrice and Sidney Webb: Fabian Socialists*, Macmillan, London, 1984.
Reader, Keith A., 'The Intellectuals: Notes towards a comparative study of their position in the social formations of France and Britain', *Media, Culture and Society*, 1982.
Ree, Jonathan, *Proletarian Philosophers*, Oxford University Press, Oxford, 1984.
— 'Socialism and the Educated Working Class', in Levy, Carl (ed), *Socialism and the Intelligentsia 1880–1914*, Routledge and Kegan Paul, London, 1987.
Rieff, Phillip (ed), *On Intellectuals*, Doubleday, New York, 1969.
Robins, L. J., *The Reluctant Party: Labour and the EEC 1961–1975*, G. W. and A. Hesketh, Ormskirk, Lancashire, 1979.
Rodgers, William, *The Politics of Change*, Secker and Warburg, London, 1982.
— 'Labour's Predicament: Decline or Recovery', *Political Quarterly*, Volume 50, 1979.
— 'Socialism without Abundance', *Socialist Commentary*, July–August 1977.
— *Hugh Gaitskell*, Thames and Hudson, London, 1964.
Rose, Hilary, 'Up Against the Welfare State', *Socialist Register*, 1973.
Ross, Alan, S. C., 'U and non-U', *Encounter*, November 1955.
Rossanda, Rossana, 'Revolutionary Intellectuals and the Soviet Union', *Socialist Register*, 1974.
Rothman, S., 'British Labour's New Left', *Political Science Quarterly*, Volume 76, 1961.
Rowbotham, Sheila, Segal, Lynne and Wainwright, Hilary, *Beyond the Fragments: Feminism and the Making of Socialism*, Alyson Publications, Boston, 1981.
Royal Commission on Trade Unions and Employers' Associations 1965–1968, Report, Chairman: Rt. Hon., Lord Donovan, HMSO, London, 1968.

Rustin, Michael, *For a Pluralist Socialism*, Verso, London, 1985.
— 'Different Conceptions of Party: Labour's Constitutional Debates', *New Left Review*, March–April 1981.
— 'The New Left and the Present Crisis', *New Left Review*, May–June 1980.
Samuel, Raphael, 'The Lost World of British Communism', *New Left Review*, November–December 1985.
— and Gareth Stedman-Jones, 'Labour and Social Democracy', *History Workshop Journal*, Number 12, Autumn 1981.
Samuels, Stuart, 'English Intellectuals and Politics in the 1930s', in Phillip Rieff (ed), *On Intellectuals*, Anchor Books, New York, 1970.
Saran, Mary, *Never Give Up: Memoirs*, Oswald Wolff, London, 1976.
Saville, John, *The Labour Movement in Britain*, Faber and Faber, London, 1988.
— 'Hugh Gaitskell: An Assessment', *Socialist Register*, 1980.
— 'Labourism and the Labour Government', *Socialist Register*, 1967.
— 'The Politics of Encounter', *Socialist Register*, 1964
Scanlon, Hugh, Interview, *New Left Review*, November–December 1967.
Scargill, Arthur, 'The New Unionism', *New Left Review*, July–August 1975.
Scharpf, Fritz, *Crisis and Choice in European Social Democracy*, tr. Ruth Crowley and Fred Thompson, Cornell University Press, Ithaca, 1991.
Schlesinger, Philip, 'In Search of the Intellectuals: Some comments on recent theory', *Media, Culture and Society*, Volume 4, Number 3, 1982.
Schneer, Jonathan, *Labour's Conscience: The Labour Left 1945–51*, Unwin Hyman, London, 1988.
Schorske, Carl E., *German Social Democracy 1905–1917: The Development of the Great Schism*, Harvard University Press, Cambridge, 1955.
Schumpeter, Joseph, *Capitalism, Socialism and Democracy*, Harper and Brothers, New York, 1947.
Sedgwick, Peter, 'The Two New Lefts', *International Socialism*, Number 17, Summer 1964.
Semmel, Bernard, *Imperialism and Social Reform: English Social Imperial Thought 1895–1914*, Allen and Unwin, London, 1960.
Seyd, Patrick, *The Rise and Fall of the Labour Left*, Macmillan Educational, Houndmills, 1987.
— 'Labour Party Reform', *Political Quarterly*, Volume 49, 1978.
— 'Fabians and the Labour Party', *Political Quarterly*, Volume 44, 1973.
Seymour-Ure, Colin, 'The SDP and the Media', *Political Quarterly*, Volume 53, 1982.
Shanks, Michael, *The Stagnant Society*, Penguin, Harmondsworth, 1961.
Shaw, Bernard, *The Fabian Society: What it has done and how has it done it*, Fabian Society, London, 1892.
Shils, Edward, 'Remembering the Congress for Cultural Freedom', *Encounter*, November 1990.
— 'British Intellectuals in the Mid-Twentieth Century', *The Intellectuals and the Powers and Other Essays*, University of Chicago Press, Chicago 1972
— 'The Intellectuals and the Powers: Some Perspectives for Comparative Analysis', in *The Intellectuals and the Powers and Other Essays*, University of Chicago Press, Chicago, 1972.
— 'Intellectuals in Great Britain', *Encounter*, April 1955.

Skidelsky, Robert, *Politicians and the Slump*, Macmillan, London, 1967.

Social Democratic Party, 'Twelve Tasks for Social Democrats', *The Times*, 27 March 1981.

Socialist Union, *20th Century Socialism*, Penguin, Harmondsworth, 1956.

— *Socialism and Foreign Policy*, Bookhouse, London, 1953.

— *Socialism: A New Statement of Principles*, Lincoln-Praeger, London, 1952.

Stead, W. T., 'The Labour Party and the Books that Helped to Make It', *Review of Reviews*, (33), June 1906.

Stedman-Jones, Gareth, *Languages of Class*, Cambridge University Press, Cambridge, 1983.

— 'The Pathology of English History', *New Left Review*, November–December 1967.

Steel, David, *The House Divided: The Lib-Lab Pact and the Future of British Politics*, Weidenfeld and Nicholson, London, 1980.

Stephenson, Hugh, *Claret and Chips: The Rise of the SDP*, Michael Joseph, London, 1982.

Stokes, Eric, *The English Utilitarians and India*, Clarendon Press, Oxford, 1959.

Strachey, John, *The End of Empire*, Gollancz, London, 1959.

— *Contemporary Capitalism*, Gollancz, London, 1956.

— *Why You Should be a Socialist*, Gollancz, London, 1938.

— *The Coming Struggle for Power*, Gollancz, London, 1934.

— 'The Education of a Communist', *Left Review*, December 1934.

Taverne, Dick, *The Future of the Left: Lincoln and After*, Jonathan Cape, London, 1974.

Tawney, R. H., *Equality*, George Allen and Unwin, London, 1952.

— 'The Choice before the Labour Party', *Political Quarterly*, Number 3, 1932.

Therborn, Göran, *The Ideology of Power and the Power of Ideology*, New Left Books, London, 1980.

— 'The Rule of Capital and the Rise of Democracy', *New Left Review*, May–June 1977.

— *Science, Class and Society*, New Left Books, London, 1976.

Thomas, Hugh, *John Strachey*, Methuen, London, 1973.

— (ed), *The Establishment: A Symposium*, Blond, London, 1959.

Thomas, William, *The Philosophic Radicals: Nine Studies in Theory and Practice 1817–1841*, Clarendon Press, Oxford, 1979.

Thompson, E. P., *The Making of the English Working Class*, Pelican, Harmondsworth, 1962.

— 'The Peculiarities of the English', *Socialist Register*, 1965.

— *Out of Apathy*, Stevens and Sons, London, 1960.

Tomlinson, Jim, 'Why Was There Never a "Keynesian Revolution" in Economic Policy?', *Economy and Society*, February 1981.

de Toqueville, Alexis, *The Old Regime and the French Revolution*, Doubleday and Co., Garden City, New York, 1955.

Torrance, John, 'The Emergence of Sociology in Austria', *European Journal of Sociology*, Volume XVII, Number 2, 1976.

Townsend, P. and Bosanquet, N. (eds), *Labour and Inequality*, Fabian Society, London, 1972.

Tracy, Noel, *The Origins of the Social Democratic Party*, Croom Helm, London, 1983.

Trevelyan, C. P., *From Liberalism to Labour*, George Allen and Unwin, London, 1921.

Van Duzer, Charles, *The Contribution of the Ideologues to French Revolutionary Thought*, Johns Hopkins Press, Baltimore, 1935.

Wainwright, Hilary, *Arguments for a New Left: Answering the Free Market Right*, Basil Blackwell, London, 1994.

— 'For An Imaginary Party: Notes on Principles of Organisation for the Radical Left', Mimeo, 1989.

— *Labour: A Tale of Two Parties*, The Hogarth Press, London, 1987.

— *The Greater London Council's Economic Programme*, Canadian Centre for Policy Alternatives, Ottawa, 1985.

Watkins, Alan, 'The State of the Labour Party', *Political Quarterly*, Volume 43, 1972.

Watson, George, 'Were the Intellectuals Duped?: The 1930s Revisited', *Encounter*, December 1973.

Waugh, Evelyn, 'An Open Letter to the Hon. Mrs. Peter Rodd (Nancy Mitford)', *Encounter*, December 1955.

Webb, Beatrice, *Our Partnership*, Longmans Green, New York, 1948.

— 'The Disappearance of the Governing Class', *Political Quarterly*, 1930.

— *My Apprenticeship*, Longmans Green, New York, 1926.

Weiner, Martin, *English Culture and the Decline of the Industrial Spirit 1850–1980*, Cambridge University Press, Cambridge, 1981.

Westergaard, John, and Henrietta Resler, *Class in Capitalist Society*, Heinemann, London, 1975.

Whitaker, Ben (ed), *A Radical Future*, Jonathan Cape, London, 1967.

Whiteley, Paul, *The Labour Party in Crisis*, Methuen, London, 1983.

— 'Who Are the Labour Activists?', *Political Quarterly*, Volume 52, 1981.

Widgery, David, *The Left in Britain 1956–68*, Penguin, Harmondsworth, 1976.

Williams, Gwyn, 'The Concept of "Egomania" in the Thought of Antonio Gramsci: Some Notes on Interpretation', *Journal of the History of Ideas*, Number 21, 1960.

Williams, Geoffrey Lee and Williams, Alan Lee, *Labour's Decline and the Social Democrats' Fall*, Macmillan, London, 1989.

Williams, Philip, *Hugh Gaitskell*, Oxford University Press, Oxford, 1982.

— 'Changing Styles of Political Leadership', in *The Politics of the Labour Party*, Denis Kavanagh (ed), George Allen and Unwin, London, 1982.

Williams, Raymond, *Politics and Letters*, Verso, London, 1979.

— 'An Alternative Politics', *Socialist Register*, 1981.

— 'Notes on Marxism in Britain since 1945', in *Problems in Materialism and Culture*, Verso, London, 1980.

— 'The Politics of Nuclear Disarmament', *New Left Review*, November–December 1980.

— *May Day Manifesto*, Penguin, Harmondsworth, 1968.

— 'The British Left', *New Left Review*, March–April 1965.

— *Culture and Society 1780–1950*, Chatto and Windus, London, 1960.

Williams, Shirley, *A Job to Live: The Impact of Tomorrow's Technology on Work and Society*, Penguin, Harmondsworth, 1985.

— 'On Modernising Britain', in *The Re-birth of Britain*, Kennett, Wayland (ed), Weidenfeld and Nicholson, London, 1982.

— *Politics Is for People*, Harvard University Press, Cambridge, Massachusetts, 1981.

— *Technology, Employment and Change*, Cambridge University Press, Cambridge, 1980.

— *Britain and the Free Trade Area*, Fabian Society, London, 1959.

— *The Common Market and Its Forerunners*, Fabian Society, London, 1958.

— 'Uneasy Courtship', *Socialist Commentary*, April 1958.

— 'Crossing the Channel', *Socialist Commentary*, September 1957.

Windlesham, (Lord) David, *Communication and Political Power*, Jonathan Cape, London, 1966.

Wolfe, Alan, 'Radical Intellectuals in a Conservative Time', *New Political Science*, Nos. 5–6, 1974.

— *From Radicalism to Socialism*, Yale University Press, New Haven, 1975.

Wood, Neal, *Communism and British Intellectuals*, Columbia University Press, New York, 1959.

Wright, Anthony, *British Socialism: Socialist Thought From the 1880s to the 1960s*, Longman, London, 1983.

Wright, Erik O., 'Intellectuals and the Class Struggle of Capitalist Society', in Pat Walker (ed), *Between Labor and Capital*, Black Rose Books, Montreal, 1978.

Wyatt, Woodrow, *What's Left of the Labour Party?* Sidgwick and Jackson, London, 1977.

Yeo, Stephen, 'Notes on Three Socialisms – Collectivism, Statism and Associationism – mainly in late nineteenth and early twentieth century Britain', in Levy, Carl (ed), *Socialism and the Intelligentsia 1880–1914*, Routledge and Kegan Paul, London, 1987.

Young, Michael, *Bigness Is the Enemy of Humanity*, SDP, London, 1981.

— *The Rise of Meritocracy, An Essay on Education and Equality*, Thames and Hudson, London, 1958.

Zeitlin, Irving, *Ideology and the Development of Social Theory*, Prentice-Hall, Englewood Cliffs, N.J., 1968.

Zentner, Peter, *Social Democracy in Britain: Must Labour Lose?* John Martin Publishing, London, 1982.

Index